DIY Utopia

DIY Utopia

Cultural Imagination and the Remaking of the Possible

Edited by
Amber Day

LEXINGTON BOOKS
Lanham • Boulder • New York • London

Published by Lexington Books
An imprint of The Rowman & Littlefield Publishing Group, Inc.
4501 Forbes Boulevard, Suite 200, Lanham, Maryland 20706
www.rowman.com

Unit A, Whitacre Mews, 26-34 Stannary Street, London SE11 4AB

British Library Cataloguing in Publication Information Available

Library of Congress Cataloging-in-Publication Data Available

ISBN 978-1-4985-2388-2 (cloth : alk. paper)
ISBN 978-1-4985-2389-9 (electronic)

∞™ The paper used in this publication meets the minimum requirements of American National Standard for Information Sciences—Permanence of Paper for Printed Library Materials, ANSI/NISO Z39.48-1992.

Printed in the United States of America

Contents

Introduction

Creative Play and Collective Imagination

We are in what, on the surface, appear to be fairly gloomy times in terms of belief in progress and collective change for the good. Contemporary predictions about the future tend to be characterized by some flavor of doom or dystopian vision. This is overwhelmingly true for imagined narratives, those most prevalent in film, television, and literature, but it is also true of the predictions coming out of, say, environmental science or geopolitics. For this reason, it seems particularly important that we be invested in collectively working toward solutions and correctives, but that is not a function that is all that supported by the dominant culture at present. Party politics is largely regarded with cynicism more than soaring ideals, while our fantasy worlds are frequently circumscribed. However, that does not mean that the desire to dream is entirely absent. Rather, within alternative culture, there appears to be a flowering of utopian imaginings and of the creation of spaces designed for collective discussion and creativity. The desires evidenced by these movements can tell us much about ourselves and our moment.

I am hardly alone in noticing the wider popular cultural lack of optimism or belief in future improvements. As Ruth Levitas explains, images of decline are now much more prevalent than those of progress, creating "a climate conducive to dystopia, the warning of what will happen if . . . —and there is often little conviction that averting action can be assured."[1] Indeed, one is hard pressed to find any contemporary popular cultural narratives in film, television, or literature premised on the assumption that collective effort can solve perceived problems or create cultural improvements. Rather, we seem captivated by images of apocalypse, only occasionally averted by the actions of a lone hero.

As a noteworthy response to such an environment, in September 2012, Arizona State University launched their Center for Science and Imagination, a unique think tank of science-fiction writers, engineers, scientists, and illustrators. In their own writings and interviews, the center describes itself as created in reaction to the dual observations that exclusively dark visions of the future seem to dominate contemporary science fiction, and that there is an apparent lack of grand scientific and technological ambition in comparison to past eras.[2] Hypothesizing that there might be a link between the two, the center aims to serve as "a network hub for audacious moonshot ideas and a cultural engine for thoughtful optimism."[3] According to Edward Finn, the director of the center, "the goal is to install in us a sense of 'agency' about the future, 'to make us realise that we are all making choices that create the future.'"[4] It is worth noting that such an effort crosses traditional disciplinary lines, and even the firm boundaries erected between fiction and science in a broader effort to emphasize creativity and vision. In a remarkably similar manner, many of the artists and activists represented in this volume articulate the bedrock goal of spurring others to see themselves as creators—both of current problems and of potential solutions.

Simultaneously, small-scale projects as well as larger movements are springing up with strikingly analogous goals. This volume focuses on a range of artist- or activist-inspired projects, as well as the efforts of various subcultural communities of interest. More playfully self-conscious than past utopian movements, today's are often whimsical or ironic, but are still entirely earnest. Artists invite us to re-author city maps, or archive individual ideas for the future, while maker collectives urge us to rethink our relationship to consumer goods. All seem to have grown out of a similar do-it-yourself (DIY) ethos and alternative culture.

The mushrooming DIY subculture is one that has developed largely in opposition to mainstream consumer culture. It encompasses a wide variety of activities, from crafting, to building, to farming, leading to the growing visibility of anarchist knitting circles and co-operative "hack-labs." In some respects, it may seem easy to dismiss the hipster preciousness around many such endeavors, but the DIY movement also has a political bent, positioning itself as an alternative to the dominant culture of conspicuous consumerism, corporate mass production, and ecological destruction. It is this broad subculture that has laid the groundwork for many of the utopian imaginings discussed in this volume.

These utopian projects take a variety of forms, emerging from the worlds of art and activism, interpersonal skill-sharing and open source web collaboration. Similar to the other DIY pursuits, their starting point is often a desire to fill in elements that one might feel are missing from mainstream culture or political life. Far removed from the rigidly prescriptive utopian movements of the past, these projects tend to be characterized by a sense of play, a self-referential wink, or a desire for each participant to make it his/her own.

Utopia here may not be seen as ultimately attainable, but as anthology contributor Steven Duncombe puts it, an opportunity to pose the question "what if?" Duncombe has created a digitized version of Thomas More's *Utopia*, complete with an annotatable "social" text for readers to comment on More's ideas and then share these comments with others. He explains that "by envisioning impossibilities Utopia creates an opening to ask 'What If?' without closing down this free space by seriously answering 'This is what!' With such visions, the future imagined can never be fixed."[5] Many of these projects are invested in utopia as process, in simply getting people thinking creatively and collectively, and in about sharing earnestly held desires.

It should be noted that some of the creators, collectives, and movements assembled here might not necessarily use the descriptor "utopian" themselves. Indeed, the concept of "utopia" is one with which many hesitate to be associated, as it is something we are taught to regard with suspicion. As Levitas explains, even dictionary definitions of the term utopia contain derogatory hints, employing words like "unrealistic" or "idealistic." As she puts it, "colloquial usage thus tends to dismiss speculation about the good society as intrinsically impractical."[6] There is also a widespread assumption that utopian thought is necessarily totalizing and thus dangerous if taken seriously. As Lucy Sargisson makes clear, the root of this fear "is a mistaken association between utopianism and perfection, and between utopianism and fundamentalism."[7] She goes on to say that some utopian ideals are intended as blueprints, and thus should be approached with an abundance of caution. Nevertheless, argues Sargisson, utopianism remains not just desirable but essential, as "politics without Utopia would be bleak indeed. Utopias (in the sense of visions of a better way of being) give politics a sense of where it wants to be. In this sense, Utopia lies at the heart of politics."[8] Indeed, Sargisson is not alone in pointing to the importance of understanding and valuing human desires for what *could* be. Levitas points out that there is now a growing academic field known as utopian studies, at the heart of which is the assumption that "utopia is not escapist nonsense but a significant part of human culture."[9] I too am interested in our grand ideals and most fervent desires, as well as in what our art, culture, humor, and play tell us about ourselves. And I believe that by conceptualizing the material collected here as homemade strivings for utopia, we can examine a diverse array of contemporary phenomena at once, taking a wide angle on our moment in history.

CAPITALISM AND ITS DISCONTENTS

Taken as a whole, the case studies contained in this volume demonstrate just how hard it is for us to envision anything outside of neoliberal capitalism, and yet that we have a powerful desire to take it apart in piecemeal ways. The DIY impulse is rooted firmly in a drive to bring people back into touch with the material world, in a nostalgia for lost skills and trades, and often in a desire for collective engagement, elements that are frequently in direct opposition to the flows of power within late capitalism. Aspects of this tension are visible in each of the essays collected here. The articles by Catherine D'Ignazio, Martha Kuhlman, and Rob Walker all point our attention to the struggle over public space, examining projects that playfully challenge corporate and governmental control over city spaces and that ask passersby to consider how a city *might* be used by its inhabitants. Both Lorenzo Giannini and Jeremy Hunsinger focus on organized "hacker" and "fixer" cultures, communities that critically question the contemporary relationship between production and consumption, while the artists and activists profiled by Linda Doyle and Jessica Foley similarly seek to draw attention to the competing interests of the users and the owners of Wi-Fi radio technology.

It should be noted, however, that capitalism exerts an incredibly powerful force capable of pulling nearly everything back into its center. As Deborah Philips points out in her examination of British home improvement television, the DIY movement in particular can be fairly easily reabsorbed into dominant paradigms, used both to sell advertisements and to shore up existing systems of power, thereby casting utopia as the acquisition of things. Likewise, McAlister and Aiello's description of *Dwell* magazine and its critique in *Unhappy Hipsters* implies that the utopian prescriptions of modern architecture and design are profoundly enmeshed in privileged forms of cultural capital. Indeed, these case studies serve as examples of the phenomenon pinpointed by Raffaella Baccolini when she argues that "in these unquestionably anti-utopian times, Utopia has been conflated with materialist satisfaction and thus has been commodified and devalued."[10] There is certainly nothing about the DIY aesthetic that would make it automatically resistant to reabsorption. Indeed, Hunsinger demonstrates the way in which the DIY electronics community's "mental ecology" is in tension with its growing consumerist tendencies.

Clovis Bergère's chapter on the DIY creation of youth-centered spaces (or bureaux) in Guinea hits on some of these competing strains of confrontation and replication of power. As he explains, the bureaux allow young people to fill in what is missing in the services provided by municipalities, collectively finding a way of making-do that is itself utopian in its mundaneness, creating their own model for networking and forging community support systems under otherwise semi-dysfunctional circumstances. However, as Bergère points out, these organically developed spaces do inevitably end up reproducing many existing structures of power, including hierarchies of gender, class, and ethnicity. In a similar manner, Lisa Daily draws our attention to the perplexing fact that utopian solutions proposed within the existing system of capitalism are always already limited. She argues that the often attractive proposals of ethical capitalism, for instance, naturalize "a faulty form of ready-made solutions that inevitably secures the continuation of excessive consumption (often without the consideration for the production of environmental destruction), perpetuates the myth of individualized private sector solutions to structural inequalities, and cements existing hierarchical social relations despite appearances of empowerment and solidarity through the rhetoric of freedom, voluntary exchange, and competition."[11] As she points out, even utopia must be historicized when put into action—linked to both history and politics—otherwise it becomes de-politicized, inevitably shoring up the status quo.

It is, indeed, incredibly difficult to think beyond the present system, as it is a skill in which most of us have little practice or training. In the introductory material to his Open Utopia project on the web, which he profiles in this collection, Duncombe points out that the dominant system dominates not because it is the one we all agree is best, but because we are convinced that there is no alternative. Citing a number of polls in which inhabitants of capitalist countries overwhelmingly respond that free market capitalism is not working well, he argues that, on its own, this lack of belief is of little threat to the system, as "when ideology becomes truly hegemonic, you no longer need to believe. The reigning ideology is everything: the sun, the moon, the stars; there is simply nothing outside—no alternative—to imagine."[12] As such, then, to encourage daydreaming of alternatives (or practicing them), as many of the groups profiled here do, is simultaneously subversive, difficult, and necessary. The existence of utopian thinking is itself substantive. As Frederic Jameson has argued, "it is the very principle of the radical break as such, its possibility, which is reinforced by the Utopian form, which insists that its radical difference is possible and that a break is necessary."[13] Creating the space for people to form community around collective imagining is a political act. And the proliferation of such projects ultimately demonstrates that there is a great deal of desire to challenge the way things are, to create miniature versions of alternate worlds, and to push back against existing flows of power.

ART, CULTURE, AND THE POLITICAL IMAGINARY

This anthology makes the case that the majority of these projects and communities are doing political work by encouraging the desire for alternatives. However, that does not necessarily mean that they are flawlessly emancipatory or inclusive. The DIY community, for example, has historically been critiqued for its blindness to struggles beyond the environmental and anti-corporate. In his study of 1990s DIY culture in Britain, for example, George McKay argues that the community has had a tendency to ignore class, race, gender, and disability, or has introduced them tokenistically, the danger being "that DIY culture quietens marginalised voices and erases difference, and that, paradoxically, it achieves both of these by a loud rhetoric of inclusivity"[14] That is not necessarily the case across the board, of course, but is important to keep in mind. Likewise, it should be noted that to gather these case studies together is not to equate them with one another. The stakes are notably very different for the Black Lives Matter protesters than they are for tinkerers at a fixer lab. To put them side by side is not to suggest that their goals are necessarily always compatible. Nevertheless, this collection is premised on the belief that there is value in pulling together disparate examples that share some family resemblances. As Ruth Levitas argues, "we learn a lot about the experience of living under any set of conditions by reflecting upon the desires which those conditions generate and yet leave unfulfilled. For that is the space which utopia occupies."[15]

And, though I would advise against equating the activists with, say, the writers behind the parody site *Unhappy Hipsters* (Chapter 11), it would likewise be a mistake to dismiss any of the artists, hackers, or fixers as being merely hobbyist and thus peripheral from real-world stakes. To do so would be to fall into the long-standing trap of seeing art and culture as somehow removed from serious political thought. On the contrary, the spheres of art, entertainment, and sociability are arguably where societies work through their norms, ideals, and aspirations. Stuart Hall describes popular culture in general as "the arena of consent and resistance," arguing "it is partly where hegemony arises and where it is secured."[16] In reference to utopian thinking in particular, a number of theorists have pointed out that it is art that often does the best job of connecting us to these longings or of allowing us to envision something other than the here and now. Drawing on the thinking of German philosopher Ernst Bloch, José Muñoz describes "the anticipatory illumination of art, which can be characterized as the process of identifying certain properties that can be detected in representational practices helping us to see the not-yet-conscious."[17] Given these specialized capabilities, as Benjamin Kunkel explains, "the experience of art continues to radicalize many sensibilities more decisively, if obscurely, than political argument."[18] What matters in each example, whether an open source art project, fixer collective, or activist demonstration, is the beginning of a new narrative or imagined community.

As noted, however, none of the utopian ideals collected here attempt to provide a prescriptive blueprint. Far removed from the rigidly totalizing utopian plans of bygone eras, many of these projects are deliberately fanciful. The artist-produced projects in particular are not designed to ever take shape in material form. The Institute for Infinitely Small Things has not sent their renamed map of Cambridge streets to city hall for consideration. The artists working with Rob Walker are not actively constructing a "snooze tower." However, there is nothing cynical about the sentiment behind these projects, as all are imbued with real sentiment, hope, or desire. They all seek to affect those who come into contact with the projects, aiming to spark questions, ideas, or idle daydreaming about alternatives. As Jameson argues, what is utopian is not the commitment to specifics but to the act of imagining possible utopias in "their greatest variety of forms," as the "utopian is no longer the invention and defense of a specific floorplan, but rather the story of all the arguments about how Utopia should be constructed in the first place."[19] Instead of blueprints, we have provocations.

ALIENATION AND DESIRE

The questions are: what exactly is the appeal or pleasure in utopian practice? And how might we think about its goals and effects? One of the descriptions that emerges from many of the case studies gathered here is of throwing everyday practices or norms into relief. In his chapter, Rob Walker remarks that "good stories—funny, provocative, weird, or disturbing—have value in the real world" as they prod us to actually see the culture in which we live. Indeed, this is the most basic goal of all forms of political art. It is what Bertolt Brecht famously characterized as the "alienation effect" in his life-long quest to get audiences to suddenly focus on an element of their world that is so taken-for-granted as to be almost invisible, and to begin to question why it is so. As he puts it, "a representation that alienates is one which allows us to recognize its subject, but at the same time makes it seem unfamiliar."[20] A variation on this description recurs throughout this collection, as the authors write of the desire to spur others to cast a critical eye on their surroundings. Indeed, we could not begin to contemplate alternatives to the present if we cannot actually see the present.

Another consistent theme is the desire to counteract cynicism and inertia, the forces normally aligned to block this sort of thinking. As discussed, the dominant system dominates because most of us are convinced there are no alternatives, or that it would be too difficult to effect change, and we assume that our own agency is insignificant in its atomized singularity. Part of the purpose of these utopian projects is to demonstrate that there are many people with shared concerns, and to provide a sense of affirmation and strength in numbers. While the street corner bureaux described by Bergère function as literal community centers, much of the appeal of the maker or fixer events, as well, is the community they provide, creating the space for shared practice as well as the development of a shared code of ethics. Similarly, the Open Utopia project or the map of The City Formally Known as Cambridge invite strangers to interact and exchange ideas with one another, connecting through play and the contemplation of possibilities. Finally, as Kumanyika explains, the practice of livestreaming throughout protests has allowed people to coalesce around the Black Lives Matter movement, helping to create a networked community both real and imagined.

Indeed, as I have argued elsewhere,[21] this feeling of affirmation and community is a crucial one for any social or political movement. Such engagement is often dismissed as "preaching to the converted," but we would do better to think of it as a form of rallying the troops. While we all have a multitude of diffuse feelings and opinions rattling around our heads, most remain at the level of background noise. It is another thing entirely for one of those feelings to be brought to the surface, to feel the pleasure of having it affirmed, and to experience the sense of community in opposition. José Muñoz reminds us that this process is particularly important for marginalized groups. As he argues, "minoritarian subjects are cast as hopeless in a world without utopia."[22] But there is potential power in the communal experience of unhappiness, as it is "from shared critical dissatisfaction we arrive at collective potentiality."[23] I would add that political change is never truly spontaneous. Rather, the desire and will for change must have had the chance for incubation and discussion; thus, providing the space and opportunity for such communion is itself vitally important.

Finally, there is the actual creation of ideas. In true DIY form, these collectives, activists, and artists seek to fill in gaps in the dominant culture or speak to unmet needs. As Ronald Deibert describes it, "DIY means taking matters into your own hands, not leaving it for others to do it for you. It means making decisions without the gaze of those in power saying what's right and what's wrong, what's allowed or what's not."[24] When the world does not exist as we would like it to, it is the forging of alternatives in miniature form. And, indeed, many of these projects involve generating real ideas. Whether practical or fanciful, detailed or abstract, they are designed to exercise our creative muscles and ideally remind us that we do have agency and we do have imagination.

CHAPTER OVERVIEWS

The collection is divided into four sections. We open with a variety of projects pointedly but playfully devised to spark reflection, spurring participants and passersby to contemplate the open-ended question "what if…?" Stephen Duncombe starts us off with a discussion of the importance of utopia, while outlining his own project of digitizing Thomas More's *Utopia*. In making the text open access and partially user-generated, including features such as "Wikitopia" Duncombe provides a platform for collective idea generation and kibitzing. Catherine D'Ignazio introduces us to her collective, the Institute for Infinitely Small Things, and its project to communally rename the streets of Cambridge, Massachusetts with a random assortment of passersby. Using this seemingly useless map as her focal point, D'Ignazio explains how "cultivating civic imagination can create new worlds," prompting reflection on mundane systems of power and broadening the sphere of who participates in civic life. Rob Walker then offers a brief history of "architecture fiction," while describing his own project, the Hypothetical Development Organization, which involved the creation of fantastical development ideas for neglected buildings. He refers to the renderings of these hypothetical developments as a "form of urban storytelling," designed to spur others to suddenly notice the building he or she may have walked by a hundred times before, making it "exist again in a new way." Each of these author/creators is invested in the importance of having us stop to think critically about the actual in relationship to the theoretical.

In Part II we survey several DIY countercultural communities. Lorenzo Giannini takes us into the world of "fixers" and the repair events they have engendered. As he describes them, these events are explicitly created as a way to take back some control over the commodities in our lives, and to draw critical attention to the contemporary relationship between production and consumption. Similarly, Doyle and Foley introduce us to radio as a world of DIY experimentation, profiling a number of practitioners currently working to challenge the status quo of spectrum allocation and management. Doyle and Foley argue that "a rhetoric of scarcity and tragedy continues to inform the way that spectrum is managed" and they question the appropriateness of this imaginary, asking how it might be changed. Finally, Jeremy Hunsinger examines the ongoing metamorphosis of DIY electronics communities, uncovering a layer of complexity and contradiction. He points to the ideological conflict at play in the "mental ecology" of such communities, as the central informative websites construct need by tying knowledge and the capacity to create to the ability to purchase things. Most important for this collection, Hunsinger argues that this "path to quick success shortchanges the imaginal possibilities of DIY electronics enthusiasts and, in kind, it frames our subjective capacities, and shortchanges our future." Together, these chapters provide a helpful snapshot of the DIY ethos and its relationship to utopian strivings.

In the third section, we move further outside circles of power as we examine protest movements and improvised marginal communities. Clovis Bergère takes us to the urban centers of Guinea and the informal, unofficial youth gathering spaces known as "bureaux." Bergère describes these temporary autonomous zones as "key sites of rehearsal where alternative ontologies can be tested and tried," examining the ways in which they meet the needs of young people in the face of dysfunctional local services. Martha Kuhlman then takes us on a tour of a number of local art projects in Providence, Rhode Island, all designed to challenge official uses of public space and to "lay claim to the city in the name of the community." She conceptualizes these small gestures as a "utopian micropolitics of everyday life," while gesturing as well to the class and racial politics that makes some of these projects more threatening to existing power structures than others.

Chenjerai Kumanyika focuses on the practice of livestreaming within the Black Lives Matter protests. Drawing from his own experiences with this form of DIY media-making, he describes the ways in which streaming helped construct Black Lives Matter as a networked community of protesters, creating the experience of togetherness in moments of resistance. While he celebrates this function, he also explores the downsides to the technology's centrality in the movement, including the lack of fully equitable access, the potential exploitation of vulnerable streamers by more well-resourced media companies, and the fact that "streaming can be complicit in compelling organizers into a seductive politics of reaction, and endless awareness raising." He persuasively examines both the pitfalls and potential of DIY media production within social justice movements.

In the final section, we move from the smaller-scale projects of artists and activists into the mass-produced world of popular culture and business. Here, we have the complicated push and pull of DIY and utopian ideals absorbed into the market and the neoliberal status quo. Deborah Philips examines British crafting and home improvement television programming marketed by nostalgically referencing the World War II-era austerity measures termed "Make Do and Mend" that the Conservative government had brought back into parlance in the wake of the 2008 financial crash. Focusing on one home improvement guru in particular, Kirstie Allsopp, Philips argues that her programs perform a profoundly gendered and ideological role. As opposed to the earlier collective effort to save resources that one of her shows explicitly references, the focus of this program is entirely on the private and the domestic, while "the response to the economic downturn is to retreat into the home, where it becomes the woman's responsibility to 'make do and mend' in order to rescue the family finances," often paradoxically through buying a great many products.

Joan Faber McAlister and Giorgia Aiello examine the tension between the design magazine *Dwell* and the website created to poke fun of it, *Unhappy Hipsters*. They point to the way in which modernist utopias seem comically out of place in an era now accustomed to critiques of the imperialist interest of globalization, which the parody website gamely exploits. Further, they are interested in the ways in which "globalizing visions featuring everyday utopias prompt local responses in the form of technological dystopias—creating a critical exchange that may be crucial for social imaginaries to spark social change." Finally, Lisa Daily examines the paradoxes of ethical capitalism: products and services sold through an appeal to consumers to do good through their purchases. Daily argues that "by subjecting public benefit and the vision of a better world to the whims of capitalism, the real needs of communities and individuals are limited to the imagination of what is entrepreneurial and marketable." In her view, a utopian futurity must be able to see beyond existing capitalism and attempt to buck "the ideological training of our imaginations that incessantly look for ready-made solutions to complex problems within simplistic acts of economization." While these essays remind us of how easily both DIY gumption and utopian ideals can be neutered and domesticated, they also gesture outward to the utopian impulse that might step outside these limitations.

CONCLUSION

A given cultural moment always contains competing currents of thought and incompatible ideals that jostle for prominence. At this moment, on the one hand, the dominant narratives put forward by our entertainment put little faith in collective change. However, alternative culture tells a different story. It is rife with examples of longing for new social and political narratives, new forms of communion and sociability, and new imaginings of the possible. These are longings that are currently unmet by mainstream culture, but that are taking expression in myriad ways at the local level. Granted, most of these are the individual projects of small-scale artists, collectives, and activists, tiny works in the grand scheme of things, but these sorts of projects are becoming visible all over alternative culture. And they have been met by a great deal of localized enthusiasm and engagement by those encountering them. Indeed, it speaks to the outsize importance of these small-scale projects. In a culture struggling to articulate what we even dare to wish for, alternative, participatory forms of culture offer a key locus for collective imagination and energy.

NOTES

1. Ruth Levitas, *The Concept of Utopia* (Syracuse: Syracuse University Press, 1990), 225.

2. Mark Piesing, "Countering Dystopian Science Fiction's 'Wet Blanket Effect' On Innovation," *Wired*, June 26, 2013, http://www.wired.co.uk/news/archive/2013-06/26/dystopian-science-fiction

3. "About Us" Center for Science and the Imagination, accessed February 18, 2016, http://csi.asu.edu/about-us/

4. Piesing, "Countering Dystopian Science Fiction's 'Wet Blanket Effect' On Innovation."

5. Duncombe, this volume.

6. Levitas, *The Concept of Utopia*, 3.

7. Lucy Sargisson, "The Curious Relationship Between Politics and Utopia," in *Utopia, Method, Vision: The Use Value of Social Dreaming,* eds. Tom Moylan and Raffaella Baccolini (Germany: Peter Lang, 2007), 27.

8. Sargisson, "The Curious Relationship Between Politics and Utopia," 42.

9. Levitas, *The Concept of Utopia*, 1.

10. Raffaella Baccolini, "Finding Utopia in Dystopia: Feminism, Memory, Nostalgia, and Hope," in *Utopia, Method, Vision: The Use Value of Social Dreaming*, eds. Tom Moylan and Raffaella Baccolini (Germany: Peter Lang, 2007), 27.

11. Daily, this volume.

12. Stephen Duncombe, "Introduction: Open Utopia," *The Open Utopia*, accessed June 30, 2016, http://theopenutopia.org/full-text/introduction-open-utopia/

13. Frederic Jameson, *Archaeologies of the Future: The Desire Called Utopia and Other Science Fictions* (London; New York: Verso, 2005), 231.

14. George McKay, "DIY Culture: Notes Toward an Introduction," in *DiY Culture: Party & Protest in Nineties Britain*, ed. George McKay (London; New York: Verso, 1998), 45.

15. Levitas, *The Concept of Utopia*, 8.

16. Stuart Hall, "Notes on Deconstructing the Popular," in *Cultural Resistance Reader*, ed. Stephen Duncombe (London: New York: Verso, 2002), 192.

17. José Esteban Muñoz, *Cruising Utopia* (New York: New York University Press, 2009), 3.

18. Benjamin Kunkel, *Utopia or Bust: A Guide to the Present Crisis* (London; New York: Verso, 2014), 169.

19. Jameson, *Archaeologies of the Future*, 217.

20. Bertolt Brecht, *Brecht on Theatre: The Development of an Aesthetic*, trans John Willett (London: Eyre Methuen, 1964), 192.

21. Amber Day, *Satire and Dissent: Interventions in Contemporary Political Debate* (Indiana: Indiana University Press, 2011), 145–146.

22. Muñoz, *Cruising Utopia*, 97.

23. Ibid., 189.

24. Ronald Deibert. "Foreword," In *DIY Citizenship: Critical Making and Social Media*, eds. Matt Ratto and Megan Boler (Cambridge, MA: MIT Press, 2014), ix.

BIBLIOGRAPHY

"About Us." Center for Science and Imagination. Accessed February 16, 2016. http://csi.asu.edu/about-us/

Baccolini, Raffaella. "Finding Utopia in Dystopia: Feminism, Memory, Nostalgia, and Hope." In *Utopia Method Vision: The Use Value of Social Dreaming*, edited by Tom Moylan and Raffaella Baccolini, 25–46. Germany: Peter Lang, 2007.

Brecht, Bertolt. *Brecht on Theatre: The Development of an Aesthetic.* Translated by John Willett. London: Eyre Methuen, 1964.

Day, Amber. *Satire and Dissent: Interventions in Contemporary Political Debate.* Indiana: Indiana University Press, 2011.

Deibert, Ronald. "Foreword." In *DIY Citizenship: Critical Making and Social Media*, edited by Matt Ratto and Megan Boler, ix–x. Cambridge: MIT Press, 2014.

Duncombe, Stephen. "Introduction: Open Utopia." *The Open Utopia.* Accessed June 30, 2016. http://theopenutopia.org/full-text/introduction-open-utopia/

Hall, Stuart. "Notes on Deconstructing the Popular." In *Cultural Resistance Reader*, edited by Stephen Duncombe, 185–192. London: New York: Verso, 2002.

Jameson, Frederic. *Archaeologies of the Future: The Desire Called Utopia and Other Science Fictions.* London; New York: Verso, 2005.

Kunkel, Benjamin. *Utopia or Bust: A Guide to the Present Crisis.* London; New York: Verso, 2014.

Levitas, Ruth. *The Concept of Utopia.* Syracuse: Syracuse University Press, 1990.

McKay, George. "DiY Culture: Notes Toward an Introduction." In *DiY Culture: Party & Protest in Nineties Britain*, edited by George McKay, 1–53. London; New York: Verso, 1998.

Muñoz, José Esteban. *Cruising Utopia.* New York: New York University Press, 2009.

Piesing, Mark. "Countering Dystopian Science Fiction's 'Wet Blanket Effect' on Innovation." Wired.co.uk, June 26, 2013. http://www.wired.co.uk/news/archive/2013–06/26/dystopian-science-fiction.

Sargisson, Lucy. "The Curious Relationship Between Politics and Utopia." In *Utopia Method Vision: The Use Value of Social Dreaming*, edited by Tom Moylan and Raffaella Baccolini, 25–46. Germany: Peter Lang, 2007.

Part I

IMAGINATION AND PLAY: ASKING "WHAT IF?"

Chapter 1

Opening Up Utopia

Stephen Duncombe

A few years ago, in 2009, I was asked to give a series of lectures at Moscow State University for graduate students and junior academics from across Russia as part of the Fulbright Foundation's Summer School in the Humanities. The topic was "political imagination." As I prepared for my lectures I was acutely aware that I was stepping into a society in which political imagination had led to a horrific political reality. I decided that I had to teach the benchmark of political imagination, Thomas More's *Utopia*, but how was I going to do this in the context of Utopia's failure in the Soviet Union?

Reading *Utopia* again I realized More himself provides the answer. *Utopia* was not the story I had remembered from my first reading in university. I recalled More's *Utopia* as the tale of a far-off island in which an ideal—if somewhat boring—society existed; upon re-reading I discovered something else: an imagination machine. The book was written not only to provide a vision of a better world, but to prompt us to envision our own Utopias. *Utopia* is more than the story of a far-off land where there is no private property. It is a text that instructs us how to approach texts, be they literary or political, in an open manner: open to criticism, open to participation, open to modification, and open to re-creation. More, in a word, had created an *open* Utopia.

This idea of *Utopia* as an open text and an inherently unfinished project became the basis for my lectures in Moscow. More important, it provided the impetus for the "Utopia" I would set about creating when I returned to New York City. I was determined to build a digital platform—a virtual island—where visitors could experience More's *Utopia* as an open text, and then open it up even further on their own. But before I get there, we need to return to the source.

MORE'S *UTOPIA*

When More wrote *Utopia* in 1515–1516 he was not the first writer to have imagined a better world. The author owed a heavy literary debt to Plato's *Republic*, wherein Socrates lays out his blueprint for a just society. But he was also influenced by the political and social imaginings of classic authors like Plutarch, Sallust, Tacitus, Cicero, and Seneca, all of whom an erudite Renaissance Humanist like More would have been on intimate terms. The ideal of a far-off land operating according to foreign, and often alluring, principles was also a stock-in-trade in the tales of travel popular at the time. The travelogues of Sir John Mandeville were bestsellers (albeit among a limited literate class) in the fourteenth century, and adventurer's tales, like those of the late fifteenth and early sixteenth-century explorer Amerigo Vespucci, were familiar to More. Most important, the Bible—the master text of More's European home—provided images of mythical-historical lands flowing with milk and honey, and glimpses of a world beyond where the lion lays down with the lamb. By the time More sat down to write his book envisioning alternative worlds was a well-worn literary tradition, but his *Utopia* literally named the practice. One need not have to read his book, or even know that such a book exists, to be familiar with the word, and "Utopia" has entered the popular lexicon to represent almost any positive ideal of a society. But, given how commonly the word is used and how widely it is applied, *Utopia* is an exceedingly curious book, and much less straightforward than one might think.

Utopia is actually two books, written separately and published together in 1516 (along with a great deal of ancillary material: maps, marginalia, and dedications contributed by members of Renaissance Europe's literary establishment). Book I is the story of More meeting and entering into a discussion with the traveler Raphael Hythloday; Book II is Hythloday's description of the land to which he has traveled—the Isle of Utopia. Book I of *Utopia* opens with More introducing himself as a character and taking on the role of narrator. He tells the reader that he has been sent to Flanders on a diplomatic mission for the king of England, and introduces us to his friend Peter Giles, who is living in Antwerp. All this is based in fact: More was sent on such a mission by Henry VIII in 1515, and Peter Giles, in addition to being the author's friend, was a well-known Flemish literary figure.

Soon, however, More mixes fiction into his facts by describing a meeting with Raphael Hythloday, "a stranger, who seemed past the flower of his age; his face was tanned, he had a long beard, and his cloak was hanging carelessly about him, so that, by his looks and habit, I concluded he was a seaman."[1] While the description is vivid and matter-of-fact, there are hints that this might not be the type of voyager who solely navigates the material plane.

Figure 1.1 Woodcut by Ambrosius Holbein for the 1518 Edition of Thomas More's Utopia.

Giles, for example, explains to More that Hythloday "has not sailed as a seaman, but as a traveler, or rather a philosopher."[2] Yet it is revealed a few lines later that the (fictional) traveler has been in the company of the (factual) explorer Amerigo Vespucci, whose party he left to venture off and discover the (fictional) Island of Utopia. This promiscuous mix of reality and fantasy sets the tone for *Utopia*. From the beginning we, the readers, are thrown off balance: Who and what should we take seriously?

The second book of *Utopia* begins with Raphael Hythloday taking over the role of narrator and, like the first book, opens with a detailed description of the setting in order to situate the reader. Unlike the real Flanders described by More in Book I, however, the location that Hythloday depicts is a purely imaginary space:

> The island of Utopia is in the middle two hundred miles broad, and holds almost at the same breadth over a great part of it, but it grows narrower towards both ends. Its figure is not unlike a crescent. Between its horns the sea comes in eleven miles broad, and spreads itself into a great bay, which is environed with land to the compass of about five hundred miles, and is well secured from winds. In this bay there is no great current; the whole coast is, as it were, one continued harbor, which gives all that live in the island great convenience for mutual commerce.[3]

Like the coordinates of the Garden of Eden—located at the mythical juncture of the real rivers Pison, Gihon, Hid'dekel, and Euphrates—this description lends a physical veracity to what is a fantasy, a technique that More employs throughout. After this physical description of the island, Hythloday begins his almost encyclopedic account of the customs and constitution of Utopia. Highlights include an elected government and priesthood, freedom of speech and religion, public health and education, an economy planned for the good of all, compassionate justice and little crime, the lack of private property and, perhaps most Utopian of all, no lawyers: "a sort of people whose profession it is to disguise matters and wrest the laws."[4]

The people who populate Utopia are kind and generous, and shoulder their responsibility for the general welfare as the natural order of things. They always have work, yet also enjoy a great deal of leisure, which they spend in discussion, music, or attending public lectures (alas, gambling, beer halls, and wine bars are unknown in Utopia). There is ideological indoctrination, to be sure, but even this is idealized: the Utopians begin each communal meal with a reading on a moral topic, "but it is so short that it is not tedious."[5] (Academics and ideologues take note!) The various cities of Utopia function in harmony with one another, and if one district has a surplus of crops or other goods, these are redirected toward cities which have a deficit, "so that indeed the whole island is, as it were, one family."[6]

At the root of Utopia, the source from which everything grows, is the community of property. This quality of the society is best described thus:

> [E]very house has both a door to the street and a back door to the garden. Their doors have all two leaves, which, as they are easily opened, so they shut of their own accord; and, there being no property among them, every man may freely enter into any house whatsoever.[7]

For "though no man has any thing, yet they are all rich."[8]

Utopia is More's sixteenth-century Europe turned upside-down. This inversion of the real is best illustrated in one of the few anecdotes that Hythloday narrates—a visit to the island by a group of foreign ambassadors. The Anemolians, as they are called, have never traveled to Utopia before, and are unfamiliar with the local customs. "[T]hey, being a vainglorious rather than a wise people, resolved to set themselves out with so much pomp that they should look like gods, and strike the eyes of the poor Utopians with their splendor."[9] Dressed for success, the Anemolian ambassadors wear cloth made from gold and drape heavy gold chains around their necks, while gold rings adorn their fingers and strings of gems and pearls hang from their caps.

But in Utopia, Hythloday tells us, such wealth and finery signify differently. Gold is what the chains and shackles of slaves are made from (for no matter how enlightened More was, he was still a man of his times and could not imagine a Utopia without slavery). Jewels are considered children's playthings: pretty to look at, but valued much as marbles or dolls are by us. Utopians craft their dinnerware from everyday clay and glass, saving their gold and silver to fashion implements for another part of the nutritional process: chamber pots ("O magnificent debasement of gold!" is written in the marginalia at this point in the text).[10] Ignorant of the Utopians as they are, the Anemolian ambassadors make their public appearance bedecked in their finery. The Utopians, confused, bow to the humblest and most simply dressed of the Anemolian party and ignore the leaders, who they believe to be slaves. Anticipating the truth-telling boy in Hans Christian Andersen's "The Emperor's New Clothes," a child, spying the ambassadors, calls out to his mother: "See that great fool, that wears pearls and gems as if he were yet a child!" To which the mother answers: "Hold your peace! This, I believe, is one of the ambassadors' fools."[11]

This anecdote, along with the rest of Hythloday's description, presents the world of the Utopians in such a way that the reader confronts these radical ideas as the norm to which their own world is an aberration. More naturalizes his imagined Utopia, making it "real." But what sort of reality is this? As many know, Utopia is a word made-up by More from the Greek words *ou* (not) and *topos* (place). It is a space which is, literally, *no-place*. Furthermore, the storyteller of this magic land is named Raphael Hythloday, or "Hythlodaeus" in the Latin in which More wrote. The root of this surname is the Greek *huthlos*, a word used frequently by Plato, meaning nonsense or idle talk. So here we are, being told the story of a place which is named out of existence, by a narrator who is named as unreliable. And these are just two of the countless paradoxes, enigmas, and jokes scattered throughout the text.

And so begins the debate among *Utopia* scholars for nearly five centuries: Is More's story of an idyllic society an earnest effort to suggest and promote such ideals, as the canonical—and Catholic—reading of Edward Surtz and J. H. Hexter might suggest? Or is the entirety of *Utopia* a satire, an exercise demonstrating the absurdity of proposing political, social and economic alternatives to the status quo, as revisionist scholars like Alistair Fox argue?[12]

There is suggestive evidence for More's sincerity. More is at pains to lend a sense of veracity to the story. He very clearly situates it within the context of his own—verifiable—trip to Flanders in 1515, and scatters the names of well-known contemporaries throughout the book: Peter Giles, Archbishop Morton, Amerigo Vespucci, and others. As you will remember, More provides painstakingly detailed descriptions of Utopia, beginning with Hythloday's account of the landscape of the island. And the first printings of *Utopia* contained an illustrated map of the nation, and Giles, More's friend and fellow "witness" to Hythloday's tale, supplied a Utopian alphabet.

Again and again More goes out of his way to try to persuade his readers that Utopia is a real place. In a prefatory letter from More to his (real) friend Giles included in the first editions the author asks his friend for help in remembering the *exact* length of a bridge that Hythloday mentions in his description. More recalls hearing that the bridge was half a mile, or 500 paces long, but fears he might be in error, because he also recalls "the river contains there not above three hundred paces in breadth."[13] More wants to get his facts right.

While it stretches credulity to suggest that More expected his audience to fully believe that Utopia is real, it is reasonable to argue that he uses fantasy to articulate political, economic, and religious alternatives he *really* believes in. For instance, Hythloday mentions in Book II that the Utopians, when told about Christianity, approved of the religion as it "seemed so favorable to that community of goods, which is an opinion so particular as was well as so dear to them; since they perceived that Christ and His followers lived by that rule."[14] More, a devout Christian who once studied for the priesthood and would later give his life to honor his beliefs, had every reason to be sincere about the community of goods described in Utopia. Given who he was and what he believed, it is exceedingly difficult to imagine More satirizing Jesus and his followers.

The surname of the narrator of Utopia, Hythloday, may translate as "speaker of nonsense," but his Christian name, Raphael, finds its genesis in the Archangel Raphael, who gives sight to the blind. *Raphael* Hythloday might therefore be recognized as a guide to help the reader see a greater truth. What obvious absurdities *Utopia* does contain—chamber pots made of precious metals, for example—could be understood as a way to throw into sharp relief the corruptions of contemporary Christendom. Less charitably, such silliness could be seen as a sort of political cover for airing heretical political and religious views. By salting his tale with absurdities, More can suggest these radical ideas yet at the same time politically distance himself from them. He has his cake and eats it too.

To sum up this perspective: More was serious about *Utopia*. He was earnest in his appreciation of the manners, customs, and laws of the Utopians, and used realism in order to convey a sense of genuine possibility. Utopia was meant to be experienced by the reader as a valid alternative to the real world in which they lived.

On the other hand, there is also evidence that More meant his *Utopia* to be read as a satire. In recent years, revisionist *Utopia* scholars have claimed that, far from being a sincere vision of the society we ought to have, the author used his imagined island as an extended argument for why such utopian visions are, literally, a joke. In addition to the destabilizing names given to the place and the narrator, More, in his description of the island of Utopia, makes attractive possibilities that he—given his personal, economic, political, and religious position in life—would be expected to be dead set against. He was a man, lawyer, property holder, future king's councilor, Lord Chancellor, and dogmatic defender of the faith, yet the island he describes has female equality, communal property, democratic governance, religious freedom, and no lawyers. This seems quite a contradiction. In this light, More's conscious use of the absurd in *Utopia* can be interpreted as undercutting the radical ideas advanced in his book, and the silliness of many of the customs and characteristics of Utopia taint any such idea of an ideal society. By inserting a political vision of an ideal world within a society that also uses chamber pots made of gold and silver, for instance, More effectively ridicules *all* political idealization.

The detailed descriptions of Utopian landmarks that give the account its sense of realism are likewise undermined by More's use of humor. In the same prefatory letter to Peter Giles in which he worries that he might not have his facts straight about the length of a bridge, More arrives at a solution to his dilemma: He asks his friend, "to talk with Hythloday, if you can face to face, or else write letters to him" so that in "my book, there may be neither anything be found that is untrue, neither anything be lacking which is true."[15] The humor here comes in the realization that Hythloday will never contradict anything More writes, because Hythloday is a fictional character; there will be no fact checking of *Utopia*, because there is no one to contact to check the facts. Approaching *Utopia* satirically changes the meaning of More's words. The tokens of veracity I describe above—the debate over the bridge, the Utopian alphabet, the maps, and so forth—far from being evidence for More's sincerity, can be seen from this perspective as supporting materials for one big prank.

But there are more than two sides to the story of *Utopia*. While good arguments for both the satirical and sincere interpretations of the text can be made, I believe this binary debate obfuscates rather than clarifies the meaning of More's work, and misses the political genius of *Utopia* entirely. The brilliance of More's *Utopia* is that it is simultaneously satirical *and* sincere, absurd *and* earnest, and it is through the combination of these seemingly opposite ways of presenting ideals that a more fruitful way of thinking about political imagination can start to take shape. It is the presentation of Utopia as *no-place*, and its narrator as *nonsense*, that creates a space for the reader's imagination to wonder what an alternative someplace might be like. In enabling this dialectical operation *Utopia* opens up Utopia, encouraging the reader to imagine one for themselves.

Utopia is no-place. Yet *Utopia*'s presentation—not only its copious claims to facticity, but the realism of the descriptions—gives the reader a world to imagine; that is, it is also *some-place*. It thus works as springboard for imagination. More is not telling us to simply think about a different social order, but instead conjures up a vision for us, drawing us into the alternative through characters, scenes, and settings in this phantasmagoric far-off land. We do not imagine an alternative abstractly, but inhabit it concretely, albeit vicariously. Through *Utopia* we are presented with a world wholly formed, like an architect's model or a designer's prototype. We experience a sense of radical alterity as we step inside of it and try it on for size. For the time of the tale's telling, we live in Utopia, its landscape seeming familiar and its customs becoming normal. This reorients our perspective. More provides us with a vision of another, better world.

And then destabilizes it.

More presents an alternative to his sixteenth-century Europe, which he then reveals to be a work of imagination. But the reader has been infected; another option has been shown. They cannot safely return to the assurances of their own present, as the naturalness of their world has been disrupted. As the opening lines of a brief poem attached to the first printings of *Utopia* read:

Will thou know what wonders strange be,
in the land that late was found?
Will thou learn thy life to lead,
by divers ways that godly be?[16]

Once an alternative—"divers ways that godly be"—has been imagined, staying where one is or to trying something else become options that demand attention and decision.

Yet the choice More offers is not an easy one. By disabling his own vision he keeps us from short-circuiting this imaginative moment into a fixed imaginary: a simple swapping of one image for another, one reality for another. More will not let us accept (or reject) his vision of the ideal society as the final destination. In another poem attached to the early editions, this one printed in the Utopian language and in the voice of the island itself, "Utopia" explains:

I one of all other without philosophy
Have shaped for many a philosophical city.[17]

In other words, Utopia does not have, nor does it provide, the reader a wholly satisfactory philosophy; its systems of logic, aesthetics, ethics, metaphysics, and epistemology are constantly undercut by its creator. But it is because the reader cannot satisfy themselves within the confines of Utopia that it can become "for many a philosophical city," a place that many can ponder and a space that makes room for all to think.

Here's how *Utopia* is meant to work with a reader, step by step:

1. I believe the world I live in is the only world possible.
2. I read *Utopia* and, through More's description, experience an alternative world.
3. I question that my world is the only world that is possible.
4. Utopia is better than my world and I want to live there.
5. More won't let me; he keeps insisting that it is No-Place.
6. I either have to go home to the world I know, knowing that something better has been imagined, and therefore wallow in despair, cynicism and bad faith, or. . .
7. I imagine a better world—a Utopia—for myself.

The difficulty with asking people to imagine "outside the box" is that, unaided, they will usually not. We may bend and shape the box, reveal its walls and pound against them, but our imagination is constrained by the tyranny of the possible. The problem with many social imaginaries is that they posit themselves as a realizable possibility. Their authors imagine a future or an alternative and present it as *the* future or *the* alternative. If accepted as a genuine social possibility, this claim leads to a number of not mutually exclusive results:

1. Brutalizing the present to bring it into line with the imagined future: Nazi genocide, Communist forced collectivization or, in this century, the apocalyptic terrorism of radical Islam.
2. Disenchantment as the future never arrives and the alternative is never realized: the Soviet Union post-Stalin or the consequent depression of the New Left after 1968.
3. A vain search for a new imaginary when the promised one fails to appear: the current revival of religious fundamentalism in the wake of the failure of secular alternatives to deliver a just society.
4. Living a lie: Stalin's "Socialism achieved" or "The American Dream."
5. Rejecting possibility altogether: dismissing Utopia, with a heartfelt distrust or an ironic wink, as a naïve impossibility.

But what if impossibility is incorporated into the social imaginary in the first place? This is exactly what More does. By positioning his imaginary someplace as no-place, he escapes the problems that typically haunt political imaginaries. Yes, the alternatives he describes are sometimes absurd but this conscious absurdity is what keeps *Utopia* from being a singular and authoritative narrative—that is, a closed act of imagination to be either accepted or rejected. By creating an alternative reality and simultaneously undermining it, he encourages the reader not be taken in by the fantasy. It is hard to fool someone with a lie if they already know it is one. This curious state of belief and not belief, being and not being, a place that is also no-place, is what gives *Utopia* its power to stimulate imagination. Between these poles an opening is created for the reader of *Utopia* to imagine, What if?

"What if?" is *the* Utopian question, one which functions both negatively and positively. The question throws us into an alternative future: *What if* there was only common property? But because we still inhabit the present, we also are forced to look back and ask: How come we have private property here and now? Utopia insists that we contrast its image with the realities of our own society, comparing one to the other, stimulating judgment and reflection. This is its critical moment. But this critical reflection is not mere refusal. That is, it is not caught in the parasitical dependency of being wed to the very system it calls into question, for its interlocutor is not only a society that one wants to tear down, but also a vision of a world that one would like to build. (This is what distinguishes the "What if?" of Utopia from the same question posed by dystopias.) Utopian criticism functions not as an end in itself, but as a break with what is for a departure toward something new. By asking "What if?" we can simultaneously criticize and imagine, imagine and criticize, and thereby begin to escape the binary politics of negating critique on the one hand and blind faith on the other.

At the end of his account of the fanciful island, Raphael Hythloday, leader of the blind and speaker of nonsense, tells More (and us) that Utopia, because of the plans adopted and the structural foundations laid, is "like to be of great continuance."[18] Indeed it will continue, for the very plan and structure of More's *Utopia* makes it a generative text, one that guarantees that imagination does not stop when the author has finished writing and the book is published. All texts are realized and continuously re-realized by those who experience them, and in this way they are forever rewritten, but More went to special pains to ensure that his imaginative act would not be the last word. Lest the reader find themselves too comfortable in this other world he has created, the author goes about unsettling his alternative society, building with one hand while disassembling with the other, fashioning a Utopia that must be engaged dialectically. *Utopia*, moving metaphors from one medium to another, functions as source code, providing the core of what can, and must, be modified by the reader in order to create a functioning Utopian program (for on its own, it continually crashes).

There is a famous passage in the Bible that those invested in political imagination like to cite. It is from Proverbs, 29:18, and the King James Version begins like this: "Where there is no vision, the people perish . . ." Usually it is only this phrase that is remembered, yet the full line continues thus: ". . . but he that keepeth the law, happy is he."[19] It is the passage in its entirety that reveals the double-edged sword of political imagination. Utopic imagination is necessary: it gives people something to believe in and hope for. Yet that moment of imagination will—and, for the authors and translators of the Bible, must—become law to be followed if a new world is to be built. In other words, what starts out as one person or a small group's creative inspiration becomes everyone's program to follow, everyone's box to be contained within. This is the Utopian history from which we are desperately trying to awake: communism, fascism, and now neoliberalism and radical Islamism. Each one starts out as imagination; each becomes law. It appears an inescapable trap.

But there is a way out: the vision, and the attendant law, must be one that can never be fixed or stabilized. This is what *Utopia* promises: imagined alternatives that insist on remaining imaginary: no-place. By envisioning impossibilities Utopia creates an opening to ask "What If?" without closing down this free space by seriously answering "This is what!" With such visions, the future imagined can never be fixed. There will never be a moment when Utopia can be definitively declared. These utopian visions are something we have imagined, and thus can re-imagine at will. Utopia is No-Place, and therefore it is left up to all of us to find it.

Utopia is not a plan, but neither is it a prank. It is a *prompt*.[20]

OPEN UTOPIA

This idea and ideal of Utopia as a prompt stayed with me after I returned from Russia. Facing a sabbatical year, and freed by tenure from the constraints of publish or perish, I decided to experiment with More's *Utopia.* As ingenuous as he was in engineering his imagination machine, More was limited by the cutting-edge communications technology of his day: the book. He may have stimulated his reader's imagination, but each reader confronted the book alone in their reading chair. While the reader's imaginings may have been fruitful, the solitary experience of reading and the unidirectional flow of information inherent in analog print communications meant there were limited possibilities for imagination to be generated, collected, and built upon. And since Utopia is, or ought to be collectively imagined and collaboratively created (for the most horrific Utopias have been the master plans of individuals or small cliques) I set myself the task of figuring out how to open up *Utopia* even further. Coming five centuries after More I had access to a communications technology that More did not, namely, the computer. As a tool, networked computers allow for bidirectional flow of communications, multi-person collaboration, and appendable archiving. In brief, the perfect platform for opening up *Utopia*. And so, in 2011, funded by a Kickstarter campaign, I began building what would become TheOpenUtopia.org.

As a primary tenet of More's *Utopia* was common property, my first task was to bring More's book into the public domain. Luckily, after five hundred years of being in print, finding a source out of copyright was not difficult. As Utopia was originally printed in Latin, I used the 1684 English translation by Gilbert Burnet, the Bishop of Salisbury, for the bulk of the text. Although this translation can sound a bit stilted to modern ears, it is the one used in the copyright-free Project Gutenberg text, and thus, out of respect for this early attempt to make an open Utopia, the one I used as the basis of Book I and Book II. Many of the supplementary letters that surrounded early editions (and give hints to the readers as to how to approach the text) I found lucidly translated in an 1895 Claredon Press edition, also out of copyright. The remaining letters and the marginalia notes on the main text I had specially translated from the original Latin text by the young Classics scholar C. Jacob Butera. With a complete text now assembled, I licensed it under Creative Commons. Next, I needed a platform on which to make this text available. Using free and open source software (Ubuntu, a Linux OS; OpenOffice word processing program; and the WordPress blogging platform) I created a website and made the complete text of *Utopia* available for free download in pdf, e-pub, txt and odt (open document) formats.

Thomas More's *Utopia* was Open! But all I had really done was transform text on a page to text on a screen. I hadn't really opened up the text to new ways of imagining.

From the very beginning, *Utopia* was more than mere words on a page: the first editions included fanciful maps and a facsimile of a Utopian alphabet. Continuing and furthering this tradition, I assembled a gallery of Utopian-themed art on the site. These illustrations range from all the original woodcut maps, to comic book covers (Rick Griffin's very trippy, 1960s era, *Man from Utopia*) to snapshots of street signs pointing the way to towns called Utopia. And, as visitors to the site have the opportunity to send in their own found or created "art," this visual archive is ever-expanding. From a gallery of still images it was a small step to creating an archive of utopian videos, including early Soviet science-fiction films, earnest and satirical looks at the "world of tomorrow," and documentation of "guerilla futures" enacted by artistic activists. Here too, visitors can suggest videos to be added.

I was also interested in enabling a very old form of communications: orality. Gathering some actor friends, I began recording readings of *Utopia* and then posting these on the site for people to listen to. (These recordings, incidentally, led to an interesting discovery. While reciting a poem in the text written in the language of the Utopians, a university colleague in Classics who I had recruited for the task broke out laughing. Confused, I asked him what was so funny. He explained that one of the words in this made-up Utopian language—itself a mash-up of Greek and Latin—was essentially unpronounceable. Yet another joke by More for his classically educated sixteenth-century readership.)

Well and good, but not good enough. To facilitate collective and collaborative imagination I needed to do more than merely post materials up online for people to—individually—download and read, see, watch, or listen to. I looked around to see what digital platforms existed that might enable non-individualized and evolving knowledge production. I didn't have far to look: Wikipedia. On Wikipedia knowledge is transformed from something that is, to something that is always being built, transformed, revised: never stable, always fluid: protean. This is not something hidden, but part of the presentation itself, with each Wikipedia entry topped by tabs revealing the article, discussion, history and "edit this page." Each entry is the result of collaborative imagination. Best of all, Wikipedia is a platform that many people use and understand.

With Wikipedia as a template I created "Wikitopia," a wiki devoted to collectively and collaboratively imagining and writing Utopias. I began with a "stub," a bare-bones entry to which others might edit, add to, and revise. For the content of my stub I selected short passages from More's *Utopia*, dividing them up under categories like Geography, History, Political Structure, Social Structure, Property, Wealth, Sex and Domestic Relations, and so on. I then opened this "definition" of Utopia up to public editing by any registered user (user registration being necessary to thwart spammers). Following More's own example, I also wanted to free people from their dependency upon a master text and provide a space for them to imagine on their own. To facilitate this, I allowed users to create their own pages on Wikitopia, where they could describe and define their own Utopia.

Users created Utopias like *Alberto*, an imaginary society "established in 1950 as a government-sanctioned community within the United States dedicated towards scientific innovation"; *Kernowtopia*, a mythical intentional community in Cornwall which, in the near future, secedes from the United Kingdom (Kernow being the Cornish word for Cornwall); and *Masters of the All*, a truly strange, first-person literary immersion into an alternate world. These, and other, user-generated Utopias, organized in a "Your Wikitopia" sidebar on the main page, are open to visitors to read, be inspired by . . . and, of course, revise and edit.

When the first edition of *Utopia* was published in 1516 it included copious marginal notes, some profound, others silly, and most likely contributed by More's friend and coconspirator in the Utopia project, Peter Giles. Since then, with the exception of a few scholarly editions, the practice of reproducing marginalia has fallen off. I wanted to restart the tradition of marginalia—and open up the practice. With help from the Institute for the Future of the Book, I created a "Social Book" of Utopia. Social Book is a program (full disclosure: it is not open source) with which readers can comment upon an original text, highlighting a word or a passage, and then creating their own marginal notes. These notes can then be viewed by other readers who can, in turn, comment upon those comments and contribute their own. It is akin to a reading discussion group online. The community of readers commenting upon the text can be as small as one: the reader herself, or it might be the size of a typical class, or even as large as the entire universe of users, depending

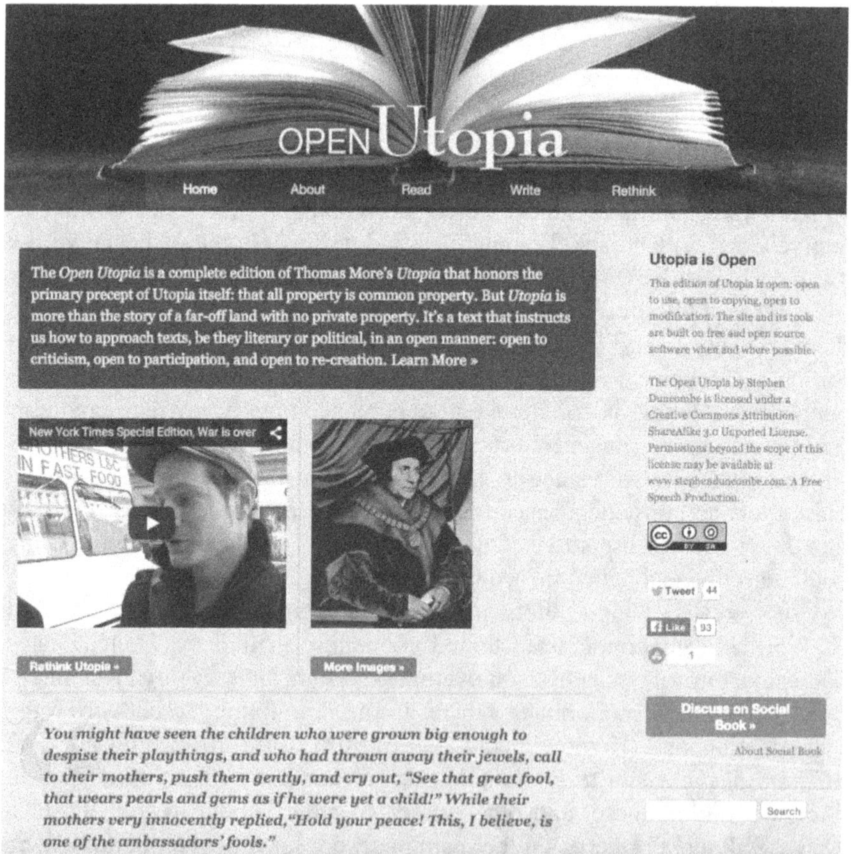

Figure 1.2 Home Page of the Open Utopia Website.

upon the groups the reader—now also writer—decides to create and join. With the implementation of Social Book, I decided I was done.

On December 5, 2012, Open Utopia went live.

SOME-PLACE

People loved *the idea* of Open Utopia. Within months of its launch it had been written about in the *Chronicle of Higher Education* and *Public Books,* and mentioned in *Education Week*, *Social Media Week*, *Tech Crunch*, and the *Walker Art Magazine*. It had even been picked up by blogs overseas.[21] I was asked to speak about Open Utopia at several academic forums on "digital humanities," and on the local public radio station, WNYC. [22] Compared to the largely silent reception of most of my other academic projects, Open Utopia was a smashing success. . . . As an idea. In practice things moved a great deal slower. The first group of visitors to discover Open Utopia were spammers, and soon Wikitopia was clogged with bogus pages hawking virility medicines rather than describing utopias (though one might argue that these, too, represented a certain fantasy ideal). With the help of a computer security expert these "early adopters" were kept at bay, and the next wave of explorers arrived. These were the curious who would browse the site, read a few pages, look at a few pictures, and then hurry on to the next virtual world yet to be explored on the web. These visitors didn't seem very interested in building a new Utopia through collective imagination and collaborative creation; they were largely there to consume: a text, an image, another mediated experience.

My dream of an autonomous community of creators of Utopia had not come to fruition. It seemed—as I, in a dark moment, said to the *Chronicle* reporter—that I had created a tool for job that didn't need to be done. Perhaps, I thought, there is a mismatch between the experience of the book, with its demands for individualized linear thinking and long-term concentration, and the "powerful infidel heteroglassia" (to use a term of Donna Haraway's) of the web: the multitasking, searching, forwarding, glancing, swapping, and sharing. Experiments like mine: transposing books online—even if it they are open, re-writable, with videos and sounds and images—were, perhaps, a move in the wrong direction. Maybe More had opened up *Utopia* as far as it could go, and books should stay as books. Many people—including the reviewer for *Public Books*—admitted that in order to really engage with the text they downloaded and printed a copy; hedging my bets I had also simultaneously released my edition of *Utopia* as an old-fashioned, paper and ink book. I concluded that a more generative use of my time would have been exploring, encouraging, and developing entirely new forms of collaborative creation that our digital age is engendering rather than re-tooling an archaic medium.[23] I had lost my way to Utopia.

And then something happened: new Utopias started popping up on Wikitopia. Only a handful, to be sure, and one of them bore the signs of an assigned class project, but they were there. Visitors had also begun editing the "stub" on the main page of Wikitopia. Many of the edits were humorous or absurd, for instance, the inclusion of "Knightly Day" because "The people of Utopia adore the actress Kiera Knightly. They view her as a deity." But then again, there was plenty of humor and absurdity in More's original text, recall the golden toilets.

Participation in Open Utopia's Social Book came on even slower. A few comments showed up in the margins here, and a few there, but most of them were from friends who I had cajoled into participating. A class on Utopia at the New School used it as a resource and the numbers of comments briefly shot up . . . and then dropped off. Here too, it seemed as if the very form of the book, whether ink on a page or characters on a screen, retarded re-creation. Confronted with the Master Text, even if that master text was one that undermines its own authority, readers bow in silent submission. And then, a year or so after my initial launch, I received a call from Bob Stein, the creator of the Social Book platform. He asked if I had been following what was happening on my site. Rather sheepishly, I admitted had not made a visit to Open Utopia in over a month. Getting off the phone I pointed my browser to the site and opened up the Social Book edition of *Utopia*.

There were thousands of comments! As I became a more dutiful steward, and revisited Open Utopia more frequently, I watched these numbers grow, as nearly every line in the book was annotated with, at most recent count, nearly 2500 comments. Some comments are erudite and philosophical: commenting on the exacting records kept in Utopia. One reader wrote: "Interesting that their past is recorded instead of remembered and retold. Archiving is indicative of self-consciousness. Makes me wonder, what creates this kind of perfection?" Some are factual queries aimed at the community, as another reader, pondering Utopia's architecture asked: "Why are the roofs flat?" And other comments are more personal and idiosyncratic: "Working with Amy everyday is my Utopia." It had taken a long time, but settlers had arrived at Open Utopia and were building their own meanings.

My experience with Open Utopia re-taught me the lesson I first learned when reading *Utopia* in preparation for my lectures in Moscow: Utopia is never complete. (And ones that claim to be are to be avoided at all costs.) Marginal comments are still being added to Social Book, and every once in a while a new entry or edit appears in Wikitopia. Periodically, someone will suggest a new image or video to add to the archive. And I still have not completed the recordings of Utopia; I probably never will. I like that

TheOpenUtopia.org is not done and dusted and sitting on a shelf. It's still open.

Keeping Utopia open, as a project continually worked on yet never completed, *is* a success. It's not the sort of success we are taught to believe in: a finished product, an accomplishment ticked off, a destination discovered, but it is a definition of success at the heart of any radical project: the constant, collective struggle to make a better world. Utopia is no-place: a world where we can never arrive, but as great, and late, Uruguayan poet-journalist Eduardo Galeano understood, it is still good for something. He writes of Utopia:

> She's on the horizon. . . . I go two steps, she moves two steps away. I walk ten steps and the horizon runs ten steps ahead. No matter how much I walk, I'll never reach her. What good is utopia? That's what: it's good for walking.[24]

Galeano, better than most, more beautifully than all, understood the importance of keeping Utopia on the horizon, forever incomplete, and always open.

www.theopenutopia.org

NOTES

1. Stephen Duncombe, ed. *Open Utopia*, by Thomas More (Wivenhoe/New York/Port Watson: Minor Compositions/Autonomedia, 2012), 29.
2. Ibid., 30.
3. Ibid., 83.
4. Ibid., 147.
5. Ibid., 107.
6. Ibid., 110.
7. Ibid., 90.
8. Ibid., 185.
9. Ibid., 115.
10. Ibid., 113.
11. Ibid., 116.
12. Edward Surtz and J. H. Hexter, eds. *Complete Works of St Thomas More, vol. IV, Utopia* (New Haven: Yale University Press, 1965); Alastair Fox, *Utopia: An Elusive Vision* (New York: Twayne/Macmillan, 1993).
13. Duncombe, *Open Utopia*, 19.
14. Ibid., 167.
15. Ibid., 20.
16. Ibid., 13.
17. Ibid., 8.
18. Ibid., 189.

19. *The Bible*, Authorized King James Version (Oxford: Oxford University Press, 1998), 748.

20. For a more complete discussion of More's text see my Introduction to *Utopia*. Duncombe, *Open Utopia,* ix–lxv.

21. Jennifer Howard, "With 'Social Reading,' Books Become Places to Meet," *The Chronicle of Higher Education*, November 26, 2012, accessed online, np; Henry S. Turner, "Books, not Moocs," *Public Books*, April 2013, accessed online, np; Catherine A. Cardno, "Slotting 'Social Reading' Into the Classroom," *Education Week*, November 29, 2012, accessed online, np; Lisa Chau, "Interview with Stephen Duncombe, SMWNYC Panelist for Literature Unbound," *Social Media Week*, February 8, 2012, accessed online, np; Jordan Crook, "NYU Professor Open Sources 'Utopia' By Sir Thomas More," *Tech Crunch*, October 2012, accessed online, np; Sarah Peters, "Utopia Is No Place, An Interview with Stephen Duncombe," *Walker Art Magazine*, August 27, 2012, accessed online, np. Overseas blogs include Mouhamadou Diallo, "The Open Utopia," *ENS de Lyon*, December 13, 2013, np; Julien Helmlinger, "Quand l'Utopie de Thomas More devient lieu de rencontre avec Open Utopia," *ActuaLitte*, November 30, 2012, np; Paula Simoes, "Web Readings Weekly Roundup," *EuroMACHS*, April 19, 2011, np.

22. WNYC, "Open Utopia," The Brian Lehrer Show, aired October 16, 2012.

23. For my next digital project I did exactly this. A part of the research mission of the Center for Artistic Activism, and working with Jacques Servin of the Yes Men, I created an open access, user-generated database of case studies of creative activism: Actipedia.org

24. Eduardo Galeano, *Walking Words* (New York: Norton, 1995); reprinted in *The Nation*, June 12, 1995, 829.

BIBLIOGRAPHY

The Bible, Authorized King James Version. Oxford: Oxford University Press, 1998.

Fox, Alastair. *Utopia: An Elusive Vision*. New York: Twayne/Macmillan, 1993.

Galeano, Eduardo. *Walking Words*. New York: Norton, 1995.

More, Thomas, *Open Utopia*. Stephen Duncombe, ed. Wivenhoe/New York/Port Watson: Minor Compositions/Autonomedia, 2012. On the web at http://theopenutopia.org/full-text/

Surtz, Edward and J. H. Hexter, eds. *Complete Works of St Thomas More, vol. IV, Utopia*. New Haven: Yale University Press, 1965.

Chapter 2

Civic Imagination and a Useless Map

Catherine D'Ignazio

The use of street names for commemorative purposes is instrumental in transforming the urban environment into a virtual political setting.

—*Maoz Azaryahu, The power of commemorative street names, 1996*

A publication of this order allows no scope for the play of the imagination, being a simple exponent of facts.

—*Boyd's Lancaster Directory (An early index of street names & numbers), 1857, as quoted in Rose-Redwood, 2008*

I want to rename 'Wood St' to 'Boodle St' because it's my dog's name.

—*Participant, The City Formerly Known as Cambridge, 2006*

In 2008, a group called the Institute for Infinitely Small Things published a useless map. From 2006–2008, the Institute held "renaming parties" where members of the public were invited to propose new names for any public place in Cambridge, Massachusetts. These submissions formed the basis of the "useless" map—so named because it would be hopeless to use it to navigate the city of Cambridge. What in Google Maps is called the "Cambridge Common" is referred to on the map as "That Place Where Freaks Gather to Hula Hoop and Do Other Circus Tricks." Harvard Square is "Cash Money Land" and Main Street is "Lafayette Under Repair St." Many places on the map are named after dogs and boyfriends and babies. I am the Director of the Institute for Infinitely Small Things[1] and this is an accounting of the provenance, process and reception of the map of *the City Formerly Known as Cambridge.*

In this essay, I will show why inviting people to rename public places in Cambridge was not merely an exercise in supreme silliness. It was also an exercise in cultivating civic imagination and practicing civic power in a semi-fictional and bounded scenario. Street names are infinitely small things—sites of historical and political power made manifest in the landscape and typically regarded as background. In making *the City Formerly Known as Cambridge*, people "tried on" the role of author in relation to their everyday landscape and reflected on history, power, and their favorite snacks in the process. I posit that these experiences of "civic art" (a term defined later in the text) build speculative collective capacity by helping people dream together in a place where the stakes are low and the potential for fun is high. While the results may be idiosyncratic, personal, even useless (as the title of this paper claims), the real utility of such endeavors is to train the collective muscle for civic dreaming so that it can be mobilized when it truly matters. Cultivating civic imagination is about extending the invitation to be an author of the world and to make new worlds in the process.

ABOUT THE INSTITUTE

The Institute for Infinitely Small Things is a performance research group that sometimes exists. We are brought into being on certain special occasions by a passion for spatial justice and rolling around in public space and a shared ethos that changing things together is the only way to truly study them. We are artists and computer programmers, architects and filmmakers, curators and students, accountants, and children. There are about 25 of us counting by an infrequently used mailing list but a project may be done in the Institute's name by as little as 0 or as many as all. By "infinitely small things," we do not mean the little odds and ends like cigarette butts that hide between urban sidewalk slabs. Rather, we mean the social and political tiny things that permeate the public spaces of our everyday lives. They are those things typically designated as "background" and regarded as neutral, natural and inevitable which nevertheless hold an enormous amount of history (and thus inequity), politics (and thus contestation), and social life (and thus promise for fun).

STREET NAMES ARE INFINITELY SMALL THINGS

Commemorative street names—those that honor historical, mythical figures or events versus simply being numbers—are a very good example of infinitely small things. Street names are "ostensibly visible, quintessentially mundane, and seemingly obvious."[2] They are in the background of our lived experience of the city (when we are not lost) and literally the background on Google Maps when we are lost. Artist Michael Rakowitz notes that the quickest way to forget someone is to name a public place after them "so that their name disappears into an address, into an architecture."[3] Azaryahu calls this "semantic displacement" and emphasizes how there is a continuous erosion of the historical meaning of a name in favor of the idiosyncratic, personal meanings of place inscribed by people conducting their everyday lives in a city. Our hypothesis is that everyone reading this chapter lives on a street with a name and that most do not know where the name comes from. Please fill out our survey at http://goo.gl/forms/qHjWa1koaI to tell us if we are wrong about this.

Street names would seem to be mundane facts. But by whom and for whom? And since when? Prior to the Revolutionary War, for example, "very few streets in Manhattan had street signs posted at intersections, and the population relied chiefly on shop signs, descriptive designations, and local familiarity when navigating through the city's streets."[4] Names, such as they existed, were vernacular and related to the particularity of a spot, for example, "Take a right at the red house." One does not need names for navigation until one has *strangers* in the landscape.[5] With the increased mobility of people and things, street names became systematized in the nineteenth century in the United States and institutionalized by the early twentieth century. Azaryahu calls this the "city-text"[6] and Rose-Redwood details this as the process of rationalization of the urban landscape through the production of "legible" urban spaces.[7] There is high economic value to legible spaces, particularly for global capitalist markets of goods and services. Legibility is a value that we in the Global North have now internalized, equate with modernity and bring as "development" to the Global South.[8] The project of naming and numbering urban space in order to make it rational and legible is one that continues today through increasingly sophisticated and ubiquitous Google everything, GIS, satellite imagery, and crowdsourced geographic information which make everything from social use to environmental data geocoded, rational and legible.[9]

The tricky thing about the systematized, legible city is that it is primarily the official government administrators that mold the symbolic infrastructure of the urban landscape. "The administrative act of naming streets is an example of the appropriation of the public domain by official agencies that have specific political agendas."[10] These agendas may not be nefarious but they are instrumental in "substantiating the ruling sociopolitical order,"[11] which is to say that those histories which are officially sanctioned, widely recognized, and not troublesome or contestational will be commemorated as places where others will not. As such, everyday personal geography is conflated with official, some might say, "hegemonic" history. And it is precisely in this conflation of history and banal everyday life, a "low-voltage interaction" from a casual encounter, that "enables an official version of history to be incorporated into spheres of social life which seem to be totally detached from political contexts or communal obligations, and to be integrated into intimate realms of human interactions and activities."[12] The background character—the infinitely smallness—of street names is precisely their power.

Yet street names are not always background, as anyone who has lived in Soweto, Berlin, Bucharest, or Moscow can tell you. Street names may especially come to the foreground of our collective attention upon the shifts of power such as the fall of Communism that usher in a drastic change in worldview that is subsequently made manifest in the landscape by the new regime in power. While most municipal names change slowly and incrementally, these are the cases where the relationship between place names and political, economic, and military power is most clear. Indeed, it was the experience of one Institute member from Podgoriça, Montenegro, that led to the seed of the idea for *the City Formerly Named as Cambridge*. He noted that all of the names in Cambridge were "Anglo-Saxon" and he would like to introduce more consonants into them (as his mother tongue adores consonants and has words like *smrt*). This started the initial investigation into the names of public places in Cambridge—where are the names from? Who are they commemorating?

PLACE NAMES IN CAMBRIDGE, MASSACHUSETTS

Who would you think names in Cambridge, Massachusetts, commemorate? It is very likely what you would guess: white guys, lots of them, mostly associated with Harvard. Figure 2.1 shows a small sample of the area around Harvard Square with important streets noted with their corresponding image of the white man for whom they are named. Indeed, if you scan the excellent online historical reference compiled by librarian Christopher Hail[13] for the history of street names in Cambridge you will find that the only streets that do not honor white men honor trees,[14] other cities,[15] or local topography.[16]

Here it may be interesting to take up a thought experiment. If you were an alien anthropologist and wanted to use the names of public places in cities to learn about the people on this planet, what might you use them for? It certainly would not be for learning about the current demographics of a city. In certain neighborhoods of Cambridge, 35 percent of the population is African-American. There are significant Brazilian, Haitian, Hispanic, and Ethiopian immigrant populations. And yet, there are no place names that commemorate these histories. One of the few place names for a non-White/Anglo person that we located was Cardinal Medeiros Avenue, named for the Portuguese

Figure 2.1 The White Men of Cambridge, Massachusetts.

American who served as the Archbishop of Boston for many years. And the funny-slash-not-funny story about that street is that the Massachusetts Alliance of Portuguese Speakers worked really hard to make that name happen. When the City came to install the street sign, it turned out they had actually spelled his name wrong and had to send it back for refabrication.

Another interesting story is the case of the Maria L. Baldwin School in North Cambridge. Until 2002, it was named the Agassiz School after Jean Louis Rodolphe Agassiz, a professor of zoology and geology at Harvard. He was also a racist who fought hard to keep Irish and Jewish students out of Harvard and expounded the idea that the human races were created with unequal attributes.[17] After learning more about the origins of his school's name, ninth-grader Nathaniel Vogel spearheaded a successful campaign to change the school's name to honor the first African-American principal of the school, Maria L. Baldwin.[18] After a lively debate, the School Committee voted for the renaming.[19] Numerous other places in Cambridge, including the surrounding neighborhood, remain named after Louis Agassiz.

In Cambridge, the names of public places tell the alien anthropologist about the make-up of the ruling class or the "default citizen"—they are white, they are men, they are of Anglo-European descent, and they have money and history on their side. In this, the names of Cambridge public places render natural the authorized, official version of history[20] and provide for "the intersection of hegemonic ideological structures with the spatial practices of everyday life."[21] This particular city-text does not necessarily incorporate the social reality of a large percentage of its current inhabitants, nor of its former inhabitants (as we must imagine that around 50 percent even in colonial times were likely women, not to mention immigrants, minorities and people of color). In order to officially change a name in Cambridge—and the process is similar in other US cities—you must go through the City Engineer's office and collect signatures of all of the abutters and indicate whether or not they agree to the change. Then, the City Council will vote on the new name. The only stipulation is that you may not name a street after a living person. So part of the reason that the names of public places do not change in step with the changes in population is that the process of gathering political will for an actual name change is somewhat difficult and time-consuming. An individual or community group needs social capital, time, and possibly financial capital to effect this kind of "authorship" on the landscape. And there is the weight of history to consider—one had better be completely sure of the name if it's going into the public record.

CIVIC IMAGINATION AND THE BEGINNINGS OF BEGINNINGS

But contesting space need not be so onerous nor happen so infrequently. Before arriving at a new name for anything, the Institute felt a broader, more open space of reflection, conversation, and contestation about names was possible. For *the City Formerly Known as Cambridge*, we wanted to challenge the names in Cambridge, and the narrative of the "default citizen" that they represented, by radically opening up the space of authorship. We were drawing specifically on our knowledge of and participation in open source communities such as Wikipedia[22] and Open Street Map,[23] where individuals contribute volunteered information to create a comprehensive system. The key difference is that we were not interested in mapping "what is" but in mobilizing what Henry Jenkins calls the "civic imagination" to create a collective vision of what could be. Jenkins et al. explain the concept of the civic imagination as ". . . the capacity to imagine alternatives to current social, political or economic conditions. One cannot change the world unless you can imagine what a better world might look like, and too often, our focus on contemporary problems makes it impossible to see beyond immediate constraints. One also can't change the world until one can imagine oneself as an active political agent."[24]

There are therefore two key components to the civic imagination. The first is that it remains in the speculative realm and is defined by the capacity to develop creative *potential, future alternatives* to current conditions. While many critical projects step back to assess injustice or inequity after the fact, projects that engage civic imagination represent generative contributions[25] that offer new ways to approach a problem together. The corollary to this first part of the definition is that the people undertaking it must have an understanding of the human-designed, historically contingent, highly malleable nature of the world. Things that seem inevitable—street names, advertising, gasoline, mass incarceration—must become denaturalized from the everyday environment and converted into objects of direct contemplation, action and design. The infinitely small things must be identified. More than anything, this is a shift in individual and collective perception of the world. It is not about the dreaded "raising awareness," a terrible, patronizing turn-of-phrase if one ever existed, but about "changing the frame," as Ivan Sigal, director of the Global Voices network, has asserted.[26]

The second component of the definition centers on empowerment. You cannot change the world until you can imagine yourself as an active political agent. Nor, we would add, until you *have hope* and *personally care* enough about a collective issue to make it worth changing. This shift—from apathy, cynicism or ironic distance to designerly investment—is possibly the most critical for cultivating civic imagination. Civic authorship is a muscle and it needs to be activated, nourished and trained.

The training of this collective civic capacity to dream is where "civic art" comes in. There is a long history of scholarship that shows that civic activity can be a gateway to political engagement.[27,28] But there has been far less research on intentionally cultivating civic imagination, and by extension political hope, personal agency, and design thinking about social and political concerns, as a gateway to civic activity. I would assert that this is, or could be, the realm of civic art. Gyorgy Kepes[29] and Doris Sommer[30] are two scholar-practitioners who have attempted to articulate why we need civic art and given compelling examples. You might see this as akin to the emerging field of "social practice art"—a subgenre of art that renewed the interest in the intersection of art, politics and everyday life for practitioners, theorists, funders and educators. Social practice art often takes "the encounter" as the medium through which art unfolds. But evaluation of this kind of work as well as the relationship of the artist to the community remain open questions.[31] Where social practice takes any kind of social relations as fodder for art (and often appropriates and aestheticizes those relations in problematic ways in the process), civic art is more exclusively concerned with processes of governance, dissent and protest, citizen participation in political processes, and the production of collective, explicitly political imaginaries.

In *Dream: Re-imagining Progressive Politics in an Age of Fantasy*,[32] Steven Duncombe makes the case that fantasy, dreaming and imagination are not peripheral to the business of politics and the public realm but constitutive of it. These highly human proclivities are *the beginnings of the beginnings* of new worlds. While traditional political advocacy, movement activism and community organizing certainly have their place, there is an opportunity to think more carefully and intentionally about cultivating civic imagination in order to include more people and perspectives in the civic process. But the beginnings of beginnings of new worlds are fragile, provisional, experimental, and it is necessarily so. Cultivating civic imagination is about offering people a low-stakes opportunity to try on a new kind of authorship, to perform a new kind of political agency, and to envision a new (possibly silly, personal, trivial, useless) world. And this is exactly what we did in Cambridge in relation to the names of public places.

How it worked

The renamings took place in a series of thirteen "renaming parties" staged in different locations around the city. At each site, the Institute erected our large white tent, a banner that said "The Institute for Infinitely Small Things" and set up two renaming stations along with a research library where people

Figure 2.2 The Institute Staged 13 Renaming Parties Across the City of Cambridge. Photo by Lino Ribeiro.

could review the history of names in Cambridge. Each event was carefully planned in conjunction with another event or reason people would be present. We were seeking what Kim Pruesse calls "the accidental audience."[33] We held renaming parties at Farmer's Markets, museums, and local festivals. We sought to stage renaming parties in places of leisure and recreation where people would have time and incentive to stop, be curious, and spend a couple minutes talking with us.

The experience of renaming worked as follows: Participants would be drawn in either by the large banner with the Institute's name or possibly by one of the Institute members asking them if they would like to rename Cambridge. An Institute member would explain that we were seeking to rename every public place in the city of Cambridge. Together they would look up the street the person lived on in our printed copy of Hail's directory of Cambridge street names.[34] For example, if you looked up Cushing Street in the binder you see that it was established in 1691 as a through street without a name that linked Belmont Street and Huron Ave. In 1847, it was named Cushing Street for John Perkins Cushing. At this point in the renaming experience the Institute member and the participant might likely check Wikipedia or one of the numerous books we had in our library for some history of Cushing. It turns out he was a merchant, opium smuggler and conservatory founder from the nineteenth century. He was very well-liked by women and the town of Belmont (adjacent to Cambridge) is named after his lavish estate. As Hail's history of buildings and street names is quite detailed, the participant might even be able to see the history of their particular building/address in the historical record.

After some discussion and possibly looking up some other names together, the Institute member might again offer to the participant to rename a place in Cambridge. The participant might browse the books, maps, and prior renamings contributed by others for a little longer in order to make a decision. Once they determined which location they wished to rename, the Institute member gave them a map where they marked the location with a star. The participant then filled out a renaming form and noted the old name of the place, the new name and the reason they wanted to bestow the new name.

People would often want to rename the same place. As the Institute did not want to curate any of the names on the map, we devised an economic system. The first name was free, that is, if no one had named the street that you wanted then you did not have to pay any money to bestow your name. If the next person came along and wanted to rename that same place they had to pay us a quarter ($0.25). The next person that came along would have to pay $0.50, and so on. As in real life, those who paid more money got their name on the map. Most places were not renamed more than once or twice, but Massachusetts Avenue was renamed 10 times and it's going "price" by the end of the project was $2.50.[35]

DESIGN GOALS FOR A SPECULATIVE CIVIC CONVERSATION

There are several conscious design decisions to note from the above description of the experience of the project. These translate into three design goals that we had for the project. First of all, we wanted to create a *fun, light-hearted, and playful* experience. This is what Duncombe calls an "ethical spectacle"—a symbolic action that is participatory, open, transparent, realistic and utopian.[36] Key to the experience being both realistic *and* utopian is the use of fun, personalization and imagination to dramatize real-world power dynamics underlying street names as well as the orientation toward the future, for example, the ability to rename any place to whatever name you choose, even if you know City Hall does not want Hancock St to be called "Land of the Evil Chipmunks."

The second goal was to produce *a meaningful conversation and learning experience with each participant* about names of public places. To this end, the renaming experience was consciously located in physical places in Cambridge, Massachusetts. Since a number of Institute members are software programmers we have often been asked, "Why didn't you digitally crowdsource it? Why couldn't people online do a renaming?" This was a very conscious design decision that we made. While we did not want to require any kind of proof of residence in Cambridge, we explicitly wanted to limit the participants to those who were currently experiencing the city. As we are the Institute for Infinitely *Small* Things, the goal was not to aggregate the largest number of new names but to focus on the quality of conversation with each person. In this, our goal was to move street names from the realm of the inevitable—the infinitely small and "quintessentially mundane"[37]—and into the focus of attention in order to produce a new way of seeing the space around them.

Finally, *we created a speculative situation to place the participant in a position of power*. Rather than "users" of the city, we created a semi-fictional space where participants could experiment with a different kind of civic agency—that of authorship in relation to the landscape. Though we hoped to create a learning experience, our goal was not to "educate" the public about history but activate people's curiosity through the ability to make space one's own and to inscribe a personal mark onto a collective landscape. This relates back to the second part of the definition of civic imagination regarding political agency. The default frame for participants in *the City Formerly Known as Cambridge* was one in which they had and were expected to exercise political agency. These three design goals were designed to re-orient the participant to the space around them, to provoke reflection about the names of public places, to "try on" a kind of civic power that they had never had and to invite creative, personal, fun, contestational responses to the everyday landscape.

A HYPOTHETICAL (BUT ENTIRELY POSSIBLE) MAP OF CAMBRIDGE

The renaming parties took place over two years—from 2006 to 2008. In total we conducted more than 300 conversations about place names in Cambridge and collected more than 330 names for the map. We published the map in 2008. All participants who had filled out their address on the renaming form received a free copy of the map in the mail. The map looks fairly conventional but includes only the new names that were submitted.

We used yellow callouts with photographs on the front of the map to highlight particularly interesting new names. For example, on the right-hand side you can see a picture of a large painted smokestack with the logo of the NECCO candy company. This is because one resident renamed the "Area 4" neighborhood to "Candyland" in order to commemorate that neighborhood's industrial past in candy manufacturing. Another callout features a photo of a gentleman who renamed Massachusetts Ave to Prince Hall Blvd. He had been working for the past couple years to effect that name change through the

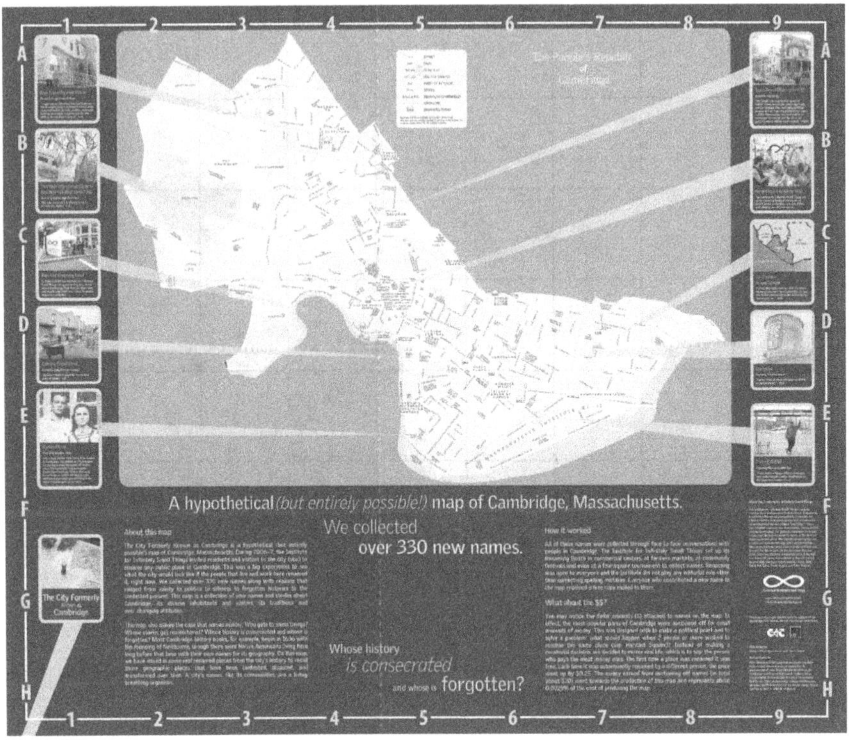

Figure 2.3 Map of the City Formerly Known as Cambridge, 2008.

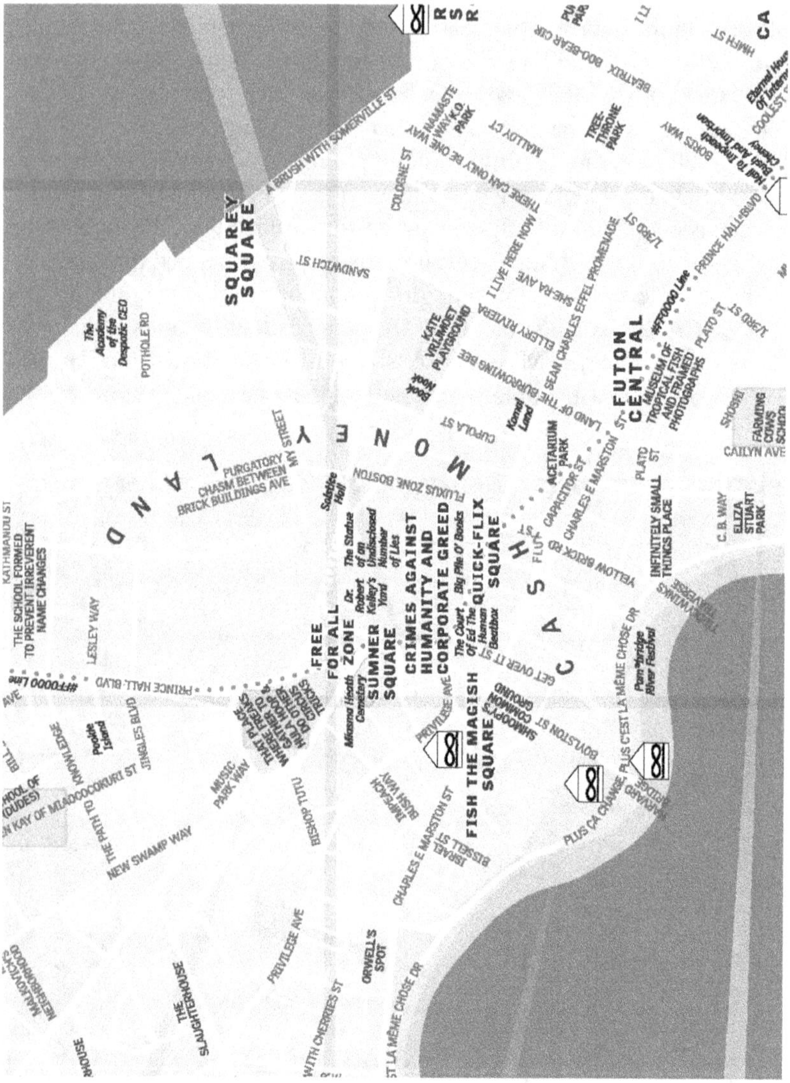

Figure 2.4 Map of the City Formerly Known as Cambridge, 2008, Detail. People had many creative and critical suggestions for the areas around Harvard Square and Central Square.

City Council and decided that doing it on our map would be a good interim step. The front of the map also describes the project and asks in large type, "Whose history is consecrated and whose is forgotten?"

The back is an alphabetical index that contains the text of every new name and every new reason submitted by participants as well as insets that discuss famous renamings, Native American names, and a how-to guide for renaming your city. The back of the map includes names that did not make it onto the front because they were outbid. For example, one woman renamed Harvard St to Ann Radcliffe St because she said "After John Harvard donated about 100 books to establish Harvard University, Ann Radcliffe was the one who gave all the money necessary to maintain the university. Now Radcliffe is only commemorated through a Harvard Institute and not through any other place in the area (no streets after Ann or Radcliffe)." This renamer actually gave us $5.00 to preserve her name. But unfortunately, she was outbid by Sean Effel who asked which name was going for the most money and then promptly gave us $7.00 to name Ann Radcliffe Street after himself to Sean Effel Promenade.

WHAT PEOPLE RENAMED AND WHY

People renamed places for a variety of reasons and exhibited various levels of attention, contestation, and silliness in the process. In order to develop the yellow callouts for the front of the map, we categorized the data in a systematic way using a thematic approach.[38] We categorized the names into eight groups: (1) Fun: Random, silly, funny renamings; (2) Personal Commemoration: Renamings that commemorated something personally meaningful such as a loved one, dog, favorite book, or home country; (3) Social Use: New names that described how a place is currently being used by people; (4) Contestational: Renamings that were either contesting something objectionable or complaining about something in the city; (5) Vanity: People renaming places for themselves; (6) History: Either celebrating or contesting history; (7) Reduce Confusion: Renamings to clear up misunderstandings and inconsistencies such as duplicate street names in neighboring towns; and (8) Aspirational: New names that sought to ascribe aspirational values, such as peace, love, and wellness, onto a space. The chart below gives specific examples of renamings from each of these categories.

A USELESS MAP, TEN YEARS LATER

What is the lasting effect, if any, of participation in such an exercise in civic imagination? Would participants remember the experience and what

Table 2.1 Example Reasons for Renaming Places

Fun	A seven-year-old renamed her school, King/Amigos, to the "Farming Cows School" because she said *"I think it would be fun to have cows at school."* Fayerweather St was renamed to "Attack of the Giant Moms St" because *"it sounds funny."* Green St was renamed to "Pink St" because *"Pink is just plain better. Thank you!"*
Personal Commemoration	A man renamed Riverside Press Park to "Kno Park." He said, *"My 'little brother', a child who I mentor, used to meet me here every weekend to go skateboarding. He made up his own skateboard team and named it 'Kno'. I'm naming it for him because our friendship was very important and influential to him. The park kind of symbolizes our friendship."* Wood St was renamed to "Boodle St" *"Because it's my dog's name."* Magoun St was renamed to "Jaybear Ave" *"Because my boyfriend lives there and this will make him blush."*
Social Use	Windsor St was renamed by a resident to Redemption Alley *"Because all the cart people use our street as a thoroughfare to redeem their cans at the Redemption Center on Columbia St."* The Cambridge Common was renamed to "That Place Where Freaks Gather to Hula Hoop and Do Other Circus Tricks" because *"that's what it is, especially on Wednesday nights."*
Contestational	Bryant St was renamed to Pothole Rd because *"This very short street is possibly the worst paved in Cambridge."* One resident renamed Dunster St to "Get Over It St" because *"I have been harassed multiple times by the same homeless man on this street for being queer. He needs to get over it."* Notably, one participant used their renaming to protest the project itself as well as the renaming of the Agassiz School. The Baldwin School was renamed to "The School Formed to Prevent Irreverent Name Changes" because *"we don't need to rename things."*
Vanity	A young woman renamed Walden St to "Ciara's St." She said, *"I chose this name because it's my name and I want something named after me!! :)"* Charles St was renamed to "Da Liberiana St." The namer said, *"I chose this name because Liberia is where my ancestors came from. I want this for my new street because that is the nickname my friends gave me."*
History	Massachusetts Ave was renamed "Prince Hall Boulevard" *"to honor the first African American Freemason and a prominent Boston citizen during the Revolutionary War."*

Reduce Confusion	One resident renamed Upland Rd to "Bruegger's Bagels St." They said, *"Nobody knows how to get to my house when I tell them to turn on Upland Rd so I have to say 'Bruegger's Bagels St'. This would make it MUCH easier for me to throw parties! Thanks!"*
Aspirational	A name that did not make it onto the map for the Charles River was "The River of Hopes and Dreams" *"Because it is a source of inspiration."*

they renamed? Did the project still resonate? Had it inspired other renaming thoughts, conversations or applications? We decided to try to evaluate the experience almost ten years later against our original design goals: (1) fun, lighthearted, and playful experience; (2) a meaningful conversation and learning experience with each participant; and (3) create a speculative situation to place the participant in a position of power.

In June 2015, ten years after the project began, we sent out a short survey to the almost 300 people who contributed new names to the map. The survey asked the participants if they remembered the project, if they had wanted to rename anything else in the city after that, and several questions about their experience.[39] We tried to keep the questions open-ended so as to not lead participants toward our goals.[40] Many of the participants' email addresses had expired and only 169 emails were delivered. Of those, twenty-two people responded to the survey. We used a thematic approach to code their responses based on our three design goals.

(1) Fun, lighthearted, and playful experience

More than 100 renamings on the published map fell into the "fun" category so participants clearly felt that they had permission to be playful and silly in their choice of names. New names such as "Nostril," "Munchkin Land," "Pookie Island," and "Humpty Dumpty Street" abound. Some survey respondents stated simply that "It was fun and funny" (Participant 13) and "This was a wonderful experience" (Participant 23). Others noted that the fun part came through the conversations with their friends, "I really enjoyed reading some of the names others had put down for places and debating with friends and others what we would rename places" (Participant 14). A couple said that they took pleasure in just thinking about what to rename (Participant 18 & 19) And several noted that the project evoked "fond memories" for them. One survey respondent even continued the playful spirit of the project to tell us other things he desired in the future, "I'd like a really hot gay boyfriend, overthrow capitalism, and have many more discotheques (that actually play classic seventies disco) open in the City of Cambridge. Oh, and affordable housing, we need a lot more of that too" (Participant 21).

We can state with fair certainty that fun was had in the course of this project. We believe this is because the project invited personal marks in a collective landscape. Participants may have even purposefully been silly as a response to the idea that we intuitively *know* that our public places are going to reify a sanctioned and sanitized notion of history and propriety. The freedom to decommemorate officialdom and personalize a bland, administrative landscape is exciting. So while it's possible to read personalization as vain and silly, another way to read it is the pleasure of speaking and being heard (and interrupting official discourse). As Duncombe says, "Perhaps the problem is not that people don't want to get involved in politics, but rather that they don't want to take part in a professionalized politics so interested in efficiency that there is no space for them."[41]

(2) A meaningful conversation and learning experience with each participant

As a baseline for creating a meaningful conversation and learning experience, we asked participants to state whether they remembered participating. Though some respondents did not remember the places that they had renamed, all respondents except for one remembered participating in the project almost ten years ago.[42] In their responses to open-ended questions, many participants remembered the experience but very few mentioned conversing specifically with members of the Institute (other than that we were "nice people"—Participant 20). Those who recalled conversations were more likely to emphasize talking with their friends, "I remember encountering the booth at the Cambridge River Festival when I was walking around with a few friends. I remember we got really excited about re-naming streets, and I remember that there were bidding wars on all the major arteries" (Participant 24). And no participants mentioned talking about or looking up prior historical names of public places in our books and binders. What several people do mention browsing were the new names that other participants had suggested, for example, "Participants could give their reasons for renaming a street or landmark. I read a number of the entries. Some of the reasons were spot on" (Participant 17). The same participant mentioned wishing for more names on the map, "I wished only that there had been even more entries, because I felt sure many other places in the City Formerly Known as Cambridge deserved to be honored with more fitting names."

So, while many respondents emphasized that the experience was fun and enjoyable, nobody mentioned learning more about Cambridge, street names or the process of renaming public places. Two people noted that while they enjoyed the experience the goals were not entirely clear. Participant 20 said that it was a "vague concept" and Participant 19 advised us to use clearer language, "As a suggestion for future projects, it would be good to keep in touch a little more frequently and to lay out in more clear language what the deal was with the project." From these responses, we gather that much of the meaning for participants came through browsing other renamings, discussing them with friends and the prompt to "make one's mark" on the landscape by coming up with their own name and not through the conversation with the Institute members, the description of the goals of the project or through the historical materials we had on hand.

However there were a few participants for whom the experience provided an inspiration and an ongoing prompt for reflection on history. Participant 10 said they had not thought about the project until they moved away. "[T]he project is more relevant to me now that I live further south and see place and street names all around me honoring, say, Confederate figures, and as I watch as the ongoing development in my current home of Washington DC rather garishly reflects an absurd concentration of disposable income." Participant 24 mentioned that they have discussed the project very frequently in the years following their participation and it directly inspired their work on local history, "Anytime we talk about the streets in Cambridge that share names with Boston streets, the project comes up . . . In part because of this project, I was inspired to start working on a podcast about local history in the Boston area."

(3) A speculative situation to place the participant in a position of power

As a baseline for participants feeling empowered, we asked people if, after participating, they saw other places in the city they would like to rename. This question was an attempt to indirectly get at whether they perceived themselves as having the agency to be able to rename public places. Participant 16 said they speak about the project often as a way of illustrating how "we personally map our own experiences onto the built environment." Participant 11 chose to use the last question of the survey to reassert the inadequacy of their current street name, "Fairmont St should be renamed for real," ostensibly because of confusion as there is both a Fairmont St and a Fairmont Ave in Cambridge. While they used this survey to advocate for their position, it isn't clear that they are doing anything about it through official channels. Interestingly, placing participants in a speculative and somewhat fictional position of power made some of them take their power fairly seriously. Many spent a lot of time reading names, deliberating (alone or with friends) and even regretted their decisions afterward. "I remember which streets I named, what I named them, and that I knew immediately afterwards that I could have chosen better names" (Participant 10). And Participant 5 said "I think I regretted my street name choice. I guess it got me thinking about how we choose names for public institutions and functions, and how they tend to last, for better or worse."

While it is hard to exactly measure a feeling of personal agency ten years after an experience, we believe these responses show that empowering people with semi-fictional civic agency has real weight and can be imbued with personal meaning and relevance that resonates long after the fact. For example, Participant 13 said that "We remind our kids of our 'real' street name all the time." Participant 10 noted that "I've never looked at the map again but when I see the place I renamed, I remember it and I remember renaming and making it mine. I don't live in Cambridge (or even in Boston) anymore but I remember the spot and often see it when I'm back." Giving participants the agency to name their space shifted their relationship to that place in a significant way. Azaryahu writes, "Renaming a street has a substantial effect not only on the city but also on its human experience and cognition. A rude intervention in routinized practices and traditional relations between ordinary people and their habitat effects a cognitive dissonance and mental and communication disarray, at least temporarily."[43] We can extend Azaryahu's position to make the case that even temporarily and speculatively renaming a street has a substantial effect on one's personal experience and cognition of place. From the standpoint of cultivating civic imagination, the speculative renaming is not so much "rude intervention" as it is a way to foster a more personal relationship and a manner of caring for the landscape that the participant had not previously had. Survey respondents referred to the places they renamed in a personal, possessive way—for example, "my street," "my renaming," "my choice"—in the same way that one refers to the street that one lives on. One's street is special and personal.

And having engaged once in renaming provides opportunities to think about doing it again. This opens a possible gateway for civic agency in the future. While not all participants alluded to this idea, Participant 10 stated that if they were to do it again today, "I think my renaming choices would now likely be more pointedly political, and would likely reflect my perceptions of the tacit intentions reflected in the developmental trajectory of a given street or square." Perhaps the value of empowering participants with semi-fictional agency is that it opens a door to true political authority, both exercising their own and evaluating that of those who literally have the power. The beginning of a beginning.

ON THE POSSIBLE UTILITY OF USELESSNESS

As an artist, I am loathe to suggest that there might be some utility to uselessness, but I have already broken the unstated rules of art by administering a survey so let us just speculate a little further. Gordon and Walter use the idea of "meaningful inefficiencies" to address the importance of designing civic systems that let participants *play* as opposed to carrying out prescribed desirable behaviors such as attending a town meeting or voting. According to them, "Meaningful inefficiencies represent the design of systems for civic action, not behaviors. They can be civic tools, systems, or events, etc. that temporarily halt normal civic processes and create a delineated time or place in which play, disorder, messiness, and the ability to experiment and fail safely are utilized in productive—though not necessarily practical—ways."[44]

Whereas the focus in government has been on "civic tech" that streamlines citizen engagement with administrative services, Gordon and Walter are making a case for creating spaces that foster playful, possibly messy, possibly critical, possibly inefficient engagement with civic life. I would posit that these meaningful inefficiencies are about intentionally cultivating civic imagination *in ways that designers cannot always and should not always anticipate*. They are also about ceding power, control, and definitions of success to the participants to fill in the blanks. What might result is a "vague concept" for some (Participant 20) but the inspiration of whole body of work from another (Participant 23). Participation in open-ended systems has a ripple effect. Rethinking street names ripples out into the world thought by thought, conversation by conversation. These thoughts and conversations lay the groundwork for mobilization at a later date in time. As Gordon and Walter state, the results of meaningful inefficiencies may be "increased civic learning, reflection, empathy, and increased awareness of civic systems and their effects—which citizens can then leverage in creating new action in the normal processes of civic life."[45] Just a month ago, for example, I received the following tweet from a stranger named Nse Umoh:

> *@kanarinka: thinking abt ur project of collaborative street renaming. #Charlestown needs that kind of intervention! http://act.colorofchange.org/sign/change-name-calhoun-street-emanuel-nine-way/*[46]

The link leads to a campaign being run by ColorOfChange.org, an online advocacy organization whose mission is to strengthen Black America's political voice. They were running a campaign to change the name of Calhoun Street in Charleston, South Carolina, to Emanuel 9 Way. John C. Calhoun was a staunch advocate of slavery. The Emanuel Church, located on Calhoun St, is one of the oldest African American churches in the country and was the site of the racially motivated slaying of nine people in 2015.

While projects such as *the City Formerly Known as Cambridge* are more playful, preliminary and diffuse than a focused renaming campaign such as this, these types of civic art projects can lay groundwork that can be initiated and activated at a later date when personal engagement, community organizing, and political will converge. At the Institute for Infinitely Small Things, we think the ability to "try out" civic systems and "try on" political agency, even in a semi-fictional context, has real-world consequences. Namely, these preliminary performances are essential to activate civic imagination, prompt reflection and initiate critical action on the naturalized, mundane power systems that maintain and structure civic life. Exercises in civic imagination also help to broaden the sphere of who participates in that civic life. There is a growing body of research that shows that political participation is unfolding in increasingly mediatized, participatory, personalized and cultural ways.[47,48,49,50] In this new climate, it is not enough to exercise the right to vote. We also need to exercise our civic imaginations and practice ways of dreaming together.

ACKNOWLEDGMENTS

For this project, the Institute for Infinitely Small Things was Shannon Coyle, Catherine D'Ignazio, Heloisa Escudero, Toby Kim Lee, Jaimes Mayhew, James Manning, Dave Raymond, Heather Ring, Katherine Urbati, Matilda Sabal, Max Sabal, Rob Sabal, Nicole Siggins, and Savić Rašović. The project was made possible with the support of the Cambridge Arts Council, the LEF Foundation, and iKatun. Furniture design by Aliza Shapiro and Fotini Lazaridou-Hatzigoga. Map design by Maegen Rzasa, Ryan Torres, and Tarek Awad. Cartography by Nat Case & Hedberg Maps.

Reuben Rose-Redwood and Derek Alderman, "Critical Interventions in Political Toponymy," *ACME: An International E-Journal for Critical Geographies* 10, no. 1 (March 2011): 1–6.

NOTES

1. The unwritten rules of governance for the Institute for Infinitely Small Things state that anyone who is affiliated with the Institute may represent themselves as the Director. And anyone may affiliate themselves with the Institute without informing anybody.
2. Maoz Azaryahu, "The Power of Commemorative Street Names," *Environment and Planning D: Society and Space* 14, no. 3 (1996): 311–30, doi:10.1068/d140311.
3. "Apr 27 Michael Rakowitz on Redirective Practice, Problem-Solving and Trouble-Making," *Videos*, accessed August 4, 2015, http://bit.ly/1GH7xZj.
4. Reuben S. Rose-Redwood, "Indexing the Great Ledger of the Community: Urban House Numbering, City Directories, and the Production of Spatial Legibility,"

Journal of Historical Geography 34, no. 2 (April 2008): 286–310, doi:10.1016/j.jhg.2007.06.003.

5. Who are the strangers? They are imagined to be of the desirable, male, capitalist type—bureaucrats, merchants, businessmen. The 1838 Philadelphia directory advertised itself as "a convenient and intelligent pocket companion for the *stranger*, *merchant*, or *businessman* in Philadelphia, by affording him a ready and desirable guide, promptly directing him where to obtain the various goods which comprise his required assortment of merchandize, with as little delay as possible: thereby economising time, and expediting his general business transactions." (as quoted in Rose-Redwood, 2008, italics added.)

6. Azaryahu, "The Power of Commemorative Street Names."

7. Reuben Rose-Redwood and Derek Alderman, "Critical Interventions in Political Toponymy," *ACME: An International E-Journal for Critical Geographies* 10, no. 1 (March 2011): 1–6.

8. Catherine Farvacque-Vitković, *Street Addressing and the Management of Cities*, Directions in Development (Washington, DC: World Bank, 2005).

9. John Pickles, *A History of Spaces: Cartographic Reason, Mapping, and the Geo-Coded World* (Psychology Press, 2004).

10. Azaryahu, "The Power of Commemorative Street Names."

11. Ibid.

12. Ibid.

13. Christopher Hail, "Harvard/Radcliffe On-Line Historical Reference Shelf: Cambridge Buildings," Reference, *Cambridge Buildings and Architects*, (November 2002), http://hul.harvard.edu/lib/archives/refshelf/cba/index.html.

14. Maple Ave—http://hul.harvard.edu/lib/archives/refshelf/cba/m.html#mapleave

15. Akron St—http://hul.harvard.edu/lib/archives/refshelf/cba/a.html#akronst

16. Reservoir St—http://hul.harvard.edu/lib/archives/refshelf/cba/r.html#reservoirst

17. Edward Lurie, "Louis Agassiz and the Races of Man." *Isis* 45, no. 3 (1954): 227–42.

18. Olivia S. Solomons, "MARIA LOUISE BALDWIN," *Negro History Bulletin* 5, no. 1 (1941): 19.

19. Lauren R. Dorgan, "Committee Renames Local Agassiz School | News | The Harvard Crimson," May 22, 2002, http://www.thecrimson.com/article/2002/5/22/committee-renames-local-agassiz-school-the/.

20. In doing research for the project all historical texts we found about Cambridge and Massachusetts started with the white people with only a token mention, if any, of the fact that native populations may have previously inhabited the area.

21. Azaryahu, "The Power of Commemorative Street Names."

22. "Wikipedia:FAQ/Contributing," *Wikipedia, the Free Encyclopedia*, July 17, 2016, https://en.wikipedia.org/w/index.php?title=Wikipedia:FAQ/Contributing&oldid=730254941.

23. "File:Osmdbstats1 Users.png—OpenStreetMap Wiki," *Open Street Map Wiki*, accessed July 25, 2016, http://wiki.openstreetmap.org/wiki/File:Osmdbstats1_users.png.

24. Henry Jenkins et al., "Superpowers to the People!: How Young Activists Are Tapping the Civic Imagination," in *Civic Media: Technology, Design, Practice*, eds. Eric Gordon and Paul Mihailidis (MIT Press, 2016).

25. Shaowen Bardzell, "Feminist HCI: Taking Stock and Outlining an Agenda for Design," in *Proceedings of the SIGCHI Conference on Human Factors in Computing Systems*, CHI '10 (New York, NY: ACM, 2010), 1301–10, doi:10.1145/1753326.1753521.

26. As quoted in Dalia Othman, Catherine D'Ignazio, and Rahul Bhargava, "Measuring Impact | Berkman Center," 2015, https://cyber.law.harvard.edu/getinvolved/studygroups/datastorytelling_impact.

27. Robert D. Putnam, *Bowling Alone: The Collapse and Revival of American Community* (New York: Simon & Schuster, 2000).

28. Alexis de Toqueville as cited in Benjamin Bowyer and Joseph Kahne, "Revisiting the Measurement of Political Participation for the Digital Age," in *Civic Media: Technology, Design, Practice*, eds. Eric Gordon and Paul Mihailidis (MIT Press, 2016).

29. Gyorgy Kepes, "Toward Civic Art," *Leonardo* 4, no. 1 (January 1, 1971): 69–73, doi:10.2307/1572235.

30. Doris Sommer, *The Work of Art in the World: Civic Agency and Public Humanities* (Durham: Duke University Press Books, 2014).

31. Carolina Miranda, "How the Art of Social Practice Is Changing the World, One Row House at a Time | ARTnews," April 7, 2014, http://www.artnews.com/2014/04/07/art-of-social-practice-is-changing-the-world-one-row-house-at-a-time/.

32. Stephen Duncombe, *Dream: Re-Imagining Progressive Politics in an Age of Fantasy* (New York: New Press; Distributed by W.W. Norton, c2007).

33. Kim Pruesse, *Accidental Audience: Urban Interventions by Artists* (Toronto: off\site collective, 1999).

34. Hail, "Cambridge Buildings and Architects."

35. Though we did have conversations with a few people who questioned this logic, we felt that a symbolic nod toward the role that money plays in the naming of places was very apt. All in all we made less than $25 this way.

36. Duncombe, *Dream*.

37. Azaryahu, "The Power of Commemorative Street Names."

38. Barney G. Glaser and Anselm L. Strauss, *The Discovery of Grounded Theory: Strategies for Qualitative Research* (Transaction Publishers, 2009).

39. Survey questions are accessible here: http://goo.gl/forms/tU6XwDpXEJ.

40. Bernard CK Choi and Anita WP Pak, "A Catalog of Biases in Questionnaires," *Preventing Chronic Disease* 2, no. 1 (2005): A13.

41. Duncombe, *Dream*.

42. This could, of course, be self-selection in who chose to respond to the email survey versus who regarded it as meaningless spam.

43. Azaryahu, "The Power of Commemorative Street Names."

44. Eric Gordon and Stephen Walter, "Meaningful Inefficiencies: Resisting the Logic of Technological Efficiency in the Design of Civic Systems," in *Civic Media: Technology, Design, Practice*, eds. Eric Gordon and Paul Mihailidis (MIT Press, 2016).

45. Ibid.

46. Nse Umoh, "@kanarinka Thinking Abt Ur Project of Collaborative Street Renaming.#Charleston Needs That Kind of Intervention! Http://act.colorofchange.org/sign/change-Name-Calhoun-Street-Emanuel-Nine-way/ …," microblog, *@nseabasiumoh*, (July 9, 2015), https://twitter.com/nseabasiumoh/status/619222634216222720.

47. Cliff Zukin et al., *A New Engagement?: Political Participation, Civic Life, and the Changing American Citizen* (Oxford University Press, 2006).

48. Russell J. Dalton, *The Good Citizen: How a Younger Generation Is Reshaping American Politics* (Washington, DC: CQ Press, c2008).

49. Bennett W. Lance and Alexandra Segerberg, "The Logic of Connective Action," in *Civic Media: Technology, Design, Practice*, eds. Eric Gordon and Paul Mihailidis (MIT Press, 2016).

50. Henry Jenkins et al., "Superpowers to the People!: How Young Activists Are Tapping The Civic Imagination."

BIBLIOGRAPHY

"Apr 27 Michael Rakowitz on Redirective Practice, Problem-Solving and Trouble-Making." *Videos*. Accessed August 4, 2015. http://bit.ly/1GH7xZj.

Azaryahu, Maoz. "The Critical Turn and Beyond: The Case of Commemorative Street Naming." *ACME: An International E-Journal for Critical Geographies* 10, no. 1 (March 2011): 28–33.

———. "The Power of Commemorative Street Names." *Environment and Planning D: Society and Space* 14, no. 3 (1996): 311–30. doi:10.1068/d140311.

Bardzell, Shaowen. "Feminist HCI: Taking Stock and Outlining an Agenda for Design." In *Proceedings of the SIGCHI Conference on Human Factors in Computing Systems*, 1301–10. CHI '10. New York, NY: ACM, 2010. doi:10.1145/1753326.1753521.

Bennett, W. Lance and Alexandra Segerberg. "The Logic of Connective Action." In *Civic Media: Technology, Design, Practice*, edited by Eric Gordon and Paul Mihailidis. MIT Press, 2016.

Bowyer, Benjamin and Joseph Kahne. "Revisiting the Measurement of Political Participation for the Digital Age." In *Civic Media: Technology, Design, Practice*, edited by Eric Gordon and Paul Mihailidis. MIT Press, 2016.

Choi, Bernard CK and Anita WP Pak. "A Catalog of Biases in Questionnaires." *Prev Chronic Dis* 2, no. 1 (2005): A13.

Dalton, Russell J. *The Good Citizen: How a Younger Generation Is Reshaping American Politics*. Washington, DC: CQ Press, c2008.

Dorgan, Lauren R. "Committee Renames Local Agassiz School | News | The Harvard Crimson." May 22, 2002. http://www.thecrimson.com/article/2002/5/22/committee-renames-local-agassiz-school-the/.

Duncombe, Stephen. *Dream: Re-Imagining Progressive Politics in an Age of Fantasy*. New York: New Press; Distributed by W.W. Norton, c2007.

Farvacque-Vitković, Catherine. *Street Addressing and the Management of Cities*. Directions in Development. Washington, DC: World Bank, 2005.

"File:Osmdbstats1 Users.png—OpenStreetMap Wiki." *Open Street Map Wiki*. Accessed July 25, 2016. http://wiki.openstreetmap.org/wiki/File:Osmdbstats1_users.png.

Glaser, Barney G., and Anselm L. Strauss. *The Discovery of Grounded Theory: Strategies for Qualitative Research*. Transaction Publishers, 2009.

Gordon, Eric and Stephen Walter. "Meaningful Inefficiencies: Resisting the Logic of Technological Efficiency in the Design of Civic Systems." In *Civic Media: Technology, Design, Practice*, edited by Eric Gordon and Paul Mihailidis. MIT Press, 2016.

Hail, Christopher. "Harvard/Radcliffe On-Line Historical Reference Shelf: Cambridge Buildings." Reference. *Cambridge Buildings and Architects*, November 2002. http://hul.harvard.edu/lib/archives/refshelf/cba/index.html.

Henry Jenkins, Sangita Shresthova, Liana Gamber-Thompson, and Neta Kligler-Vilenchik. "Superpowers to the People!: How Young Activists Are Tapping The Civic Imagination." In *Civic Media: Technology, Design, Practice*, edited by Eric Gordon and Paul Mihailidis. MIT Press, 2016.

Kepes, Gyorgy. "Toward Civic Art." *Leonardo* 4, no. 1 (January 1, 1971): 69–73. doi:10.2307/1572235.

Lurie, Edward. "Louis Agassiz and the Races of Man." *Isis* 45, no. 3 (1954): 227–42.

Miranda, Carolina. "How the Art of Social Practice Is Changing the World, One Row House at a Time | ARTnews," April 7, 2014. http://www.artnews.com/2014/04/07/art-of-social-practice-is-changing-the-world-one-row-house-at-a-time/.

Othman, Dalia, Catherine D'Ignazio, and Rahul Bhargava. "Measuring Impact | Berkman Center," 2015. https://cyber.law.harvard.edu/getinvolved/studygroups/datastorytelling_impact.

Pickles, John. *A History of Spaces: Cartographic Reason, Mapping, and the Geo-Coded World*. Psychology Press, 2004.

Pruesse, Kim. *Accidental Audience: Urban Interventions by Artists*. Toronto: off\site collective, 1999.

Putnam, Robert D. *Bowling Alone: The Collapse and Revival of American Community*. New York: Simon & Schuster, 2000.

Reuben S. Rose-Redwood. "Indexing the Great Ledger of the Community: Urban House Numbering, City Directories, and the Production of Spatial Legibility." *Journal of Historical Geography* 34, no. 2 (April 2008): 286–310. doi:10.1016/j.jhg.2007.06.003.

Rose-Redwood, Reuben and Derek Alderman. "Critical Interventions in Political Toponymy." *ACME: An International E-Journal for Critical Geographies* 10, no. 1 (March 2011): 1–6.

Solomons, Olivia S. "MARIA LOUISE BALDWIN." *Negro History Bulletin* 5, no. 1 (1941): 19.

Sommer, Doris. *The Work of Art in the World: Civic Agency and Public Humanities*. Durham: Duke University Press Books, 2014.

Umoh, Nse. "@kanarinka Thinking Abt Ur Project of Collaborative Street Renaming . #Charleston Needs That Kind of Intervention! Http://act.colorofchange.org/sign/change-Name-Calhoun-Street-Emanuel-Nine-way/?source=mailing4516&t=5&akid=4524.907913.aeiRs5 …." Microblog. *@nseabasiumoh*, July 9, 2015. https://twitter.com/nseabasiumoh/status/619222634216222720.

"Wikipedia: FAQ/Contributing." *Wikipedia, the Free Encyclopedia*, July 17, 2016. https://en.wikipedia.org/w/index.php?title=Wikipedia:FAQ/Contributing&oldid=730254941.

Zukin, Cliff, Scott Keeter, Molly Andolina, Krista Jenkins, and Michael X. Delli Carpini. *A New Engagement?: Political Participation, Civic Life, and the Changing American Citizen*. Oxford University Press, 2006.

Chapter 3

Implausible Futures for Unpopular Places

Rob Walker

Beginning in 2010, the Hypothetical Development Organization, founded by G. K. Darby, Ellen Susan, and I, set out to recognize, and expand upon, a form of urban storytelling. It works like this:

First, we identify a suitable building: Something that appears neglected, and seems to have no immediate prospects for a future use. In short, we choose an unpopular place. Next we devise a hypothetical future for that structure. Specifically, we strive to make this future blatantly implausible: maybe provocative, maybe funny; above all engaging. Then an artist creates a rendering based on the imaginary concept. This is printed onto a 3′ x 5′ sign, modeled on those used by real developers. That sign, finally, goes onto the building.

In December 2010, our stories began to appear around New Orleans. By March 2011 we had presented ten of them to the public at large. This effort concluded with a display of duplicates of each of the HDO's initial creations at an art gallery in New Orleans. The project was realized thanks to the efforts of an astonishing crew of contributing artists, with the financial support of far-flung strangers.

Strictly speaking, nothing more need be said. But my purpose here is to tell the stories behind these stories, because this project raised a number of questions among those who have come into contact with it. In some instances the answers are interesting.

Here, then, is an account, and an explanation, of this enterprise, its history, and its aims.

IT STARTED LIKE THIS

One day I went for a routine walk. My wife and I live in Savannah, GA, in an area that's mostly residential, but interspersed with commercial and public buildings. It's a nice stroll to an excellent bakery, my bank, a convenience store, the main branch of the public library.

Our neighborhood is the sort that people describe as "transitional," and some of the property, both residential and commercial, is vacant. On one nearby commercial structure, vacant for the four-plus years we've lived in the area, I noticed a sign during this particular walk. You've seen similar signs, and I'd seen this one probably a hundred times, without ever really thinking about it. It was a rendering of a development, a future, involving a small, empty building. It suddenly struck me that, given how long this sign has been here, what it depicted was, at best, a *hypothetical* future—and arguably a fictitious one.

Since whenever this sign was first posted, the real estate market has collapsed, the old go-go economy has evaporated, and as it happens this building has been put up for sale. Any development that may take place someday would depend on someone buying it, and on what that party might want to do. Until then, it's just another empty building that happens to have a sign on it. The disparity between the rendering and reality is considerable: In the rendering, in fact, the actual extant structure has been folded into a much bigger building, which in point of fact exists nowhere besides that rendering. In real life, it's a vacant lot.

It further struck me that there are vacant buildings much like this one, with no definitive future, all over town—all over *lots* of towns. In a sense, then, our city streets are full of fiction, or something very much like it. The stories, mostly visual, are told in the form of colorful signs attached to drab or neglected structures, presenting speculations about how the very same physical place might look in some unspecified future. The abandoned office tower could house airy condos. The long-shuttered auto shop might morph into a gleaming boutique. The factory built for some bankrupt enterprise will, perhaps, burst with life again, its cheery mixed uses enjoyed by stock-image people representing a cross section of pleasant citizenry. Sometimes these ideas are punctuated by the name of a development company and its Web address. But the story flows mostly from the beguiling picture, showing what could hypothetically happen, right here.

The fact of the fiction, however, is often given away by a nearby "For Sale" sign, or the weathering visible on the rendering, or the flagrantly neglected state of the structure to which it is attached, hinting at how long ago this future was first presented to passersby. Possibly, in some more upbeat economic era, whoever spun these morning-in-America tales believed them. We cannot say, because that time has passed. Only the tales remain.

That somewhat gloomy line of thought led me to consider all the neglected buildings, in my town and others, that *lack* such signs: Evidently no one can even dream up a hypothetical future for these decidedly unpopular places. Rather sad, no? I thought so, and had an idea: Wouldn't it be cool to create completely fictional, but imaginative and exciting "renderings" of *their* hypothetical futures, too? I was thinking of Claes Oldenburg and his drawings such as "Study for Feasible Monument: Lipstick." (I should underscore that it was his *drawings* I was thinking of. I always found them, and maybe the use of the word "feasible," more interesting than the structures that he has actually managed to get built in real life—as the Lipstick Monument was, in 1969.) What if renderings with a similarly absurd and amusing spirit were posted on the actual vacant buildings?

Frankly, I wanted someone else to take on this task, because I assumed it would be pretty hard to pull it off. But Ellen Susan (that's my wife) and G. K. Darby, a friend of ours in New Orleans, convinced me that we should do it.

"ARCHITECTURE FICTION"

But before I go any further about our project, I'd like to take a detour to address the notion of "architecture fiction." This is something I had never heard of when I took that walk. But it is a wonderful genre, and I believe The Hypothetical Development Organization fits into it—and makes a pleasing contribution to it, too.

Definitions of the term seem to vary, but the coinage belongs to Bruce Sterling. He introduced it in 2006, after reading an imaginative and insightful essay by J. G. Ballard, published in *The Guardian*, about modernist architecture.[1] "Now there's some top-end sci-fi architecture criticism," Sterling observed, adding this thought: "It's entirely possible to write 'architecture fiction' instead of 'science fiction.' Like, say, Archigram did in the 60s."[2]

Archigram came to life as an "architecture telegram" (a publication, basically) put together by a group of young architects in London in 1961. Its contributors specialized in hypothetical projects. In their publications, the architects involved, including Peter Cook and Ron Herron among others, would propose fantastic schemes for completely re-imagining buildings and urban spaces, which they would illustrate in equally fantastic styles. Cook's *Plug-In City* was not made up of buildings, but was a single structure with standardized cells that could be fitted in or removed, here and there—the structure, the city, was meant to be in charge of the people, rather than the other way around. Herron's *Walking City*, a cluster of urban-ness mounted on four legs, was said to be an extension of Le Corbusier's dictum that a house is a "machine for living in." In 1963 there was a big Archigram show called

"Living Cities" at the Institute of Contemporary Arts in London, and since then the group's work has remained highly influential in certain quarters of the architecture world.

Maybe one can say that "architecture fiction" refers to stories inspired by, or imposed upon, buildings and the built environment. And since Sterling cites Archigram, I take him to mean that those buildings or environments don't have to be real, and the stories don't have to be a series of words: They can exist as plans, schematics, models, renderings.

If Archigram is the core historical reference point for the idea of architecture fiction, then the core contemporary reference point, and resource, is BLDG BLOG,[3] the popular website run by Geoff Manaugh, a writer and teacher based in Los Angeles. Mark Dery has called him "the acknowledged auteur of architecture fiction," adding: "On BLDG BLOG, Manaugh reads our built—and unbuilt—environments like a cultural radiologist, scanning them for evidence of social pathologies, symptoms of the post-apocalyptic."[4] As it happens, Manaugh was actually auditing a class about Archigram, and reading a lot of J. G. Ballard, in 2004, when he started his site.

A book based on BLDG BLOG was published in 2009,[5] collecting some of the "architectural conjecture and urban speculation" that Manaugh is interested in, and writes about so well. "Architecture will always involve telling stories—it is as much fiction as it is engineering and materials science," he writes in *The BLDGBLOG Book*'s introduction. That belief guides an extremely expansive and imaginative notion of what architecture is, even when it exists in novels and video games and other nonphysical places.

Suffice it to say I was soon obsessed with collecting examples of what may or may not qualify as architecture fiction. I'll mention just a few. For starters: "Warsaw's Polonia Hotel: The Afterlife of Buildings" was part of the Venice Biennale of Architecture in 2008. The curators presented photographs of six recent acclaimed architectural projects in Poland, along with collages that depicted how those buildings might look after a "major transformation."[6] One office building created by a prestigious firm was, for instance, depicted as it could appear in the wake of a real estate market and broader economic collapse. Specifically, it was depicted as a prison. (Apparently the building has an inner courtyard, which could work as an exercise yard with panopticon-style surveillance.)

BLDG BLOG described Canadian artist Carl Zimmerman's beautiful visions of "fictional ruins from fictional worlds" (such as a 2003 series called "Landmarks of Industrial Britain") as "a photographic series of fictional public buildings derived from small scale architectural maquettes." Zimmerman has said that his work addresses "the apparent willingness of the viewer to accept a fabricated past."[7] Ioana Iliesiu explained the fictitious "The Ruins of Twitter" as "a monument of the Death of The Internet. . . . In the server dome, tweets are recited by a mechanical voice—in real time. The server hangs, creaking, from a pulley system, hovering over an interior salt water lake."[8] Images created for the Swiss Architectural magazine *Hochparterre* showed purported "architectural misprints" or "misplots"[9]: Imagine a future process for essentially printing a house in three dimensions, to the buyer's specs—but sometimes the printer misreads the data parameters, and so the house comes out as a strange and uninhabitable blob.

Taking such thinking into the realm of the latest mobile devices, designers Irene Cheng and Brett Snyder created an app called Museum of the Phantom City, exploiting global-positioning system and augmented reality technologies. The latter layers information or images over whatever you see when you peer through your smartphone at the world around you. In this case, you get images of and information about proposed utopian projects in New York City that never came to pass.

Other examples of what might be considered architecture fiction have unfolded in reality—and have been designed, on some level, to influence reality. For example, a 2000 installation by an outfit called Heavy Trash involved eight "Coming Soon" signs installed over a 15-mile stretch of Los Angeles, announcing a new subway line that would connect downtown to the west side. This was fiction, intended to provoke discussion of the need for fresh solutions to the city's notorious transit problems.

In San Francisco, artists Packard Jennings and Steve Lambert interviewed local architects and city planers and transportation experts, asking: "What would you do if you didn't have to worry about budgets, bureaucracy, politics, or physics?"[10] Based on the answers they created illustrations printed in a series of six posters, 6' x 4', which were installed in bus shelters. (This was funded and sanctioned by the San Francisco Art Commission.)

Finally, Stuart Candy offers the intriguing framework of "Found Futures." In one of his projects, from 2007, he and his collaborators imagined what might transpire in Honolulu if that city were "ground zero of a new influenza epidemic" that occurred in 2016. They created a number of posters and signs and objects[11] designed to reflect their speculations, and put them up around Honolulu's Chinatown. A bronze plaque, for example, offered "testimony to the resilient response of the community to a hypothetical tragedy that would not occur for another ten years."[12] There were also advertisements for new businesses that could spring up in the post-pandemic environment, plus official government notices. This was part of a broader effort to spark debate about the real future of Honolulu's Chinatown. Candy borrowed a term from Australia-based futurist Jose Ramos, calling this version of architecture fiction "future jamming."[13]

OTHER SUBGENRES

Once I became aware of (and rather entranced by) architecture fiction, it was tempting to plumb the genre to reverse-engineer a highfalutin' theoretical grounding for the Hypothetical Development Organization. But as wonderful as I found these projects, I knew that this strategy was misguided. Our project's actual inspiration was embarrassingly mundane: those dull real-world development signs. And I think this origin ought to be examined, not ignored.

After all, the original idea was that such signs are, essentially, stories. It follows, then, that they are form of architecture fiction, too. Admittedly, commercial real estate signs are not a particularly *literary* sort of fiction, but this subgenre does have its own traditions and mores. Its practitioners exercise what we might consider a tentative form of realism: After all, their stories should be plausible enough to, ideally, attract capital. Thus certain rules and strictures—relating to commercial potential, practical materials, and the laws of physics—must be observed. This of course is why current manifestations of the genre tend to be so god-awful boring. And, as time goes on and the *failure* to have attracted capital becomes more pronounced, these tales tend also to be dispiriting. Or possibly just ridiculous. And that in turn is precisely why this is the set of storytelling tropes, the grammar, that the Hypothetical Development Organization borrowed.

Meanwhile, around the time that the Hypothetical Development Organization got underway in earnest—choosing our first set of buildings, devising our stories, recruiting artists to render them—I encountered what I now believe is yet *another* architecture fiction subgenre. Actually, as with those commercial development sings, it was a form I'd seen before, without properly considering it.

I happened to find myself contemplating an image, on the website of an architecture firm, depicting a proposed public space project in Memphis. Created as a competition entry, this rendering aspired to represent a future reality (for the people of Memphis, and naturally for the architecture firm that devised it). But it lost the competition. This, then, is an example of a story told not on a building, but in a portfolio or exhibition: Proposed structures and projects that no one is going to build, *ever*, and everybody knows it.

In this variety of architecture fiction, the plots all resolve in similar ways. A competition about "design solutions" for redesigning the suburbs, for instance, yields a depiction of a rezoned "Entrepreneurbia," which would turn residential neighborhoods into "innovation incubators." A parking garage would get converted into a bike storage facility; a supermarket would be transformed into a "sustainable community complex," which also includes shops and "adaptable housing for active senior citizens." Here in Savannah, there is much talk of revitalizing a strip of Martin Luther King Boulevard that was ruined by a highway overpass years ago. So we're regularly treated to stories of its future in the form of renderings printed in the local paper, imagining a new and pedestrian-friendly reinvention of the place (somehow including hundred-year-old oak trees).

In short, these are examples of the most blatantly optimistic form of architecture fiction: the blue-sky proposal, the suggestion of what ought be done, etc., given rhetorical oomph by way of a snazzy rendering. These stories never trouble or disturb. They aim to comfort.

Perhaps the most striking example I have yet encountered was from San Francisco, a story told not merely in a rendering, but in a video variation of the form, explaining how geospatial analysis would be used to reclaim city-owned but neglected sites, parcels that add up to an "archipelago of opportunity." The story offered the conjecture that "using parametric design" and "optimizing thermal and hydrological performance to enhance the whole city's ecology," the project could tap into "citizen participation to conceive a new, more public infrastructure—a robust network of urban greenways with tangible benefits to the health and safety of every citizen."

I encountered this tale by way of a blog, where someone left a comment expressing pointed skepticism about a particular passage in the video. The passage showed an "empty side street transformed into a green space that is then magically populated with people (young hipster-ish looking silhouettes, no less)," this person wrote. "If this is a side street somewhere in the industrial part of SF, where are those people coming from?"[14]

That commenter was of course being a sourpuss. Come now: *It's just a story!*

I certainly don't mean to mock or criticize such efforts. Still, as with commercial development signage, it makes sense to consider them as forms of fiction. And here I am forced to conclude that this genre tends to be implausible in a way that is not very entertaining. To the contrary, it's often fairly preachy. Moreover, by presenting itself as something that really *should* come true, but almost certainly won't, this form tends to leave its audience with a general sense of disappointment. HDO did not set out to do so, but perhaps we have performed the critic-like function of revealing these other forms of architecture fiction. Our actual goal, however, was different.

"REAL-WORLD VALUE"

When we set ourselves to the task of introducing a new variation of urban storytelling to the public at large, we agreed upon several parameters for our stories. We decided they must be self-contained, explicitly independent of a promise. (We were not trying to fool anybody.) They should exist in the real world. (As signage.) They should prod the viewer into a different way of seeing the genres of current architecture fiction described above. And they should be intrinsically engaging. In short we sought to present, to the public at large, a series of *implausible futures for unpopular places.*

Between December 2010 and March 2011, the Hypothetical Development Organization presented ten such stories to the general public, by way of signage on buildings around New Orleans. We also presented duplicates of these signs, as well as two additional hypothetical developments, at the Du Mois Gallery in that city.

Claes Oldenburg remained an influence on the hypothetical scenarios we devised, but it occurred to us later that some of our stories might show traces of our admiration for the cartoonist Ben Katchor's imaginative city fictions. In any case, the ideas we dreamed up were improved by the artists we worked with. Many were New Orleans-based, but others contributed their talents from New York, Detroit, Portland, Richmond, Virginia, and elsewhere. In some cases we arrived at concepts in collaboration with other entities: notably The Center for American Placelessness (a theoretical cultural institution devoted to the synthesis of community and placemaking) and the School of Visual Arts, Masters of Professional Studies in Branding, Class of 2011.

To offset hard costs associated with the enterprise, we used Kickstarter.com to drum up $4,197 from 80 generous backers. The public appeal involved in the Kickstarter process resulted in reactions to what we intended

Figure 3.1 Museum of the Self. This hypothetical development, rendered by Dave Pinter, proposed the conversion of a vacant building into "the home of a museum dedicated to the most important figure of our time: the self."

to do, before we had actually done it. By and large, these responses were encouraging—and as a result, we were encouraged.

But for my purposes here, the most useful response was an email from someone who *didn't* like the idea. "What does your organization hope to achieve in real world value?" someone named Glenn demanded. "The buildings you feature in New Orleans are for the greatest part not available to you (or anyone else) and are under the jurisdiction of the historic district landmarks commission. I don't see the point." I can't speak to the landmarks angle, but Glenn is wholly correct that we are not in a position to actually buy and redevelop these buildings—or any buildings. That is screamingly obvious and not worth discussing. What I'm really interested in is the question: "What does your organization hope to achieve in real world value?" I have an answer for you on that one, Glenn. Stick with me.

In writing about the Jennings and Lambert project in San Francisco—the one that presented the dreams of architects and urban planners on bus shelter posters—scholar Stephen Duncombe observed: "There is no duplicity, no selling the people a false bill of goods. It's a dream that people are aware is just a dream. Yet at the same time these impossible dreams open up spaces to imagine new possibilities. . . . [their] impossible solutions are means to imagine new ones."[15]

It is plausible that on some level the Hypothetical Development Organization's stories might have a somewhat similar function. In another response

Figure 3.2 Theater of Escape. A neglected building with "beguiling portals" could be, Michael Doyle's rendering suggests, "refitted to deliver you wherever you want to go, by way of nonexistent technology."

to our efforts, *Good* suggested: "Perhaps this street art project could turn into authentic grassroots activism."[16] Perhaps. I'm certainly open to others' interpretations of our stories, but I can't say that I wholly accept that reading. I don't believe you can honestly call any of our ideas "solutions." On the other hand, nothing we offer here falls into the category of the false utopian promise. And quite a few of our stories do carry within them provocative assessments of the contemporary urban environment.

Personally, I am most inclined to agree with an assessment on another site, Aesthetics of Joy, written by Ingrid Fetell. She asserted that the project takes "germs of imagined futures and makes them visible. Juxtaposed against the forlorn emptiness of abandoned structures, these silly fantasies feel delightful—they are uninhibited manifestations of creative energy, filtered through a lens of hope. That they are implausible is their charm, but I half-hope that one of them will be compelling enough to stick."[17]

I like that it's only a *half*-hope. It would be remarkable if some billionaire bought one of these buildings and converted it into, let's say, a New Orleans Loitering Centre, just like the one in Mark Clayton's rendering. Or if local residents rallied for a Mobile Cornucopia, inspired by the one Candy Chang depicts. Or if some governmental agency elected to construct the Snooze Towers pod structures, precisely as imagined for us by John Becker. Such an outcome would, indeed, be stranger than fiction. But ultimately, *fiction* is what the Hypothetical Development Organization has to offer. These are stories. And I do not offer that thought as an apology, an admission, or a

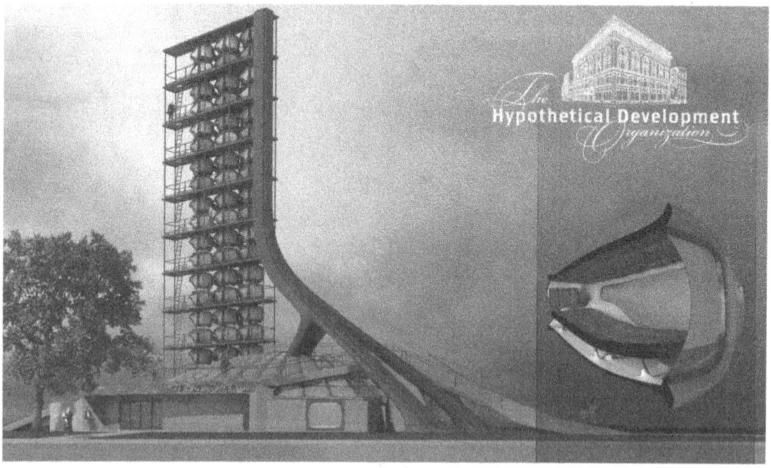

Figure 3.3 Sleep Pod. An "absurdly impractical solution" to the universal need for a place to sleep: "A stacked series of high-tech snooze pods, rising from the roof of a domed structure." Rendered by John Becker

concession. Good stories—funny, provocative, weird, or disturbing—have value in the real world.

First, these stories strike a blow for the vital habit of *actually seeing* the world we live in. By borrowing an overlooked form, the traditional development sign, obviously on some level we satirize it, exposing how preposterous many of these commercial stories are if you'd just stop and genuinely evaluate the situation. Certainly I'll never look at one of those signs in the same way again. Similarly, I don't look at—or rather overlook—neglected buildings quite so easily now. (I still walk past that vacant commercial structure that inspired all this on my routine neighborhood walks. Nothing has changed, except for the way I see it.)

Second, I don't think a story needs to be considered a means to an end. A story is an end. And a sign on an abandoned building is as good a medium as I can think of for telling an entertaining tale. I'm pleased to say, in fact, that among those who have taken note of our enterprise is Bruce Sterling himself. He wrote on his blog: "This must be the closest thing to an architecture fiction 'pure play' to have yet appeared."[18] I don't pretend to speak for precisely what Sterling means, but I think "pure play" is just right, in more ways than one.

The moment that interests me most, I suppose, would be the random passerby who suddenly *notices* that building he or she has walked past a hundred times, just because there's this sign on it, this arrestingly uncanny sign that tells a story that's blatantly and intentionally absurd. I think that moment—the story, in one image, of an implausible future for an unpopular place—makes the building exist again in a new way. It changes nothing into something.

I think it makes the passerby exist in a new way, too.

So I'm happy with a double-take, I'm thrilled with a smile. Such a moment is not a call to make something happen, or a promise of something that might happen, or an exhortation that you should hope for something to happen at some point. That moment is *something happening*. And that's not hypothetical at all. It's perfectly real.

Walker, Rob. "Implausible Futures for Unpopular Places." Places Journal, July 2011. https://placesjournal.org/article/implausible-futures-for-unpopular-places/. This essay originated as a talk given at Grand Arts, in Kansas City, Missouri, in December 2010. A version of it appears in the Blurb book Implausible Futures for Unpopular Places, *which documents the Hypothetical Development Organization's manifestation in New Orleans. More images from the project and information about the contributing artists can be found at HypotheticalDevelopment.com.*

NOTES

1. J. G. Ballard, "A Handful of Dust," *The Guardian*, March 20, 2006.
2. Bruce Sterling, "Science Fiction and Architecture Fiction," *Off Center*, March 20, 2006, http://blogs.walkerart.org/offcenter/2006/03/20/science-fiction-and-architecture-fiction/
3. See http://bldgblog.blogspot.com
4. Mark Dery, "Bunker of Broken Dreams," *Change Observer*, April 12, 2010, http://changeobserver.designobserver.com/entry.html?entry=13318
5. Geoff Manaugh, *The BLDG BLOG Book* (Chronicle, 2009)
6. Regine, "Venice Biennale of Architecture: the Polish pavilion," *We Make Money Not Art*. November 6, 2008, http://we-make-money-not-art.com/archives/2008/11/venice-biennale-of-architectur-5.php
7. Geoff Manaugh, "Fictional Ruins From Fictional Worlds," *BLDG BLOG*, January 4, 2007, http://bldgblog.blogspot.com/2007/01/fictional-ruins-from-fictional-worlds.html
8. Architectural Association School of Architecture Projects Review 2010: Ioana Iliesiu, http://projectsreview2010.aaschool.ac.uk/html/units.php?unit=96&name=615
9. "Concrete Misplots," Zeitguised, November 8, 2010, http://zeitguised.wordpress.com/2010/11/08/concrete-misplots/
10. "Wish You Were Here! Postcards from our Awesome Future," VisitSteve.com, November 2007, http://visitsteve.com/work/wish-you-were-here-postcards-from-our-awesome-future-2/
11. Examples can be seen at http://futuryst.blogspot.com/2007/10/bird-cage.html
12. Stuart Candy, "The Bird Cage," *The Sceptical Futuryst*, October 26, 2007, http://futuryst.blogspot.com/2007/10/bird-cage.html
13. Mary Vorsino, "Pranksters want debate on Hawaii's Chinatown," *Honolulu Advertiser*, October 15, 2007.
14. Allison Arieff, "Space: It's Still a Frontier," Opinionator Blog, February 3, 2010, http://opinionator.blogs.nytimes.com/2010/02/03/space-its-still-a-frontier/ (The cited comment is here: http://opinionator.blogs.nytimes.com/2010/02/03/space-its-still-a-frontier/#comment25)
15. "Duncombe on 'Wish You Were Here…'," VisitSteve.com, June 2008, http://visitsteve.com/news/duncombe-on-wish-you-were-here/
16. Alissa Walker, "Ads for Imaginary Buildings Highlight Lack of Real Development," *Good Magazine Website*, September 24, 2010, http://www.good.is/post/ads-for-imaginary-buildings-will-highlight-lack-of-real-development/
17. Ingrid Fetell, "The joy of implausible possibility," *Aesthetics of Joy*, October 9, 2010, http://aestheticsofjoy.com/2010/10/the-joy-of-implausible-possibility/
18. Bruce Sterling, "Architecture Fiction: Hypothetical Development Corporation," *Beyond The Beyond*, September 25, 2010, http://www.wired.com/beyond_the_beyond/2010/09/architecture-fiction-hypothetical-development-corporation/

BIBLIOGRAPHY

Architectural Association School of Architecture Projects Review 2010: Ioana Iliesiu http://projectsreview2010.aaschool.ac.uk/html/units.php?unit=96&name=615

Arieff, Allison. "Space: It's Still a Frontier." *Opinionator Blog*, February 3, 2010. http://opinionator.blogs.nytimes.com/2010/02/03/space-its-still-a-frontier

Ballard, J. G. "A Handful of Dust." *The Guardian*, March 20, 2006.

Candy, Stuart. "The Bird Cage." *The Sceptical Futuryst*, October 26, 2007. http://futuryst.blogspot.com/2007/10/bird-cage.html

"Concrete Misplots," Zeitguised, November 8, 2010. http://zeitguised.wordpress.com/2010/11/08/concrete-misplots/

Dery, Mark. "Bunker of Broken Dreams." *Change Observer*, April 12, 2010. http://changeobserver.designobserver.com/entry.html?entry=13318

"Duncombe on 'Wish You Were Here…,'" VisitSteve.com, June 2008. http://visitsteve.com/news/duncombe-on-wish-you-were-here/

Fetell, Ingrid. "The joy of implausible possibility." *Aesthetics of Joy*, October 9, 2010. http://aestheticsofjoy.com/2010/10/the-joy-of-implausible-possibility/

Manaugh, Geoff. *The BLDG BLOG Book*. San Francisco: Chronicle Books, 2009. http://bldgblog.blogspot.com

Regine. "Venice Biennale of Architecture: the Polish pavilion." *We Make Money Not Art*, November 6, 2008. http://we-make-money-not-art.com/archives/2008/11/venice-biennale-of-architectur-5.php

Sterling, Bruce. "Science Fiction and Architecture Fiction." *Off Center*, March 20, 2006. http://blogs.walkerart.org/offcenter/2006/03/20/science-fiction-and-architecture-fiction/

———. "Architecture Fiction: Hypothetical Development Corporation." *Beyond the Beyond*, September 25, 2010. http://www.wired.com/beyond_the_beyond/2010/09/architecture-fiction-hypothetical-development-corporation/

Vorsino, Mary. "Pranksters want debate on Hawaii's Chinatown." *Honolulu Advertiser*, October 15, 2007.

Walker, Alissa. "Ads for Imaginary Buildings Highlight Lack of Real Development." *Good Magazine Website*, September 24, 2010. http://www.good.is/post/ads-for imaginary-buildings-will-highlight-lack-of-real-development/

"Wish You Were Here! Postcards from our Awesome Future," VisitSteve.com. November 2007. http://visitsteve.com/work/wish-you-were-here-postcards-from-our-awesome-future-2/

Part II

DIY SUBCULTURES

Chapter 4

Repair Events and the Fixer Movement

Fixing the World One Repair at a Time

Lorenzo Giannini

Over the past five years we have seen the emergence of a new kind of phenomenon that we can refer to as *repair events*. Repair events are community monthly events during which people can bring their broken objects and meet people with the necessary repair skills. Repairers offer their work for free. The origin and development of this phenomenon is due to the initiatives of several organizations: the Repair Café Foundation in the Netherlands, the Fixers Collective and the Fixit Clinic in the United States and the Restart Project in England. Repair groups aim to promote a culture of repair as an alternative to a throwaway culture they believe dominates contemporary consumer behavior. They try to address this cultural change by the constitution of repair events as learning environments. Each repair is in fact a collaborative learning process, where skill-sharing is an essential element.

The first part of this paper will be dedicated to the brief and recent history of repair events and repair organizations, which have many differences and some relevant similarities. This emergence of a *repair culture* and a movement of fixers finds its roots in a combination of elements shared with the do-it-yourself and the hacker subculture and the maker movement. The second part of the paper examines the meaning and themes framework with which the most active worldwide repair groups relate. This investigation has been carried out through an analysis of digital media content produced by those groups, such as articles, blog posts, status updates on social media, and their own manifestos. I employ a practice theory perspective, because of its focus on practices as a set of meanings, materials, and competences, elements which are at the core of repair events' reproduction.

The paper identifies a set of meanings and themes that repair organizations share and that appear to be the building blocks of the emerging repair culture. All of these meanings and themes are related to a wider environmentalist and critical consumption frame, spanning from an interest in planned obsolescence as a social problem to the need for a design centered on repairability. As a conclusion, the paper shows how, in this developing context, repair organizations are placing themselves in an intermediate position between the production and the consumption spheres. From a utopian studies perspective, the fixers are drawing up the fundamental characteristics, if not of an ideal society, at least of the ideal relationship between production and consumption in late capitalism. The theme of the lack of control over commodities, and of the need to take control back, appears to be the main thread that binds the experience of repairers in a coherent framework.

WHAT IS A REPAIR EVENT?

The theme of repair, here understood in the material sense of restoring a given object, damaged or broken, to its working order, or restoring its aesthetic, has gained increased media attention in recent years. Making repairs, historically included with the rest of domestic activities, becomes a topic of discussion when the development of a market for mass-produced, low-cost goods contributes to the development of a throwaway culture which favors the disposal and replacement of defective or malfunctioning goods over repairing them. In this structure of consumerism, choosing to repair can become a conspicuous cultural or political action.

Over the last few decades, the act of repairing has acquired its own status and has become the object of sociological attention. Repair has been one of the tools available to several countercultures and subcultures which began to take shape from the sixties on (DIY, hacker, bike subcultures), all of which encompass an approach oriented toward consumer independence and critical and informed consumption, transitioning away from consumption styles determined by systems of production and the promotion of standardized commodities.[1]

In this chapter, we will observe the development of what can be defined as a *repair culture*, from the viewpoint of one of its particular elements: repair events. Repair events are a rather recent phenomenon, which places the act of repair in a collective and organized dimension. Repair events began to develop around 2009; they emerged at the same time in different places on a worldwide scale and, in a few years, became a recognized practice.

Currently, there are several models of the event, the result of several organizations in the United States and Europe. Although varied, the models have a strong set of common characteristics. Based on these similarities it is possible to identify the emergence of a phenomenon with particular characteristics. It can be clearly distinguished from other initiatives linked to the repair sphere, which, in recent years, seem to be more and more widespread and have a significant echo in the media: tutorials, guides, manuals, websites, courses, and fixing services either commercial or which bring together the commercial dimension with a focus on the cultural aspects of repair.

Repair events are periodical community events (they usually take place once a month) during which a repair collective provides their local community a number of people with different skills in the repair framework: carpenters, electricians, computer and smartphone experts, experienced do-it-yourselfers, or skilled eclectic tinkerers. These individuals (*coaches* from now on) are typically recruited at a local level and they offer their work for free and only for the short period of the event. Visitors have the opportunity to bring their damaged or malfunctioning objects, hoping for a successful repair, which happens, on average, 70 percent of the time. Events are typically held free of charge.

Even if the repair is usually free, all the events share a second fundamental concept: repairing should not be a mere free service for visitors, but rather, a moment of interaction and, in particular, an opportunity for sharing knowledge and competencies. Specifically, the *visitor* agrees to actively participate and tries to at least learn the basics of repairing. The coaches should act as teachers, involving visitors in the repair process and making them carry out as many steps of the repair as possible.

Finally, the convivial nature of the events is underlined and symbolized by the presence of food and drink, reserved in a special place. This has been an essential feature of repair events, since their inception.

A focus on community is an essential characteristic of repair events, and it is observable both in the way coaches are recruited and in the convivial nature of the events. The periodic nature of events and the desire to spread knowledge and skills regarding the care of daily consumer goods are also distinctive elements. We will now examine the events in detail, examining the different repair collectives and organizations involved.

MAIN ACTORS OF THE REPAIR ECOSYSTEM

Currently, there are four main organizations promoting repair events: the European Repair Café Foundation (The Netherlands), The Restart Project (England), and US Fixers Collective and Fixit Clinic. The four organizations had a different origin and development process, to which we will return shortly.

The Repair Café Foundation, Fixers Collective, and Fixit Clinic started their activities in 2009 apparently without any mutual influence, while the leaders of The Restart Project cite Fixers Collective and Fixit Clinic among their sources of inspiration. It is worth noting that the first two organizations had similar beginnings: a series of meetings to reflect collectively upon *repairing*.

Organizations can be distinguished according to the kind of objects that one can bring to their events: while The Repair Café Foundation and Fixers Collective raise no particular limitations on access, apart for large appliances such as washing machines and refrigerators, Fixit Clinic and Restart Project activities focus almost exclusively on consumer electronics, in particular Information and Communication Technologies (ICT) and small home appliances.

The organizations differ significantly in development capacities and prospects. To this point, the Repair Café Foundation can count more than 700 Repair Cafés open worldwide, while The Restart Project is the only other organization with such a significant growth rate, with 17 affiliated groups in 5 countries currently at work and the prospect of opening up 193 affiliated groups on every continent. The two organizations establish clear rules for affiliation: using the name of the organization and of the repair event model require compliance with the rules posted on their websites, rules that define the correct development of a repair event.

Many of the requests for affiliation come from associations which are already active in the fields of social and/or cultural promotion; repair events add to their existing activities. The groups and associations that gravitate toward the phenomenon of repair events tell us something about the points where different frameworks of values overlap. The use of space is indicative too, because if it is true that some groups have their own structure, others rely on structures provided by other associations, organizations and public authorities. All groups also participate in events and festivals of various kinds.

The developing repair ecosystem cannot disregard initiatives produced by at least two other commercial subjects: the iFixit platform and *Make* magazine. As we will see, iFixit and in particular its founder Kyle Wiens, are important actors in the definition of a shared cultural framework for repair collectives and organizations. The platform, which has a significant reputation between fixers, is divided into two separate and parallel projects: iFixit.org, which is an activist-style platform and iFixit.com, which is a platform that provides both tutorials for the repair of ICT and access to the necessary replacement parts. Occasionally, Wiens' opinion pieces are linked to and positively commented on by repair organizations from their Facebook pages. In turn, the stories of repair collectives are mentioned in the opinion articles written by the authors of iFixit.org.

The second business entity that has played a role in developing a repair culture is O'Reilly Media, publisher of the magazine *Make*. *Make* played a crucial role in the birth of what is now recognized as the *maker movement*.

Chris Anderson, who extensively wrote about the rising maker culture, places the movement's birth at the launch of the magazine in 2005 and the following year at the release of the first *Maker Faires*, which occurred a few years before the repair events began surfacing. The term, as Anderson himself admits, is little more than a "broad description that encompasses a wide variety of activities, from traditional crafting to high-tech electronics, many of which have been around for ages."[2] The role of the magazine and of the *Maker Faires* (the exhibitions connected to the magazine) was precisely to have worked as a place of collective identification for a number of very different practices.

The *Maker's Bill of Rights* was published in one of the first issues of *Make*. Mister Jalopy, its author, is now a point of reference for the movement.[3] As he puts it: "Asserting that an individual should be able to open, repair and modify the products that they buy, the Maker's Bill of Rights gave a clear voice to the Maker Movement's frustration with increasingly disposable products that lock out consumers."[4] As we will see, this document voiced a sensitivity that had not yet been properly expressed, and which therefore played a role in starting a discussion on the repair theme.

Platform21 and Repair Café Foundation

When Joanna van der Zanden, Dutch independent curator and creative director had the opportunity to manage what would become the Platform21, she likely never imagined that a few years later, her work would represent one of the turning points for the development of a repair culture and a rising movement of repairers.

Platform21 was born as a temporary incubator for reflection on the construction of a new design center for the Zuidas district in Amsterdam. The proposal came from AMO, a think tank within the architectural firm OMA (Office for Metropolitan Architecture) founded by Rem Koolhaas. AMO's report included the provocative statement: "The world does not need another design center."[5] In a period of proliferation of global design centers, the challenge for the curator was to represent in a nonorthodox way the link between the design domain and the consumption domain, trying to capture the spirit of the time. As van der Zanden states:

> Design is especially appealing as a subject because of its breadth. Everything has a design, but not every design has the same value for everyone. We surround ourselves with stuff because we can give it numerous different meanings—functional, emotional, cultural, economic, symbolic. Seen through the eyes of different people, a single product can yield those stories; you only need to be interested in them. An apparently insignificant object can be of great personal

> value and tell us more about a given culture or period than a star designer's masterpiece.[6]

In the four years of its existence, Platform21 has been host to a series of workshops on a variety of topics. The organizational objective behind the management of the project was to bring together people of different backgrounds to reflect on shared themes. The words of Van Der Zanden reveal the intention to draw from local participation and skills, rather than putting things exclusively into the hands of specialists, setting forth passion as a catalyzing element, instead of the profession: "You can join a different group of people if they share a passion for a subject. And in this way, you can bring together high and low art, professionalism and hobbyism, design and science, on an equal footing and in a productive way, and generate new conversations."[7]

In spring–summer 2009, *Platform21 = repairing* workshop was launched, during which events involving designers, students, amateurs and more generally the public, were organized for a collective reflection on the theme of repair. One day, in particular, was marked by an event of collective repair and included a number of experts to whom visitors could bring their own items to be repaired. The event was to be the prototype of future repair events.

One of the most significant outcomes of Platform21 was its role in the design of the *repair café*, the Dutch version of repair events;[8] Martine Postma, a Dutch journalist, attended Platform21 and the next autumn held her first repair café, an initiative that brought the workshop's attempted repair to another level: visitors had to be actively engaged in the repair process, leading to the establishment of the *Repair Café Foundation*.

The second relevant outcome of the project was the publication of *Platform21's repair manifesto*, an eleven item list, which tries to define the relevance of repair practices in contemporary culture. The manifesto was uploaded online and beyond the organizers expectations it was downloaded over a million times and appeared in several blogs related to sustainability; it was also linked by environmental groups, designers' and architects' blogs.[9] The manifesto was eventually translated into more than ten languages and it was indicated as a source of inspiration in the writing of other manifestos related to the repair ecosystem.

In the manifesto, the relevance of repair is highlighted from different points of view. In some cases, the text speaks directly to consumers: "Make your products live longer! Repairing is not anti-consumption. It is anti-needlessly throwing things away." Other points directly address producers and raise questions about their manufacturing strategies: "Things should be designed so that they can be repaired. Product designers: make your products repairable. Share clear, understandable information about DIY repairs." At the same time, they try to instill in consumers a critical and informed attitude, which is useful to put pressure on manufacturers: "Consumers: buy things you know can be repaired."[10]

Repair cafés and *Platform21's repair manifesto* popularity is a sign that, at both material and symbolic level, an answer was given to an underlying social need that had not yet been addressed. We will return later to the contents of the manifesto.

Proteus Gowanus and the Fixers Collective

Proteus Gowanus was founded in Brooklyn (New York) as an interdisciplinary gallery and reading room, shortly before Platform21's establishment. The Proteus Gowanus was born as an art project by the Russian artist Sasha Chavchavadze.[11] Proteus Gowanus was developed under the same premise as Platform21: starting a collaborative process that could break the gap between specialists and nonspecialists. As it is stated in the project website, it "seeks to create an alternative, culturally rich environment designed to stimulate the creative process; a place where the boundaries between the artist and non-artist fade, where images and ideas from disparate disciplines are juxtaposed to create new meanings."[12]

The gallery had run a series of yearlong workshops, each one following a given theme, during which it hosted art exhibitions, artifacts, books, plays and performances. In the period between 2008 and 2009, the chosen theme was *mend*, a multipurpose meaning word: referring both to the care of material goods, as well as personal care. *Mend* is part of the semantic of *repair* and the gallery was open to the participation of anyone who wanted to propose activities or productions that had a bearing on the topic.

The *Fixers Collective* is one of the most significant initiatives born as a result of this period of reflection and cocreation. It is an association that periodically, drawing on the experiences of the *mend* year, organizes repair events called *fixing sessions*.[13] During 2009, therefore, the autonomous path of *fixing sessions* began, by regular repair sessions with characteristics that are similar to those of a *repair café*.

Fixit Clinic

The Fixit Clinic was born with a focus on consumer electronics. Its founder Peter Mui is an engineer with long experience in ICT, who grew up inside the Massachusetts Institute of Technology in Cambridge, the environment of which is historically and culturally connected to the development of the hacker ethic.[14]

After giving birth to a number of projects related to the development of entrepreneurship, Mui founded the Fixit Clinic in late 2009.[15] The *fixit clinics* are repair sessions, assisted by expert repairers, with a focus on consumer electronics and small appliances, although in some places the sphere of repairable items have been enlarged to clothing.

The approach taken by the founder of the organization to run the events is definitely education-oriented, as he himself says: "while the primary objective of Fixit Clinic is to demystify consumer technology and empower people to disassemble and repair their broken stuff, the secondary, somewhat surreptitious goal is to improve science and technology literacy in the population overall, so we can choose officials to make good policy decisions."[16] The main location where the fixit clinics are performed is the San Francisco Bay Area.

The Restart Project

The Restart Project, the last organization considered, was founded in London in June 2012 by Janet Gunter, who describes herself as an American/British activist and anthropologist and Ugo Vallauri who describes himself as an Italian researcher with a MPhil in Geography and a working experience for the Slow Food Movement and Computer Aid International, the latter being an organization that collects and refurbishes electronic equipment for distribution in developing countries.

The Restart Project has a strong environmentalist drive. As they put it, "electronic waste is one of the fastest growing waste streams in many countries including the UK. While recycling is important, we intervene before disposal—inspiring people to buy for longevity and to divert electronics from waste."[17] While the name The Restart Project choose for its events' model is *restart party*, the event's structure and features mirror that of *repair café*, *fixing sessions,* and *fixit clinics.*

A SHARED FRAMEWORK OF MEANINGS IN THE MAKING

This analysis addresses the phenomenon of repair events and the phenomenology related to the repair domain observing repair events as practices. The theoretical framework for the use of the concept of practice is what emerges from the perspective of *practice theory*.[18] According to this theoretical perspective, practices may be considered as a particular configuration of three elements: materials, meanings, and skills.

A focus on *elements* means not only to evaluate their role in practice reproduction, but also to understand their path before and beyond it. Elements have autonomous trajectories, they can be analyzed, questioned and compared beyond observed practice and as constitutive parts of different practices.[19]

The use, circulation and sharing of materials, meanings and skills are clearly observable processes in the reproduction of repair events.

This paper focuses on the role of meanings in the reproduction of these specific practices, while an analysis of the role of materials and skills is left to future publications: what is the shared framework of meanings that rhetorically is built around the practice of repair events? Can it represent the formation of a shared cultural framework?

The sample is twofold and made up of contents produced by the groups on social media (Facebook in particular) and their own websites and documents published by the various organizations, on the style of manifestos, charters, declarations of independence etc. . . The different organizations promote their activities and manage their online identity through social media like Facebook and Twitter, and regularly publish content on dedicated sites and blogs.

Published content might relate to repair events (calls to action or reporting of events); activities or initiatives of others which the organization may or may have not joined (this content marks a connection between organizations or between organizations and other institutions or associations); a link to other web content (e.g., a blog post, news, reportage, etc). The leaders of the organizations (Kyle Wiens of iFixit, Gunter and Vallauri of The Restart Project especially) also write pieces for major international newspapers and reviews (*The Guardian, The Atlantic, or Wired*, only to name a few).

Analysis of this media content reveals something about the groups' identity, the image of themselves they want to promote, the issues and ideas they want to be associated with and the systems of relationships in which they are involved. Following the practice theory approach, all the sentences that represent the ends or purposes that the groups are striving for, or sentences that clarify groups' identity, can be identified as *meanings*, as well as those sentences that clarify or define the groups' position about certain issues. Moreover, one can consider as *meanings* all the sentences that are related to the motivations of participation.

Maker's Bill of Rights, *Platform21's repair manifesto* and *iFixit's Self-repair manifesto* were published between 2005 and 2010, shortly before the emergence of the phenomenon, and they already include most of the themes that will structure the repair groups' cultural framework during the following years.

This correspondence means on the one hand that these documents have been able to capture and shape a sensibility that was already present and on the other that they have actually had an influence on the formation of repair culture's key meanings.

The first document we can include in the repair ecosystem is the *Maker's Bill of Rights*, published in an early issue of *Make*, the magazine of reference for the so-called *maker movement*, in 2005. In the *Maker's Bill of Rights* repair is present as a background value in almost all the sentences. The *bill* comes several years before the *Platform21's repair manifesto* and seeks to provide a place of recognition to consumers frustrated at manufacturing choices made by leading brands of ICT. Each passage of the *Bill of Rights* is an indictment and points out the shortcomings in the current system of production of consumer electronics: "Meaningful and specific parts lists shall be included. Cases shall be easy to open. Battery shall be replaceable. Special tools are allowed only for darn good reasons. Profiting by selling expensive special tools is wrong, and not making special tools available is even worse."[20]

The *Bill of Rights* implies the idea that the producers illegitimately profit at the expense of the consumers and stresses the fact that manufacturers keep consumers uninformed about the functioning of devices' inner parts. Meaningfully, a focus on consumers' *duties* and on the consumption domain in general will appear in *Platform21's repair manifesto* first and in all the following manifestos and documents and every time repairing, as an issue, comes into play.

In 2010, iFixit.org, the cultural branch of the platform iFixit, published the *Self-Repair Manifesto*. The document had a clear environmentalist mark: "repair saves the planet. Earth has limited resources and we can't run a linear manufacturing process forever. The best way to be efficient is to reuse what we already have!,"[21] but it does not fail to touch on the issues of ownership: "If you can't fix it, you don't own it";[22] of repairing as a means to personal empowerment: "Repair empowers and emboldens individuals";[23] and to stress the relationship between, on the one hand, the lack of information regarding electronic devices (for which manufacturers are considered responsible): "we have the right to repair documentation for everything, to troubleshooting instructions and flowcharts"[24] and on the other hand the need that control over devices returns to consumers: "we have the right to choose our own repair technician, to replace any and all consumable ourselves, to hardware that doesn't require proprietary tools to repair."[25]

In 2013, within a year of its foundation, The Restart Project published its own document, asking ICT consumers to take a pledge: "The time has come for us to recreate our relationship to electronics. Nobody is going to do it for us, we need to take back control of the stuff we own."[26] The theme of the lack of control and of the need to take control back is one of the threads that binds the experience of repairers in a coherent framework. A second thread is the environmental sustainability of consumption patterns and production techniques: "I will not be seduced by phony green arguments about buying new devices—keeping in mind more than half of the energy used in a laptop's lifetime is spent in its manufacture."[27] The document goes on with a series of precepts aimed at the promotion of critical and informed consumption that, in that sense, becomes a means to put pressure on technology manufacturers.

Regarding Facebook and organizations' websites, while Repair Café Foundation can count on the highest number of affiliated groups and events, it has the lowest online activity rate and doesn't manage a blog at all, but only a website, which is rarely updated. In contrast, The Restart Project has by far the most important production of online content, both on Facebook and on the organization's blog, the latter being updated constantly since autumn of 2011. Fixit Clinic's usage of online media, is almost exclusively about the promoting and reporting of events, whereas the few times in which the group chooses to link and comment on other web content, the pieces linked are extensively about the identified shared framework of meanings.

Regardless of the number of status updates or blog posts which any organization has written across platforms, a core of shared and recurring meanings can be found.[28] These meanings are coherent with the set of themes proposed by organizations' manifestos and documents.

As a result of the analysis, I collected the meanings in a series of categories with homogeneous contents. These categories represent an attempt to identify the building blocks of the emerging repair culture. At a more general level the identified meanings can be divided into those which relate to the sphere of production, with particular reference to the production choices of the most popular technology companies and those which relate to consumption, with a focus on consumption culture and styles. In both areas, it's possible to make a further distinction between meanings that imply a critical, conflictual, and dissatisfied attitude and meanings that imply a proactive and collaborative attitude. Four main categories are thus identified: (a) meanings that refer to production in a critical manner, (b) meanings that relate to production in a proactive manner, (c) meanings that relate to consumption in a critical manner, and (d) meanings that relate to consumption in a proactive manner.

It is useful to specify that in the case of the Repair Café Foundation, a wide articulation of meanings is observable even in a small number of published content: the core of shared and recurring meanings is present, even only in its website *about page*. In contrast, the Restart Project has a greater commitment to the production of online content and touches a range of meanings wider than those shared by all the repair collectives, thus promoting a set of topics that are pushing the boundaries of what can be included in the repair culture domain. Finally, if we take into consideration the case of the Fixit Clinic alone, at least one category (b) is clearly under-represented. While this means that there is, as part of the collective, a lack of interest for this dimension, I am of the opinion that this does not undermine the soundness of the general categorization.

Critical Approach to the Production Sphere

The first category includes all the statements and passages in which the producers—in particular ICT producers—are accused of extending control over the devices they produce, to the detriment of full ownership by the consumers. This is well represented in the following excerpt from a piece Kyle Wiens wrote for *Popular Mechanics*, which has been linked by Fixers Collective in their Facebook page:

> I started out repairing products made by Apple, a company that doesn't exactly encourage customers to take their gadgets apart. In fact, Apple uses proprietary screws to keep tinkerers out. And where Apple leads, others follow. With the exception of companies like Dell and Lenovo, most computer brands have stopped releasing repair information or replacement parts to the public.[29]

The producers are accused of adopting production techniques and strategies that result in electrical appliances and (especially) smartphones and computers that are particularly difficult to repair, unless the consumer turns to an authorized maintenance center.

According to the repairers, consumers are systematically denied the opportunity to change, alter, repair and customize their own items. In these passages a representation of the ICT corporation as an opponent is built.

Here the fixers revive a rhetoric which, in the version applying to ICT, has been part of the hacker ethic from its outset[30] placing, in its conflictuality, on the one side, a production domain identified by its will to promote proprietary forms of knowledge and responsible for the production of black boxes inaccessible to those consumers who refuse to be regulated by the prescribed uses, and on the other side, collectives or groups identified by their will to promote an open culture. According to Steven Levy:

> Hackers believe that essential lessons can be learned about the systems—about the world—from taking things apart, seeing how they work, and using this knowledge to create new and even more interesting things. They resent any person, physical barrier, or law that tries to keep them from doing this. This is especially true when a hacker wants to fix something that (from his point of view) is broken or needs improvement.[31]

The topic of planned obsolescence can be fully seen as one of the key elements to this conflict. Formalized by a Manhattan real estate broker,[32] Bernard London, in the 1930s as a tool for sustaining demand during the Great Depression, the concept states that the process of decline and replacement of commodities must already be planned for in the production phase.[33] This concept is making a comeback as one of the main catalysts for the constitution of a shared framework of meanings between repair collectives, who blame producers of consumer electronics (from laptops to washing machines, from smartphones to refrigerators) of strategically using this process at the expense of consumers, forcing them to partake in an accelerated replacement process which is also a detriment to environmental sustainability. The Restart Project is one of the most active groups in trying to raise awareness about planned obsolescence, as in this sentence: "Say NO to planned obsolescence—'kill chips' and other tricks are simply unethical and no longer acceptable, and designers must push back" (The Restart Project).[34]

Proactive Approach to the Production Sphere

In the second category, the fixers see their relationship with production as pro-active and collaborative. Here are gathered all the statements the fixers use to discuss the possibility of the adoption of different production standards, orientated more toward repairability and, consequently, toward environmental sustainability, as discussed in this excerpt from The Restart Project's blog:

> Last year we launched mini-campaign with a simple message: the most ethical smartphone is the one you already have. The same applies to printers as well as toasters. Manufacturers should contribute to this vision and focus on long-term, loyal relationships with consumers based on openness of repair information, repairability, upgradeability and availability of spare parts.[35]

This objective can be pursued by pressuring the producers collectively as consumers. In this case, fixers frequently refer to the production model that emerges from a circular economy, that is, the "cradle to cradle" design.[36]

Recently a coalition was created, of which the Repair Café Foundation and iFixit platform are a part, which published a joint mission statement.[37] The document stresses the need for the production of commodities with a higher degree of repairability in order to extend their life cycle and gain environmental, economic and social benefits.

Critical Approach to the Consumption Sphere

In a third category I collected sentences in which repairers take a critical approach toward the sphere of consumption, as shown in this sentence from the Repair Café Foundation website: "We throw away vast amounts of stuff. Even things with almost nothing wrong, and which could get a new lease of life after a simple repair."[38] Here criticism prevails against what the repairers define as a throwaway culture, a model of consumption prevalent in contemporary society. The same intention, but with a focus on new technologies, can be found in The Restart Project's writings: "Watching people discard devices because they ran "slow." Watching people upgrade by simply buying new phones every nine months. Have we become passive, flabby consumers of technology—like the future humans in *Wall-E*? Have we have lost our "repair muscle mass"?"[39] While the maker culture had a role in the development of a repair culture, a critical approach to the consumption sphere is an element that clearly distinguishes the latter from the former. The collective ideally writes to the maker community, pointing out their approach to the production and consumption processes and asking them to become aware of the problems inherent in the production of gadgets that are destined to be thrown away:

> And now we get to where some of our disquiet with the throw-away culture overlaps with maker culture. Over the past year especially, with budget miniature computers, the price of sensors and wearable technology dropping, and everything getting reduced in size, we see a danger of the multiplication of disposable, use once and throw-away gadgets [. . .]. We see disposable electronics celebrated, and 3D printers lauded for churning out the same frivolous crap that was mass-produced last year by invisible workers in China.[40]

Proactive Approach to the Consumption Sphere

The fourth, and last category, includes all the passages in which a proactive approach is used with reference to the sphere of consumption. This is the semantic space of repair events. In the following excerpt the Repair Café Foundation describes some of repair events' main goals: "The Repair Café teaches people to see their possessions in a new light. And, once again, to appreciate their value. The Repair Café helps change people's mindset. This is essential to kindle people's enthusiasm for a sustainable society."[41]

If it is true, as stated above, that production styles and strategies tend to subtract ownership from the consumers, here the fixers reflect on the role of repair events in increasing the level of consumer empowerment and, consequently, their level of control and ownership over the possessed goods. Repair events, from this standpoint, are a venue for the transmission and sharing of skills and should be included in the category of the so-called sharing economy and collaborative consumerism.[42]

Organizing and participating in repair events is, therefore, a form of empowering and alternative critical consumption. This is the way a member of the Fixers Collective defines the project objective: "the goal of the Fixers Collective is to increase material literacy in our community by fostering an ethic of creative caring toward the objects in our lives"[43]; in addition, for fixers, running repair events also means having a particular interest in the community, whether it deals with encouraging relations of solidarity within the community or with the role that events have in recovering or rebuilding a crumbling community. As the Repair Café Foundation puts in its website:

> Knowing how to make repairs is a skill quickly lost. Society doesn't always show much appreciation for the people who still have this practical knowledge, and against their will they are often left standing on the sidelines. Their experience is never used, or hardly ever. The Repair Café changes all that! People who might otherwise be sidelined are getting involved again. Valuable practical knowledge is getting passed on.[44]

The *control* issue cuts across the measured categories, drawing a connection between, on the one hand, the meanings that relate to the conflictual relationship of repairers with the production domain and, on the other, the contribution that repairers themselves think they can give to the development of a different culture of consumption. In this framework, as in a zero-sum game between the producer and the consumer, the control of the commodity is always placed mainly on one side, at the expense of the other. In a fixer's representation, the control of an item is the result of real and full ownership, for which the mere purchase or the appropriation processes as they are classically defined by the sociology of consumption are not enough.

The theme of appropriation has been central to the sociology of consumption for several decades.[45] Full appropriation of consumer goods takes place through the activation of possession rituals, which perform a double function: that of overcoming the alien nature of mass-produced goods as well as assimilating it into the consumer's cultural world. The fixers implicitly suggest a re-elaboration of the canonical appropriation/ownership processes.

In short, a further-reaching and fuller ownership takes place only when the consumer has full knowledge of the goods possessed, of its functional mechanism, knows how to modify and repair it. This possibility, however, is increasingly and systematically denied by the design styles implemented by manufacturers.

In the framework of meanings shared by the fixers, the design styles implemented by manufacturers are meant to limit the consumer's ability to modify, repair or upgrade the good possessed. Leaving on the producers' side these elements crucial for commodity knowability and full appropriation, reinforces the inherent alienating character of the mass-produced commodity.[46] According to the fixers, the application of these production styles excludes the consumer from full ownership. From this standpoint, repair events have the role of allowing the consumers to re-appropriate shares of control over the possessed goods: they are agents of empowerment.

The more general points to this conflictual pattern mark the bond between the growing repair culture with the DIY culture[47] and, in turn, with cultures linked to the bike subculture,[48] the hacker ethic,[49] and the maker movement.

Wolf and McQuitty, who developed a conceptual model that considers the motivators and outcomes of DIY behavior, maintain that an elevated sense of control is one of the principal outcomes of engaging in DIY projects: "Control most often is associated with personal mastery of situations, which means that one is effective at fulfilling goals [. . .] DIY allows people to take charge of a part of their environment that typically is controlled by others."[50]

These and other themes shifted from the DIY culture, to the bicycling subculture, and now they are part of the growing repair culture. Bike co-ops have been places of development of discourses, values and meanings that are now part of the fixers' cultural framework. Bicycles and bicycle maintenance skills are, after all, key elements in repair events not focused on ICT. *Hackerspaces* and *fab labs* (coworking sites related to the *hacker subculture* and to the *fixer movement*) are often available for repair groups, while on occasion hackers and makers organize their own repair events, too.

CONCLUSIONS

In what we might define as an emerging repair culture, repairing—which has lost its importance among the ordinary consumption practices—is making its comeback as a cultural and political tool, in conjunction with the development of specific manufacturing styles and of a specific consumption culture.

There are numerous actors in this phenomenon, but all, as a rule, are working on both a symbolic/literary and a material level. In the first case, the work of the groups belonging to this emerging movement are drawing up—through manifestos, declarations and bills of rights—the fundamental characteristics, if not of an ideal society, at least of the ideal relationship between production and consumption. It is a cultural process founded on a critique of the existing system and on its missing elements; a critique of the prevalent production and consumption styles alike, and of the problematic relationship between the two.

To observe this cultural process through the lens of utopian studies, we must turn to a perspective capable of interpreting phenomena associated with advanced capitalism, in order to analyze contemporary utopias which address or critique capitalism and consumer society.

The primacy of multinational corporations and borderless economies is linked to the development of a new stage of capitalism, as is the return of utopian discourse in literature and cultural studies, but only after its classic concept—historically the model for understanding the national condition of modernity—has been abandoned.[51]

Technological progress and economic uncertainty require new forms of utopia. Utopia, in today's configuration, explains Robert Tally through a re-elaboration of Fredric Jameson's viewpoint, "may only be a method by which one can attempt to apprehend the system itself,"[52] "a critical tool for making sense of the postnational condition, in our postmodern age of globalization,"[53] and "a means of mapping the world"[54] in an age when representations are in crisis.

From this standpoint, the theme of inherent conflict between producers and consumers, as raised by the fixers, and centered on competing capabilities to exercise control over commodities, represents the form of cognitive mapping which Jameson believes to be the contemporary form of utopia.

To put it another way, the idea that there's a control issue in the relation between producers and consumers is one of the possible metaphors which can be used (and that fixers use) to represent society in the times of advanced capitalism, to give a sense of the transformations in the flux of transnational power and respond to the key theme of uncertainty.

The cultural work of the fixers is an attempt to draw a map of the contemporary world system, on the one hand a way to master complexity in an age of expansion of contingency and on the other, a critique of the existing situation.

From this viewpoint, utopia always implies criticism, rooted in a particular context which reveals a significant social problem which must be resolved: "in identifying and disclosing such problems, utopian discourse has already fulfilled one of its fundamental offices, which is to serve as a critique of the existing system."[55]

The theme of lack of control resounds in the extensive research carried out by Chris Carlsson[56] on what he defined as *nowtopian* subcultures, an analysis of different subversive and resistant subcultures inspired by the DIY culture.

One of the main drives to participate in this type of subculture is the will to respond to the sensation of having no control over one's social role, in the sense that one's role is carried out through one's work, its social objectives and its political content, which implies the sensation of having no control over the type of world that is created through one's work.[57]

The emerging repair culture provides an interpretation of this condition of uncertainty, attributing the responsibilities to the development of production and consumption styles and identifying the repair events as possible social cure venues. Therefore, on a material level, the success of repair events, which as nowtopic projects represent projects of local commitment, strongly rooted in daily life, can be explained in light of their ability to restore to the actors a sensation of regaining control. Given their increasing diffusion and hence their collective reach, repair events can be considered as events where people work (and are engaged) for the reassertion of popular control, in the light of an inherent conflict between producers and consumers.

NOTES

1. Steven Levy, *Hackers: Heroes of the Computer Revolution* (New York: Bantam Doubleday, 1984); Chris Carlsson, *Nowtopia: How Pirate Programmers, Outlaw Bycyclists, and Vacant-lot Gardeners Are Inventing the Future Today* (Oakland: AK Press, 2008); Matthew B Crawford, *Shop Class as Soulcraft: An Inquiry into the Value of Work* (New York: The Penguin Press, 2009).

2. Chris Anderson, *Makers: The New Industrial Revolution* (New York: Crown Business, 2012), 20.

3. Lawrence Downes, "Mister Jalopy Wants to Make a Better World," *The New York Times*, August 25, 2008, accessed July 17, 2015, http://www.nytimes.com/2008/08/25/opinion/25mon4.html

4. "Mister Jalopy," Mister Jalopy, accessed July 17, 2015, http://www.misterjalopy.com

5. Joanna van der Zanden, ed. *Curatorial Cooking // The Design Practice of Platform21* (Arnhem: ArtEZ Press, 2011), 2.

6. van der Zanden, *Curatorial Cooking,* 3.

7. Ibid., 5.

8. Sally McGrane, "An Effort to Bury a Throwaway Culture One Repair at a Time," *The New York Times*, May 8, 2012, accessed July 19, 2015; Daniela K. Rosner, "Making Citizens, Reassembling Devices: On Gender and the Development of Contemporary Public Sites of Repair in Northern California," *Public Culture* 26, no.1 (2013): 51–77.

9. Joanna van der Zanden, "Creative Strategies for Locally-Oriented Knowledge Exchange," lecture presented at the workshop *Curating as Social Practice*, Open Society Georgia Foundation and Tbilisi State Academy of Arts, Tbilisi/Batumi, Republic of Georgia, March 11–12, 2012, https://www.youtube.com/watch?v=oueJtWGSqqg

10. "Platform21's Repair Manifesto," Platform21, accessed July 19, 2015, http://www.platform21.nl/page/4375/en

11. Lilli Frances. "Proteus Gowanus. The Old Man of the Canal," *Carroll Gardens Patch*, February 4, 2011, accessed July 19, 2015, http://patch.com/new-york/carrollgardens/proteus-gowanus-the-old-man-of-the-canal

12. "About us," Proteus Gowanus, accessed July 19, 2015, http://proteusgowanus.org/about

13. "Fixers Collective," Proteus Gowanus, accessed July 19, 2015, http://proteusgowanus.org/fixers-collective/

14. Levy, *Hackers.*

15. Camilla Brinkman, "Education, empowerment and enlightenment through guided disassembly of your broken stuff," *MIT News*, February 7, 2012, accessed July 20, 2015, http://newsoffice.mit.edu/2012/education-empowerment-and-enlightenment-through-guided-disassembly-of-your-broken-stuff

16. Brinkman, "Education, empowerment and enlightenment through guided disassembly of your broken stuff."

17. "About," The Restart Project, accessed July 20, 2015, http://therestartproject.org/about/

18. Andreas Reckwitz, "Toward a Theory of Social Practices. A development in culturalist theorizing," *European Journal of Social Theory* 5, no. 2 (2002); Theodore R. Schatzki, Karin Knorr Cetina and Eike von Savigny, ed. *The Practice Turn in Contemporary Theory* (New York: Routledge, 2001); Elizabeth Shove, Mika Pantzar and Mark Watson, *The Dynamics of Social Practices: Everyday Life and How It Changes* (London: Sage publications, 2012).

19. Shove, Pantzar and Watson, *The Dynamics of Social Practice*.

20. "The Maker's Bill of Rights (PDF)," *Make*, accessed July 21, 2015, http://makezine.com/2006/12/01/the-makers-bill-of-rights/

21. "Self-repair Manifesto," iFixit.com, accessed February 7, 2015, https://www.ifixit.com/Manifesto

22. Ibid.

23. Ibid.

24. Ibid.

25. Ibid.

26. "The Pledge," The Restart Project, accessed July 22, 2015, https://restartproject.files.wordpress.com/2012/10/restartpledgedraft.pdf

27. "The Pledge."

28. For example, Fixit Clinic's use of Facebook, during analyzed period, is almost exclusively about the promoting and reporting of events, whereas the few times in which the group chooses to link and comment someone else's content, the pieces it links are extensively about the shared framework of meanings that has been identified.

29. Kyle Wiens, "Why We Fix: A DIY Manifesto," Popular mechanics, May 31, 2014, accessed May 24, 2015, http://www.popularmechanics.com/home/skills/auto-home-improvement-diy/why-we-fix-a-diy-manifesto-16846653?click=pm_latest; Fixers Collective linked the article in their Facebook page on June 1, 2014, commenting: "wonderful opinion piece by iFixit.com's very own Kyle Wiens."

30. Levy, *Hackers*.

31. Ibid., 28.

32. Giles Slade, *Made to Break. Technology and Obsolescence in America* (Cambridge: Harvard University Press, 2006).

33. Bernard London, *Ending the Depression through Planned Obsolescence* (New York: Self-published, 1934), https://upload.wikimedia.org/wikipedia/commons/2/27/London_%281932%29_Ending_the_depression_through_planned_obsolescence.pdf

34. "Repairing with Young Product Designers," *The Restart Project*, March 8, 2013, accessed October 12, 2015, http://therestartproject.org/design/repairing-with-young-product-designers/

35. "Let's give repair a chance!," *The Restart Project*, March 3, 2014, accessed October 6, 2015, http://therestartproject.org/consumption/lets-give-repair-a-chance/

36. William McDonough and Michael Braungart, *Cradle to Cradle: Remaking the Way We Make Things* (New York: North Point Press, 2002).

37. "Joint Mission Statement. Sustainable Consumption and Production: Improving Product Durability and Reparability," Repair Café, accessed May 16, 2015, http://repaircafe.org/wp-content/uploads/2015/03/Mission_Statement_Reparability_and_Durability_of_Products.pdf

38. "About the Repair Café," Repair Café, accessed July 22, 2015, http://repair-cafe.org/about-repair-cafe/

39. "#firstworldproblems." *The Restart Project*, August 2, 2012, accessed October 12, 2015, http://therestartproject.org/restart-project/firstworldproblems/

40. "Dear Makers," The Restart Project, August 8, 2013, accessed October 2, 2015, http://therestartproject.org/repair-elsewhere/dear-makers/

41. "About the Repair Café," Repair Café, accessed July 22, 2015, http://repair-cafe.org/about-repair-cafe/

42. Rachel Botsman and Roo Rogers, *What's Mine is Yours. The Rise of Collaborative Consumption* (New York: HarperCollins, 2010).

43. Nick Normal, "The curiosity is there: Interview with Vincent Lai from the Fixers Collective," *Make*, June 13, 2012, accessed May 14, 2015, http://makezine.com/2012/06/13/the-curiosity-is-there-interview-with-vincent-lai-from-the-fixers-collective/

44. "About the Repair Café," Repair Café, accessed May 16, 2015, http://repair-cafe.org/about-repair-cafe/

45. Grant McCracken, *Culture and Consumption* (Bloomington: Indiana University Press, 1988); Colin Campbell, "The Craft Consumer Culture. Craft and Consumption in a Postmodern Society," *Journal of Consumer Culture* 5, no. 1 (2005).

46. ICT brands use a variety of rhetoric to justify this situation (safety in particular).

47. Marco Wolf and Shaun McQuitty, "Understanding the Do-It-Yourself Consumer: DIY Motivations and Outcomes," *AMS Review* 1 (2011).

48. Chris Carlsson, *Nowtopia.*

49. Levy, Steven, *Hackers*; Pekka Himanen, *The Hacker Ethic and the Spirit of the Information Age* (New York: Random House, 2001).

50. Wolf and McQuitty, "Understanding the Do-It-Yourself Consumer," 164.

51. Robert T. Tally Jr., *Utopia in the Age of Globalization. Space, Representation, and the World-System* (New York: Palgrave Macmillan, 2013).

52. Ibid., ix.

53. Ibid., xiii.

54. Ibid., ix.

55. Ibid., 16.

56. Chris Carlsson, *Nowtopia.*

57. Ibid.

BIBLIOGRAPHY

Anderson, Chris. *Makers. The New Industrial Revolution.* New York: Crown Business, 2012.

Botsman, Rachel and Roo Rogers. *What's Mine is Yours. The Rise of Collaborative Consumption*. New York: Harper Collins, 2010.

Brinkman, Camilla. "Education, empowerment and enlightenment through guided disassembly of your broken stuff." *MIT News*, February 7, 2012. Accessed July 20, 2015. http://newsoffice.mit.edu/2012/education-empowerment-and-enlightenment-through-guided-disassembly-of-your-broken-stuff

Campbell, Colin. "The Craft Consumer Culture. Craft and Consumption in a Postmodern Society." *Journal of Consumer Culture* 5, no. 1 (2005): 23–42. doi:10.1177/1469540505049843.

Carlsson, Chris. *Nowtopia. How Pirate Programmers, Outlaw Bycyclists, and Vacant-lot Gardeners Are Inventing the Future Today*. Oakland: AK Press, 2008.

Crawford, Matthew B. *Shop Class as Soulcraft: An Inquiry into the Value of Work*. New York: The Penguin Press, 2009.

Downes, Lawrence. "Mister Jalopy Wants to Make a Better World." *The New York Times*, August 25, 2008. Accessed July 17, 2015. http://www.nytimes.com/2008/08/25/opinion/25mon4.html?_r=0

Frances, Lilli. "Proteus Gowanus. The Old Man of the Canal." *Carroll Gardens Patch*, February 4, 2011. Accessed July 19, 2015. http://patch.com/new-york/carrollgardens/proteus-gowanus-the-old-man-of-the-canal

Himanen, Pekka. *The Hacker Ethic and the Spirit of the Information Age*. New York: Random House, 2001.

Levy, Steven. *Hackers. Heroes of the Computer Revolution*. New York: Bantam Doubleday, 1984.

London, Bernard. *Ending the Depression through Planned Obsolescence*. New York: self-published, 1934. https://upload.wikimedia.org/wikipedia/commons/2/27/London_%281932%29_Ending_the_depression_through_planned_obsolescence.pdf

McCracken, Grant. *Culture and Consumption*. Bloomington: Indiana University Press, 1988.

McDonough, William and Michael Braungart. *Cradle to Cradle: Remaking the Way We Make Things*. New York: North Point Press, 2002.

McGrane, Sally. "An Effort to Bury a Throwaway Culture One Repair at a Time." *The New York Times*, May 8, 2012. Accessed July 19, 2015. http://www.nytimes.com/2012/05/09/world/europe/amsterdam-tries-to-change-culture-with-repair-cafes.html?pagewanted=all&_r=0

Reckwitz, Andreas. "Toward a Theory of Social Practices. A development in culturalist theorizing." *European Journal of Social Theory* 5, no. 2 (2002): 245–265. doi:10.1177/13684310222225432.

Rosner, Daniela K. "Making Citizens, Reassembling Devices: On Gender and the Development of Contemporary Public Sites of Repair in Northern California." *Public Culture* 26, no. 1 (2013): 51–77. doi: 10.1215/08992363-2346250.

Schatzki, Theodore R., Cetina, Karin Knorr, von Savigny, Eike, ed. *The Practice Turn in Contemporary Theory*. New York: Routledge, 2001.

Sharpe, Katherine. "Sip Lattés and Fix Busted Stuff at the Repair Café." *Wired*, May 31, 2012. Accessed July 17, 2015. http://www.wired.com/design/2012/05/fixer-collectives

Shove, Elizabeth, Mika Pantzar and Mark Watson. *The Dynamics of Social Practices: Everyday Life and How it Changes*. London: Sage publications, 2012.

Slade, Giles. *Made to Break. Technology and Obsolescence in America*. Cambridge: Harvard University Press, 2006.

Tally, Robert T. Jr. *Utopia in the Age of Globalization. Space, Representation, and the World-System*. New York: Palgrave Macmillan, 2013.

van der Zanden, Joanna, ed. *Curatorial Cooking // The Design Practice of Platform21*. Arnhem: ArtEZ Press, 2011.

van der Zanden, Joanna. "Creative Strategies for Locally-Oriented Knowledge Exchange." Lecture presented at the workshop *Curating as Social Practice*, Open Society Georgia Foundation and Tbilisi State Academy of Arts, Tbilisi/Batumi, Republic of Georgia, March 11–12, 2012. https://www.youtube.com/watch?v=oueJtWGSqqg

Wiens, Kyle. "Why We Fix: A DIY Manifesto." *Popular mechanics*, May 31, 2014. Accessed 24 may 2015. http://www.popularmechanics.com/home/skills/auto-home-improvement-diy/why-we-fix-a-diy-manifesto-16846653?click=pm_latest

Wolf, Marco and McQuitty, Shaun. "Understanding the do-it-yourself consumer: DIY motivations and outcomes." *AMS Review* 1 (2011): 154–170. doi:10.1215/08992363-2346250

Chapter 5

Our Knowledge Is Our Market

Consuming the DIY World

Jeremy Hunsinger

'Where can I buy an Arduino?' is not a question commonly heard unless you are participating in certain do-it-yourself (DIY) knowledge communities and practical communities. An Arduino is an open prototyping platform that is used as the basis of many DIY electronics projects. Fundamentally it started as an inexpensive electronic board with inputs and outputs.[1] These inputs and outputs pass through a microprocessor running a simplified programming language. Children can use an Arduino, as can almost anyone else. Their website believably claims it has been used on thousands of projects. To buy an Arduino is to enter into a set of relationships that define the possibility of using the Arduino and building something with it. It is one way of entering into a broader community of DIY electronics enthusiasts.

This chapter deals primarily with DIY electronics enthusiasts and the commercial world in which they participate. However, that I am analyzing this group does not necessarily delimit the issues they face from being found in similar groups. DIY cultures all have similarities and differences that are worthy of deep study, and with this chapter, I am only probing one aspect of one subculture. This subculture is the one that tends to buy and use electronic devices like the Arduino in their DIY projects. The research population that this engages is a large and diverse set of communities likely several million people strong, and in that it has several structural divisions with class, gender, and race being significant to note though they do vary somewhat internationally. This chapter is not going to explore the demographics in depth, but does openly admit that the demographics and structural divisions in these communities are not necessarily representative of the broader communities in which they operate, though sometimes they are. It should also be noted that these communities and the people in them are not stable but fluid like most human life; people come and go for a wide variety of reasons. The technologies they use likewise change and develop and the ones mentioned in this paper are current, but also are being updated. The Arduino for instance has had many updates.

The Arduino is one competing platform in the commercial DIY electronics ecosystem that exists in our world of production.[2] This ecosystem is global and competitive with materials being produced around the world and across all fields and modes of life. Various parts integrate with Legos, others integrating with houses, home brewing equipment, automobiles, and even with industrial production lines. The commercial DIY ecosystem provides the basis for a large secondary DIY economy in which people mix their knowledge and labor with these technologies to build, repair, or improve various things in their lives.

DIY is a practice-based mindset about the relationships between people, their capacities, and their things. This set of meaningful relations exist broadly in both ecological and ideological relations. This set of meaningful relations defines, in part, a mental ecology through which people approach their world.[3] This mental ecology is the key issue in DIY, as it frames the thinking and imagination of the participants.

Let us take a minute to consider what this mental ecology entails. In the first part it is not merely a subjective experience, but is part of our distributed subjectivity. We share parts of our mental ecology with other people through all kinds of demonstrative and communicative means. Knowledge, sensemaking, and creativity and imagination are three possible elements of a mental ecology, though there are others. Our mental ecology is extensive, and as such it is important to consider what limits it, and this chapter engages how our mental ecology is limited in part because of the commercialization of DIY electronics. From Felix Guattari, we also know that the social ecology and environmental ecology are facets of the same broader lived world ecology as is the mental ecology.[4] The DIY mental ecology that I am describing is not universally held, but is shared by some electronics enthusiasts for any number of reasons and for any number of desires. Classically, DIY starts with wanting to do something, to make something, to have something, or to 'scratch an itch' so to speak.[5,6] This desire manifests in knowledge seeking and sensemaking activities around the project. This involves searching for information around the project, talking to people, reading things, etc. Frequently, these activities lead DIY electronics enthusiasts to find one of the websites discussed later in this paper, and to decide that using some pre-built kit or other device would aid them in completing their project. So, we can see that there is a space being created in the imagination of the person, which is part of their mental ecology for their project and they are slotting in elements of processes and things to bring about a resolution to their 'itch'. As they may have originally intended to build this object completely on their own, and finding simpler, purchasable solutions may have changed their imagination of the project, we can see that the mental ecology is a fluid and changing system, like all ecologies, only stable in abstraction. As the person's mental ecology changes to accommodate the new knowledges and understandings of their project, and their imagination of the project changes, their mental ecology changes.

Elements of this mental ecology are confused and conflated by the existence of a commodity-relation which tends to parallel most other elements in our commercial world, a recent transformation that might make this more obvious is the commercialization or commodification of water as product as opposed to prior constructions of water as vital service.[7,8] As water became a product unto itself, and not just something supplied because it was necessary then new limiting relations around cost came into being and people started thinking of it differently, thus our mental ecology was changed by commodity-relation. This sort of commodity-relation overlaps with the DIY mentality, but clearly exists in contradiction to elements of it. In the confusing and conflating of the commodity-relation with the broader DIY ecology, DIY communities become more commercially oriented and more complicit in the formations of late capitalism with its myriad of problems such as precarity of employment, underemployment, etc. Late capitalism requires a commodity-relation between people and things, but also people and the other people who provide services to those people. This means that money, or capital, always mediates our relationships and constructs elements of the system of value and justification in those relationships. Within that understanding of late capitalism, it is easy to see where humans who have immense capacity for modes of valuation become devalued when all of our valuations are made commensurate through capital because we become subject to the capital valuations of others. DIY as a whole resists late capitalism, but is also complicit in it as it commodifies and consumes its materials and knowledges.

However, the mental ecology surrounding DIY is not about consuming the commodity as much as it is about transforming the commodity with our own capacities. This transformation is essentially a function of production or re/production in which the commodity is changed beyond its prior capacity, such as extending the life-span of something, or building something from other things that 'scratches an itch' or otherwise resolves a desire.[9]

This understanding of DIY as a subjective capacity to transform something requires the form of knowledge that enables one to perform those tasks necessary to the transformation.[10,11,12] In other words, you have to learn how to do it yourself. Sometimes this knowledge can be had easily by reading, but most DIY knowledges require some sort of apprenticeship or practical learning in order to become proficient. This apprenticeship can be formal or informal; performed in a group such as in a classroom or individually with a master or mentor. In either case, it is a practice-based mode of learning that teaches the skills to more than just the mind, but also to the body. This learning becomes a modulation of the body and mind, modifying them in relation to the practices under study.

Thinking more deeply about DIY as a set of subjective capacities that transform not only things, but also ourselves in the world, allows us to start to consider the basis of this chapter which argues that DIY communities inhabit relations to DIY technics in an ecology of commercial relations. These communities exist in tension with the commercial ecologies' ideologies some of which they explicitly resist, others of which they complicitly accept. Those ideologies function as systems that justify and normalize our actions, and as such the tensions bring contradictions into our everyday lives. With ideological-based contradictions we are left with DIY becoming a primarily commercial path. As that path is narrowed, DIY making as practice becomes more normalized and less innovative/creative.

Whether DIY communities resist or accept their commercialism, commercialism still permeates DIY communities, their modes of production, and their modes of creativity. In recognizing this permeation in DIY, we also should note that as a subaltern set of practices to the primary productive practices of current commercial machinics, DIY communities are not unique.[13,14] There are innumerable modes of resistance and complicity available to those interested in resisting, but the fascinating aspect of DIY communities is that while a few do actively imagine and enact their resistance, most people with the DIY mindset and knowledges are actively engaging commercial ecologies and enacting commercial ideologies through their DIY activities.

DIY communities do end up consuming, though they resist some forms of consumptions. Their active resistance is found in the cultural constructions around their production. DIY communities generally produce in relation to the things they own individually and that they share communally. They produce in order to improve or customize the object owned and thus increase its personal value. That personal value may not be commensurate with any realizable market value, but market value is rarely the point.

The point, insofar as there is one to DIY communities is the improvement of goods, and relationally the improvement of the individual and communal subjects through the acquisition and dissemination of knowledge in all of its forms, but primarily in the productive form. In this form, people learn how to produce things, and learn the heuristics for producing and problem solving around things. This process relies fundamentally on the commercial systems that provide access to the things that they are using, but also provide access to the knowledge of the things they are using. This tension between owning and learning is at the heart of the consummative relations of DIY communities.

THE STUDY

Originally this research derived from the analysis of a study of weblogs about hackerspaces, and makerspaces. The study originated to pursue the question of innovation, but quickly grew into a critical study of the complicity and development of relations between those who see themselves as innovating and the systems that they require to innovate and the ideologies they need to legitimate their work as innovative.[15,16]

Hackerspaces and makerspaces are physical spaces that people share as a place to have tools, to have community, to build things, and to otherwise socialize around their interests. Mostly those interests surround DIY activities as the theme of most hackerspaces and makerspaces is making and fixing things. This requires them to acquire, as a whole, a vast body of knowledge and a vast set of equipment and things. Hackerspaces and makerspaces allow them to share both the knowledge and things within a physical space.

The project compiles the content of over 200 blogs with their linked wikis and other linked materials as they were found online from 2010 to 2012. It captured the websites using a simple web-based spider to capture all publicly available documents. The original idea was to do a sampling of these sites to build a corpus for a critical discourse analysis. Note though, this chapter is not that work, which will be arriving in book form in the next few years. It is necessary to do sampling because the data comprises around 30,000 documents including plain text, Microsoft Word documents, pdf texts, assorted images, and assorted other files. According to analytical software it comprises over 888000 unique words and is over 19 million words in total. Even after cleaning up the data, there is still much overlap, as one would expect.

This chapter unlike the larger work derives from thinking about this corpus of data in relation to postmarxist critical theory; it should not be thought of as a discourse analysis, but as critical analysis and theory development. The primary goal of this chapter is to engage and begin to explain the mediations of commerce and consumption in DIY communities in relation to how DIY electronics enthusiasts know and how they produce/consume.

The specific generation of this chapter was in a finding of that study. While analyzing the textual corpus for active verbs in order to discern the activities that the various weblogs describe, I found that one of the primary sets of active verbs was not around programming or designing, but around waiting. 'Waiting' and its permutations were in the top five of active verbs across the textual corpus. This led me to question why that was. It was in seeking an answer to that question, that this chapter arose.

The simple answer is that they were waiting on one of two categories of action. They were either waiting on people, to help, to learn from, etc. or they were waiting for things, things that they purchased, things that they were borrowing, or similar things that have yet to arrive. That the mobility of things and peoples is a significant part of DIY communities such as hackerspaces and makerspaces should not be surprising, but what to me seemed to be a tension was how much waiting was being described.

Thus 'waiting' indicated to me a situation in the DIY community comprised of hackerspaces and makerspaces. It indicated that it was not as DIY as one might think and that fundamentally it relies on the structures of late capitalism to ensure timely and enthusiastic engagement with the hobby. Waiting, you see, was occasionally referred to in the blogs as a 'time suck' which is a thing that eats your time and also tends to eat your enthusiasm for your current project. It is clear that the 'just in time delivery' of late capitalism is not oriented toward the DIY community, which we already know, because 'just in time' is really centered on centralized industrialization instead of distributed maker communities like hackerspaces and makerspaces. This is not to say that the only structure causing the 'waiting' is the lack of a structural solution to delivery of just in time goods, because there is a second system at work and that is knowledge production and consumption which relies not only on the delivery of goods like manuals, but also the capacity of other people to be present. As noted earlier, sometimes people were waiting on other people.

The inquiry opened questions and opened a set of relationships that this chapter engages; providing a starting point, through which we can consider the larger contexts of DIY communities.

CONSUMER REALITIES IN HISTORICAL CONTEXT

DIY communities exist within a commercial ecosystem which can provide their material, but also occasionally provide their knowledges. This is not new by any means. The documentation of knowledge around craft and creativity didn't start with Diderot's *Encyclopedia* (*Encyclopédie*, circa 1751), but that early book did provide some formalization to the possibility of documenting it in books, providing a way for elements of the knowledge of crafts to be formalized into print media. The practice of knowledge was already formalized in guilds and the training regimes of apprentices in crafts and professions. Similarly guilds provided access to goods and material that would allow for everyone from students to masters to learn more about their craft or profession. This communal structure started in relation to the development of commerce and markets.[17]

This historical positionality of the relations of goods and knowledge in relation to commerce and markets does not limit those ideas to only commercial and market relations though. There are infinite permutations that need not have those relations. However, the possibility of those permutations is increasingly encroached upon and enclosed within commercial structures. This enclosure movement around knowledge and goods at the start of capitalism has been commented on at length elsewhere.[18,19] The reason that I refer to it here is because it is the process of enclosure that continuously transforms the modes of knowledge sharing from an ideology of shared goods and shared common goods, to one of private goods which are traded and commercialized. Guilds did enclose knowledge within their physical walls and communal rules, but the structures of enclosure are different from commercial enclosure.

We should not lose sight of this historical process of enclosure and commercialization because it is similar to the processes that occur today. However, digressing too far into history is not the idea of this section; the idea is to provide the context for understanding our current set of relations around DIY communities in relation to knowledge and goods. The current context is prefigured by the last few generations of makers and DIY communities which exist in the dialectical arena of freeing and enclosing knowledge.

A quick history around the hacker/maker movement in electronics engages interesting historical anomalies like the origin of Microsoft, Apple Computer, the Berkeley Computer Club, the Model Railroad Club of MIT, and similar stories where several knowledge communities come together in relation to several technologies and from them we get our current mass computerization regime, but what came before them was equally important with the development of electric and diesel motors, electrification of the home and the lightbulb, each of these generations of technological innovation are sets of relations between communities, knowledges, and commercializations.[20,21,22]

These commercializations entailed everything from educational institutions that would teach you about the new technologies, to magazines, to new social clubs around the technologies. The number of opportunities for people interested in electricity, electric motors, and internal combustion engines exploded. Magazines such as *Popular Mechanics* (founded in 1902) and later *Popular Electronics* (founded in 1954) provided avenues to discover, learn about, order catalogues, and purchase these technologies. They popularized the technologies as well as provided avenues for commercialization.

The media's function of popularization of the technologies is an extremely important aspect of DIY electronics because while we do have the internet today, innumerable magazines and books exist to aid and provide ideas.

LATE CAPITALISM

DIY communities are emblematic of late capitalism. Late capitalism is the formulation of capitalism demarcated by a switch to generalized universal industrialization, service economies, increased commodity orientation, increased individuation, generalized precarity, the acceleration of innovation, the instrumentalization/deskilling of labor, and thus generalized anxiety.[23,24,25,26] DIY is emblematic of these characteristics because it tends to be centered on the commodity that is being improved/repaired/maintained through individualized creation and production. This self-orientation in the service economy does tend to lower costs for the individual in some cases, but it also removes transactions from the shared economy. DIY enthusiasts don't usually pay for an oil change, nor pay for a computer repair; unless they have to do so. This removal of exchange transforms the relationships that ground community and capitalism. In part this is the change in opportunity to build relationships, but it is also more of a constitutive change in the possible relationships a person could have. While this constitutive change is part of the larger cultural changes of late capitalism, elements of DIY mental ecologies and social ecologies, in particular the self-reliant aspects, exacerbate this change and bring about some of the desiring aspects that lead to the new communal formations of hackerspaces and makerspaces. In short, DIY enthusiasts start to desire different ways of doing things that require different communities in which to participate. For instance, the Arduino required a community of developers and designers to unite with producers to bring it into existence. Sometimes the communities already exist, but sometimes the desires of a wide variety of people bring them together in new ways.

COMMODIFYING AND COMPLICIT DISSENT

To be clearer about the tensions between DIY and capitalist ideologies, we should explore a few examples. In this section of the paper, I'd like to consider the textual and paratextual materials surrounding popular maker and hackerspace websites in order to discuss how those websites construct and limit this specific set of DIY mental ecologies to fit into the commercial models of late capitalism.

As part of the broader commercial sphere of magazines and gray literature was already introduced above, starting with *Make* magazine's commercial outlet called Maker Shed is a likely place to begin. While *Make* magazine and Maker Shed did not start the maker movement, they have significantly enabled thousands of people to learn more and buy more in relation to DIY culture than before they arose. Before they arose, the makerspace/hackerspace movement was less centralized and more dispersed across a wide variety of providers. However, with the creation of the Make brand, the commercial system had a model that was becoming successful. With that growing success, more commercial entities arose. While Maker Shed is the first discussed, Adafruit Industries, SparkFun, and Evil Mad Scientist will also be discussed below.

In the discussion and description of these websites, particular attention should be paid to their design and layout as they define the paratext for the texts themselves. The paratext constructs the environment of the text, and allows us to infer relations in their texts. As we can see in reading below, each of these websites structures the relationship between commodity, community, and knowledge with varying degrees of priority. However, they are all trying to engage actively with DIY mental ecologies, and help to define those ecologies by engaging with them.

Maker Shed is a website-based shopping experience for the DIY maker community.[27] It is simple and easy to use following the best practices of shopping sites. As of this writing, the main menu which is horizontal indicates the possibilities for finding things on the site which are 'shop', 'what's new', 'best sellers', 'sale', a search window, 'my account', and an iconic shopping cart. Below that is a graphic window that says in large bold; 'Ready. Set. Make'. which has the subtitle of 'Your homebase for fun, doable projects'. on one line and 'We've got something for everyone'. on a second line. Below that in a red box with white text, it says, 'Stay in the know'. The website also has 'Let's Explore' with graphically oriented tabs with text that categorizes as follows: 'Lighting Things Up', 'Wearables', 'Soldering', 'STEM', 'IOT', which is then followed by 'New in the Shed' with images of new products. Below this is a 'view more' for the 'New in the Shed' area. That ends the shopping area and below that is the erratum of shipping, returns, affiliation, careers, about the company and social media/email linking campaign tools. It is an image intense and deeply indicative website. It structures knowledge as subordinate to the shopping experience, but also frames the relationships of politically important aspects of DIY culture as areas that it explicitly serves.

Adafruit industries is organized much the same as the prior two as it has a shopping cart and sign in as its topmost right items, with its name anchoring the right side of the top of the screen followed by a list of menus.[28] The menus include from left to right, 'shop', 'blog', 'learn', 'forums', 'video', and there is a search icon justified right. Below this set up of pull-down menus, is the banner of content. This week it is highlighting an open source 3D printed LED helmet that looks like something from Doctor Who; the helmet banner is emblazoned with 'Doin' it right open source 3D printed LED helmet'. Just below the banner and in about 1/4 of the font size there is a news feed which is currently announcing the next HOPE conference and the arrival of Bluetooth 5. It affiliates HOPE with the magazine *2600*, which is a notorious and somewhat old-school hacker magazine. The final news item that flashed up was to watch the Whitehouse news feed featuring Limor Fried, a founder of Adafruit industries. She has been recognized as a champion of change according to the feed. Below the newsfeed begins the posting of objects to buy, information about making, and related topics in familiar 1/2 page width rectangles. For instance, the two featured objects are the Arduino Uno R3 and the Adafruit Neopixel RGB LED strip. Below them is 'all about batteries', an article on the PiGRRRL, and other articles. It should be noted that the banner and articles do change when you change the page. It should also be noted that a significant part of the front page is about how to make things more than what to buy. At the bottom of the page are the usual errata of contact us, jobs, etc. Notably, there is also 'engineered in NYC Adafruit' and a quote by Steve Martin, 'Be so good they can't ignore you'. These affectations likely have appeal to certain groups of buyers.

SparkFun Electronics is another significant website that sells supplies for electronic making and it is similar to the others, though it has slight differences.[29] Like the other websites, much of its basic functionality as a store is at the top of the screen with the shopping cart on the top right, a logo then a menu to the right. The menu contains shop, learn, AVC, forum, and data. A slight change is then SparkFun has a second line directly below that starts with 'Start a Project' on the left, which is followed by products, blog, tutorials, videos, wish lists, distributors, and support. Down the whole left side of the page is a listing of general things like 'new products', specific things like the 'Getting Started with the Blynk board', what's on sale, then a list of categories from which to shop. At the top center of the main content is a banner which is dealing with their product the Blynk board, underneath that, there is a three-wide listing of new products, followed by an extensive blog post about how to do a specific project and the kit that comes with it. In this case, it is the Johnny-five robot kit. To the right of the blog post is a listing of new tutorials, with four tutorials on how to do various DIY things electronically. At the bottom of the page, they have the usual errata, but also the following paragraph:

> SparkFun is an online retail store that sells the bits and pieces to make your electronics projects possible. Whether it's a robot that can cook your breakfast or a GPS cat tracking device, our products and resources are designed to make the world of electronics more accessible.

This claim exemplifies the DIY mental ecology to the extent that it is tied to the purchasing of things to perform DIY that then ties back to your own identity as a DIY oriented person.

Finally, Evil Mad Scientist Laboratories is slightly different from the rest as it integrates shopping as a separate site and primarily focuses on the blog functions as its main site.[30]

This means that there is a header with the brand logo on the upper left and a title in the main banner area in the upper center. Below that is a menu with products, blog, forums, and contact. The products menu takes you to a separate site that is the store, but links to the store are within the blog postings also. In the same menu, aligned right is the search function for the blog. From that point on it is a traditional type blog with deep descriptions of how to do things, notifying information about things such as the 10th anniversary of the site, and such. It takes the mode of a blog and information provider for the communities that it serves. Evil Mad Scientist Laboratories has the blog tagline of 'Making the world a better place, one Evil Mad Scientist at a time'. A brief analysis of the shopping page which is a whole other URL shows that it follows much on the themes of the other primarily shopping oriented sites with pictures and names of kits and things to buy. It has an emphasis on recent products and popular products, but is otherwise quite like the other ones. The shopping side does not have as much integrated knowledge about how to do things, but given the expansive blog posts on the primary site, this makes sense.

ANALYSIS

These websites all have several functions around purchasing, information provision, community provision, and knowledge sharing. In particular, we should consider how they portray knowledge and community in relation to their other goals. While there are stylistic differences, it is easy to see that they are all using knowledge about products and DIY knowledges with products as a way to sell products. This is not unlike other products, but it isn't like the DIY you might find in a house repairer's use of a lumber yard either; there is a construction of expertise around commodified objects of knowledge in these websites that is different than buying the same objects on Amazon or Alibaba. They are attempting to appeal to experts by providing well-documented information about the products with extensive fact sheets and occasionally even circuit designs on the websites, but they are also using how-to guides and simplified instructions to develop a sense that you don't have to become an expert in these things, or you can begin to desire becoming an expert in these things. In this analysis of the websites we can consider also the tendency for individualizations tied to that expertise, because in their design almost all of the websites discussed above have community forums, but these forums are not prioritized. The priorities in all but one of the websites is clearly the products and information about the product. The exception, Evil Mad Scientist Laboratories, emphasizes stories and then embeds the products secondarily, but they still sell products and commodities through and in relation to the knowledge around those products.

On one level this commoditization is absolutely normal in a commercial economy. It is part of a commercial ecology in which we exist. It is not necessarily a hugely competitive ecology, though, as much of DIY electronics is related to communal knowledge sharing and is open source. This is demonstrated in part by the information provided on their websites, but also by the fact that they usually sell each other's products, if they have self-developed and/or self-branded products. There are a few exceptions to this tendency to sell each other's materials and it usually centers around owning a brand and marketing. For instance, some of the materials that another site called Seeed-Studio sells can only be bought there and this is likely because of licensing and branding issues. However, you can buy many SparkFun kits at almost any of the stores, just like you can get them at Amazon. However, buying from Amazon would tend to be what an outsider of the DIY community would do, whereas buying from one of the stores that I have analyzed is more of what an insider or a person who wants to become an insider would do.

I should be clear, I am not presenting a strong critique of the capital orientation of DIY culture. DIY requires material. What I am attempting to do is to draw attention to an ideological conflict and implicit tension that occurs in the mental ecology. This tension and conflict exists within the ease in which commercial projects have transformed the doing it yourself into buying parts and assembling it yourself. This is parallel to using a mix when baking a cake versus baking it from scratch; the question arises only as to the level at which one must purchase. What is happening is that DIY cultures and their ecologies are becoming more and more commercialized, so that everything is becoming more like baking from a kit and less like baking from scratch. With this, they are also moving the capacity to know away from the making and closer to the buying. The websites as I have presented them allow you to see that through their construction and marketing aspects they are tying knowledge and capacity to make to the ability to purchase things. You need these things to make your project easier, newer, more intricate, more interesting, more everything that your project should be. The construction of need in the websites very clearly allies itself with the construction of need in general culture, especially around issues of novelty and creativity in capitalism. We construct systems of needs and desire in relation to objects and their affordances in our culture in order to provide ways of relating among humans and among widely diverse series of interests. Much like there are fans of baseball teams, there are fans of development teams and their products. This is not to say it is not a unique fandom or to simplify any fandom issues, but it is to say that fans exist as do technological fetishists, and each has relations of desire and need to things outside themselves.

I chose each of these websites also because they do have what I have discussed elsewhere as the binary of 'in' and 'within' communities.[31] 'Within' communities are the developers that make things, they design new things that they sell on these websites—they are the people governed by the rules of the company and contract, whereas the 'in' communities are the users, the people outside of the company and contract which have strong relations to the companies or products. The 'in' are not governed by the company or contract, but still use the material of the company. This distinction is useful to considering the relations of the product to the user community because it distinguishes a line where people have done things for the company as part of their work, and people who do things with the company because of other reasons. In thinking about the other reasons that are described in this paper primarily as constructions of desire and need, I should be clear that knowledge always has constructions of desire and need around it. As such that does not distinguish between these two communities, but what does distinguish between these two communities is the capital flow of knowledge and money. Money tends to flow toward the 'within' and knowledge in this community tends to flow more from the 'within' toward the 'in'. This capital concentration in relation to knowledge production is normal, but seemingly at odds with DIY mental ecologies discussed above.

CONCLUSION

This chapter seeks to make an argument about how DIY mental ecologies are in tension with consumerist tendencies in DIY electronics communities as found in late capitalism. DIY electronic communities are now buying more and more of their materials from vendors who are providing easy access to almost completed kits. The desire of DIY enthusiasts to make something their own and with their own hands, to 'scratch an itch' is being replaced by the increasing commercialized space in which you can scratch your itch so long as it roughly maps onto the millions of other itchy people's desires. Not only is the normalization occurring in relations to the objects, but it is also occurring in relation to the knowledge and its acquisition. This tension is shown through the relationships of the construction of knowledge, desire, and community in these communities through a theoretical analysis of some of their shopping websites in the context of a larger research project. The conclusions entail that the tension is one between the privatization of knowledge and community as a for profit entity and the communal nature of knowledge and desire in those mental ecologies. I do not argue that this is a harmful issue, though clearly it could have deleterious effects on the nature of community, much like capitalism tends to have on the nature of communities as a whole.

Instead, what I would like to encourage with this paper is an awareness of the possibility of a plurality of modes of being in the DIY electronic sphere, and that perhaps the relations that tend to develop between groups within the sphere exist in permanent tension. That is to say that these websites, in the name of sales, have seemingly created a space where experts and newer DIY electronics users can both interact with their products without issues or challenges. In short, what they have done is created a consumerist ecology where it is ok to not only ask, 'where can I buy an Arduino?', but also one where you can ask, 'should I buy an Arduino?' which is a slightly safer place than some purchasing arenas. They have made the commercial mode of DIY become the comfortable option for the vast array of DIY electronics enthusiasts. In making this the comfortable and normal option, they have transformed the worlds and mental ecologies of DIY enthusiasts. They have created and resolved what I argue above should be a point of ideological tensions, but has become merely an accepted set of practices and purchases. This has narrowed the field of possibilities of the DIY enthusiasts because now they mostly begin to imagine and construct their projects in relation to the commercial objects. In short, the commercial objects have become paths to quick success. That path to quick success shortchanges the imaginal possibilities of DIY electronics enthusiasts and, in kind, it frames our subjective capacities, and shortchanges our future.

NOTES

1. 'What is Arduino?' 2016, https://www.arduino.cc/en/Guide/Introduction
2. Michael Storper and Robert Salais, 1997. *Worlds of Production: The Action Frameworks of the Economy* (Cambridge, Mass: Harvard University Press).
3. Felix Guattari, 2000. *The Three Ecologies* (London: Athlone Press).
4. Ibid.
5. Eric S. Raymond, 2001. *The Cathedral & the Bazaar: Musings on Linux and Open Source By an Accidental Revolutionary* (O'Reilly Media).
6. Linus Torvalds and David Diamond, 2002. *Just for Fun: The Story of an Accidental Revolutionary* (New York: HarperBusiness).
7. Georg Lukács, 1971. 'Reification and the Consciousness of the Proletariat'. *History and Class Consciousness: Studies in Marxist Dialectics,* 137.
8. Jean Baudrillard, 1981. *For a Critique of the Political Economy of the Sign*. St. Louis, MO: Telos Press.
9. Raymond, *The Cathedral & the Bazaar.*
10. Laurent Thévenot, 1984. 'Rules and Implements: Investment in Forms'. *Social Science Information* 23 (1): 1–45.
11. Luc Boltanski and Laurent Thévenot. 1999. 'The Sociology of Critical Capacity'. *European Journal of Social Theory* 2 (3): 359–77.

12. Laurent Thévenot, 2002. 'Conventions of Co-Ordination and the Framing of Uncertainty'. In *Intersubjectivty in Economics*, edited by Edward Fullbrook, 181–97 (New York, NY: Routledge).

13. William Bogard, 1998. 'Sense and Segmentarity: Some Markers of a Deleuzian-Guattarian Sociology'. *Sociological Theory* 16 (1): 52–74.

14. Felix Guattari, 1996. *Soft Subversions*. Semiotext(e).

15. Jeremy Hunsinger, 2011. 'The Social Workshop as Ple: Lessons From Hacklabs'. pp. 1–10. In: Proceedings of The PLE Conference 2011, July 10–12, 2011, Southampton, UK.

16. Jeremy Hunsinger and Andrew Schrock, 2016. 'The Democratization of Hacking and Making'. *New Media & Society* 18 (4): 535–38.

17. Fernand Braudel, 1982. *Civilization and Capitalism, 15th–18th Century: The Wheels of Commerce* (Univ of California Press).

18. James Boyle, 2003. 'The Second Enclosure Movement and the Construction of the Public Domain'. *Law and Contemporary Problems* 66 (1/2): 33–74.

19. Elinor Ostrom, 1990. *Governing the Commons: The Evolution of Institutions for Collective Action (Political Economy of Institutions and Decisions).* (Cambridge University Press).

20. Steven Levy, 2010. *Hackers: Heroes of the Computer Revolution - 25th Anniversary Edition* (O'Reilly Media).

21. Peter H. Salus, 1994. *A Quarter Century of Unix* (Addison-Wesley Pub Co).

22. Peter H. Salus, 1995. *Casting the Net: From Arpanet to Internet and Beyond (Addison-Wesley Unix and Open Systems Series).* (Addison-Wesley Professional).

23. Ernest Mandel, 1978. *Late Capitalism* (London: Verso).

24. Fredric Jameson, 1992. *Signatures of the Visible* (Routledge).

25. Ben Agger, 1991. *A Critical Theory of Public Life: Knowledge, Discourse and Politics in an Age of Decline (Critical Perspectives on Literacy and Education).* (London: UK, Routledge).

26. Mark Fisher, 2009. *Capitalist Realism: Is There No Alternative?* (Zero Books).

27. 'Makershed', 2016, http://www.makershed.com

28. 'Adafruit', 2016, 'Adafruit'. https://www.adafruit.com

29. 'Sparkfun Electronics', 2016, https://www.sparkfun.com

30. 'Evil Mad Scientist Laboratories'. 2016, http://www.evilmadscientist.com

31. Hunsinger, 2013. 'Locus Communus: The Unconnected in and Within Virtual Worlds'. In *The Unconnected: Social Justice, Participation, and Engagement in the Information Society (Digital Formations).* (Peter Lang Publishing Inc).

BIBLIOGRAPHY

'Adafruit'. (2016): Accessed 2016. http://www.adafruit.com.

Agger, Ben. *A Critical Theory of Public Life: Knowledge, Discourse and Politics in an Age of Decline (Critical Perspectives on Literacy and Education).* Routledge, 1991.

Baudrillard, Jean. *For a Critique of the Political Economy of the Sign*. St. Louis, MO: Telos Press, 1981.

Bogard, William. 'Sense and Segmentarity: Some Markers of a Deleuzian-Guattarian Sociology'. *Sociological Theory* 16, no. 1 (1998): 52–74.

Boltanski, Luc and Laurent Thévenot. 'The Sociology of Critical Capacity'. *European Journal of Social Theory* 2, no. 3 (1999): 359–77.

Boyle, James. 'The Second Enclosure Movement and the Construction of the Public Domain'. *Law and contemporary problems* 66, no. 1/2 (2003): 33–74.

Braudel, Fernand. *Civilization and Capitalism, 15th-18th Century: The Wheels of Commerce*. Univ of California Press, 1982.

'Evil Mad Scientist Laboratories'. (2016): Accessed 2016. http://www.evilmadscientist.com.

Fisher, Mark. *Capitalist Realism: Is There No Alternative? (Zero Books)*. Zero Books, 2009.

Guattari, Felix. 'The Three Ecologies'. *New Formations* 8, no. Summer (1989): 131–47.

———. *Soft Subversions*. Semiotext(e), 1996.

———. *The Three Ecologies*. Translated by Gary Genosko. London: Athlone Press, 2000.

Hunsinger, Jeremy. 'The Social Workshop as Ple: Lessons From Hacklabs'. (2011):

———. 'Locus Communus: The Unconnected in and Within Virtual Worlds', In *The Unconnected: Social Justice, Participation, and Engagement in the Information Society (Digital Formations)*, Peter Lang Publishing Inc., 2013.

Hunsinger, Jeremy and Andrew Schrock. 'The Democratization of Hacking and Making'. *New Media & Society* 18, no. 4 (2016): 535–38.

Jameson, Fredric. *Signatures of the Visible*. Routledge, 1992.

Levy, Steven. *Hackers: Heroes of the Computer Revolution - 25th Anniversary Edition*. O'Reilly Media, 2010.

Lukács, Georg. 'Reification and the Consciousness of the Proletariat'. *History and Class Consciousness: Studies in Marxist Dialectics* 137 (1971): 83–222.

'Makershed'. (2016): Accessed 2016. http://www.makershed.com.

Mandel, Ernest. *Late Capitalism*. London: Verso, 1978.

Ostrom, Elinor. *Governing the Commons : The Evolution of Institutions for Collective Action (Political Economy of Institutions and Decisions)*. Cambridge University Press, 1990.

Raymond, Eric S. *The Cathedral & the Bazaar: Musings on Linux and Open Source By an Accidental Revolutionary*. O'Reilly Media, 2001.

Salus, Peter H. *Casting the Net: From Arpanet to Internet and Beyond (Addison-Wesley Unix and Open Systems Series)*. Addison-Wesley Professional, 1995.

———. *A Quarter Century of Unix*. Addison-Wesley Pub Co., 1994.

'Sparkfun Electronics'. (2016): Accessed 2016. http://www.sparkfun.com.

Storper, Michael and Robert Salais. *Worlds of Production: The Action Frameworks of the Economy*. Cambridge, Mass: Harvard University Press, 1997.

Thévenot, Laurent. 'Rules and Implements: Investment in Forms'. *Social Science Information* 23, no. 1 (1984): 1–45.

———. 'Conventions of Co-Ordination and the Framing of Uncertainty'. In *Intersubjectivty in Economics*, edited by Edward Fullbrook, 181–97. New York, NY: Routledge, 2002.

Torvalds, Linus and David Diamond. *Just for Fun: The Story of an Accidental Revolutionary*. HarperBusiness, 2002.

'What is Arduino?' (2016): Accessed 2016. https://www.arduino.cc/en/Guide/Introduction.

Chapter 6

DIY Radio Utopia

What Is So Funny About the Tragedy of the Commons

Linda Doyle and Jessica Foley

In her seminal work, *The Concept of Utopia*, Ruth Levitas makes a case for a broad analytic definition of utopia. For Levitas, utopia is the repository of desire for a better way of being. We adapt Levitas' definition slightly in this essay. We think of utopia as a dynamic repository of desire for better ways of being alive with others.[1] Our approach permits a concept of utopia as contingent and changing over time. Levitas argues that a broad definition of utopia allows for the inclusion of variety and difference while also providing a basis for identifying and understanding utopian elements throughout human culture. At the same time, Levitas acknowledges that broad definitions require more conceptual clarity and rigor and argues that "distinctions can and should still be made between different kinds of utopias on the basis of form, function, location and content. The study of utopia should . . . incorporate all of these."[2] Just as the study of utopia has expanded, so too has the practice of, or quest for, utopia expanded beyond the constitution of an "intentional community . . . who have chosen to live together to enhance their shared values or for some other mutually agreed upon purpose."[3] Utopia in the contemporary world is intra-active and networked.[4] Utopian practices have expanded across many types of social and political activity intending to bring about transformations for the better.

While the *study of* utopia and the *quest for* utopia are different they are not mutually exclusive engagements. This essay is in fact an experiment in the interplay of both. Here, the authors, one an artist and the other an engineer, seek to develop through writing an understanding of and an argument for utopia on the contemporary radio scene.[5] We are therefore engaging with political questions that concern the contemporary role of utopia in social transformation. We do so by thinking through various specific instances of DIY practices as a way of making connections between radio and utopia.

But to what purpose? Utopian scholar Lyman Sargent argues that "if a utopia is sufficiently attractive and powerful, it can transform hope and desire into belief and action to bring the utopia into being through a political or social movement."[6] The intention of this essay, therefore, is undoubtedly utopian. We seek to articulate and expand an idea of DIY radio utopia, critically, so that we might offer insight into political problems on the radio scene. Our interest lies in the concept of utopian practices as agencies capable of transformation. We question whether DIY radio utopian practices are constitutive of "not only wishful thinking but will-full action"?[7] In the following pages, we discuss a handful of contemporary DIY radio practices and seek insight on the "metamorphosis of utopia" on the radio scene today.

This chapter is organized in sections, loosely headed as *near past, near present,* and *near future.* The first section maps a connection between the formation and invention of radio science, technology, and DIY. This minor yet potent connection is developed by calling attention to an incidental and nonreciprocal relation between Michael Faraday and Jane Marcet. We seek to develop a context for understanding radio technology as a utopian and DIY practice marked by self-education and an entrepreneurial culture of publishing practical *how-to* study and making materials.

The second section, *near present*, introduces a way of understanding radio as an amateur's apparatus involving interplay between device (function), medium (form) and message (content). Here, we emphasize the importance of the *medium* on the radio scene; *the electromagnetic spectrum.* Defining radio in many ways amounts to the same difficulties as defining utopia—both refer to a complex interplay of form, function, and content, and often depend upon questions and problems that arise from "concrete" situations. For this reason, we compose a handful of vignettes from which to draw out our consideration of DIY radio utopia as a continuation of Faraday's experimental practice and Marcet's *How-to* literature. The vignettes demonstrate in various ways, and by various degrees, several *functions* of DIY radio utopian devices; criticism, expression, compensation, transformation, and/or as a catalyst of change. The vignettes insinuate the diversity of DIY radio utopian practices and demonstrate these as constitutive of subjectivities, identities and ways of being alive with others. These DIY radio utopian practices draw attention toward the intra-actions of politics, culture and technology through the actual and/or fictional formation of counter-publics.[8]

Finally, in the third section, *near future*, we take a closer look at the importance of the radio medium; electromagnetic spectrum. In particular, we question whether and how DIY radio utopian practices are catalyzing change and social transformation on a radio scene persistently in thrall to *the tragedy of the commons* and rhetorics of scarcity. And while developing an answer to this question pitches beyond the scope of this essay, by asking it publicly we seek to motivate attention toward DIY radio utopias and their agency today.

NEAR PAST—RADIO'S DIY UTOPIAN HERITAGE

Radio's agency has historically been acknowledged as social and political as much as technological, particularly through the energetic work of amateur radio makers and operators.[9] Graham Hall's concise genealogy of electromagnetism provides insight into a history of radio as a process of interrelation between experimentation and (mathematical) theory. Radio is a technology borne specifically out of a human curiosity with nonhuman nature. The prehistory of radio remains legible as a process of self-education and DIY practice featuring cycles of experimentation and understanding. For example, Amber, a resin produced from a type of pine tree, was known to the Greeks and Romans to have a power to attract light materials when rubbed, such as hair or straw. Lodestone too was understood to attract materials, but only those containing iron. The curiosity and awareness raised through engagements with these simple materials over time have in fact framed the medium of radio technology: electromagnetic spectrum.[10]

The early to middle period of the nineteenth century demonstrates an exciting period of ad hoc and DIY experimentation among natural philosophers (physicists) establishing the connection between electricity and magnetism. This was a time in science when "self-education" was the rule rather than the exception. A central figure of electromagnetic science at this time was Michael Faraday, whose experimental work eventually led to the development of the theory of radio wave propagation. Faraday's introduction to scientific endeavor was somewhat accidental. It was his work as a bookbinder's apprentice that began Faraday's DIY education as a scientist. Binding copies of *the Encyclopedia* he came across an article on electricity, which excited him to build "his first static electricity machine and Leyden jar" and repeat some simple experiments.[11] Faraday was challenged by competing theories in the field of electricity at this time. While dominant theories of electricity were based on action at a distance (Newtonian gravity), Faraday's experimental work had led him to picture an interrelationship between electricity and magnetism, which he imagined as *lines of force*.[12]

A key, yet often overlooked, influence in Faraday's formulation of this picture was the work of a woman named Jane Marcet (1769–1858). In 1806, Marcet published *Conversations on Chemistry*, a translation of lectures made by Sir Humphrey Davy on Chemistry. Marcet's elucidation of the electrochemical experiments of Sir Humphrey Davy was informed by the "two-fluid theory" of electricity. The book skillfully simplified Davy's lectures, without reduction, by editing them into experiments and narrating them through a Socratic-style dialogue. *Conversations on Chemistry* was a highly influential handbook on the experimental craft and science of chemistry: "Many young men and women had their first serious exposure to chemistry through the lively discussions of Mrs. B. Emily, and Caroline, the characters Marcet used to convey her ideas."[13] It has been argued that Marcet's *how-to* handbook of chemistry did more than confirm Faraday's own conclusions: "it opened up to him a vast area in which electricity played the central role . . . In short, before 1810 Faraday had been an amateur electrician; after 1810, he was an amateur chemist, and the course of his future education, as well as his contributions to the growth of science, was to be determined by this conversion to chemistry."[14] Marcet's determination to publish accessible texts on the scientific developments of her time was characterized by a commitment to "accuracy, precision and intellectual honesty."[15]

While Marcet's primary interest in disseminating scientific knowledge was rooted in her desire to make it more accessible to women, her practice constituted a feminist politics that served to contribute significantly to the development of radio technology and science.[16] In this sense, Marcet's subtle and skillful work as a writer of *how-to* scientific textbooks is demonstrative of a pragmatic utopian agency. Marcet worked with the powers around her to improve access to knowledge and inspire experimentation. This *how-to* mode of communication and information sharing has roots in an amateur and craft ethos that began proliferating during the industrial revolution. As a genre, "how-to" literature becomes recognizable in all sorts of forms: "Diderot's *Encyclopedia* described the luxury trades of France to a readership of aristocrats; builders' manuals taught members of the working class not only craftsmanship but also mathematics and mechanical drawing; and chemical treatises on ceramic and glass contributed to the growing literature of the scientific community."[17] Marcet's *Conversations on Chemistry* can certainly be understood under this genre, but it is her committed *practice* of feminist pedagogy under patriarchal conditions that distinguishes her work as transformational. Marcet's work did not merely fuel aspirations, it catalyzed the scientific and technological domain. Faraday's experimental work, motivated by Marcet's practical translation of chemical science, later inspired the applied mathematician James Clerk Maxwell to develop his theories, which are acknowledged as "the basis of all radio communication" today.[18] The connection between Faraday and Marcet is not relayed here as a teleological story of cause and effect, but rather as an example evocative of the reality of asymmetric and often nonreciprocal influence in science and technology practices, and of political concerns latent in the convective processes of knowledge making.

Contemporary DIY radio utopian practices can be imagined as on a Mobius-like spectrum, where one turning point features more overt political or interventionist practices with the other turning point featuring subtler practices focused upon channeling creativity and developing Poïesis of experimentation and understanding within everyday modes of being alive.[19] Practices on the DIY radio spectrum involve a critical personal and/or collective engagement with content, device and medium that offer a way for people to form publics and counter-publics, that offer ways for communities to engage with themselves. As transmission artist Anna Friz argues, such practices enable people to enter into deeper relationships that involve "not just sending across, but sharing around: a feedback loop of sociality and expression."[20] Thus, DIY radio utopian practices can potentially catalyze ways of being alive with others that are transformational.

NEAR PRESENT—RADIO AS THE AMATEUR'S APPARATUS: 4 CONTEMPORARY VIGNETTES

Radio has become a touchstone of contemporary industrialized and information societies, enabling communication and trade in myriad and complex ways. In the gradual actualization of radio science and technology it has become something of a *black-box*. This is a metaphor developed by Bruno Latour (1987) from cybernetic discourse "to signal whenever a piece of machinery or set of commands is too complex" and which "describes scientists' and engineers' approaches to 'established' facts." From this perspective, a black-box technology means that only input and output count.[21] DIY radio utopian practices complicate and counter the taken-for-granted black-box of radio. They seek to experiment and understand how radio actually works, what enables and disables it, and how it can be made to work better for selves and others. A DIY radio approach articulates ways and means of understanding radio, often in sympathetic resonance with the *how-to* tradition of craft literature.[22]

Reflecting the experimental spirit of Faraday, the feminist politics of Marcet, and the autodidactic attitude of both, the following four vignettes have been selected as examples which offer insights on various DIY radio utopian practices and studies happening at the beginning of the twenty-first century. Each vignette describes a practice and/or study in brief and is framed as an example of *how-to* critical radio making and/or study; a situated way of asking questions as much as a mode of instruction and process of understanding.[23] Each can be considered as an open-ended epigraph to contemporary DIY radio utopian practices, but each can also be considered as a way of framing particular social and political problems embedded within knowledge and communications infrastructures. Following these vignettes, we will take a closer look at the "amateur's apparatus" in relation to how contemporary radio is conceived and managed as device, message, and medium.

HOW-TO . . . SEE INFRASTRUCTURE:

Artist Ingrid Burrington is on a "Vision Quest" in search of the Internet. Burrington argues that "the public have a right to understand internet infrastructure" and, driven by a concern that "maybe we have mistaken The Cloud's fiction of infinite storage capacity for history itself," she has begun a practical pilgrimage to uncover the Internet, as hidden-in-plain-sight. Since 2014, Burrington has been exploring New York City as an "infrastructure sightseer," questioning the purpose and function of mundane aspects of the urban landscape: manhole covers, street markings, antennas, cameras, and buildings that have become a destination of internet tourism (*bit tourism* if you will).[24] As Burrington explains: "New-York's infrastructure is a lot like the city itself: messy, sprawling, and at times near-incomprehensible. However, the city's tendency toward flux is a strange blessing for the infrastructure sightseer: markings and remnants of the network are almost everywhere, *once you know how to look for them*."[25] Burrington's self-assigned contract is to develop a sophisticated multimedia and multi-platform *how-to* literature that can instruct others who have a similar desire to perceive the Internet as a dynamic entity operating on top of various legacy infrastructures (telephone cables, for example). While Burrington recognizes that this approach is like "studying rook design to understand chess," nonetheless it establishes an empowering interface and augments a consciousness of the fact that "internet infrastructure is in specific places for specific reasons: natural resources, local politics, economics and even the history of the internet itself."[26] *Infrastructure Studies* is one aspect of DIY radio utopian practices that playfully critique, through pseudo-naive inquiry, popular perceptions of the Internet as "foggy," "cloudy," or variously elusive. With serious purpose and parodic acumen, Burrington has begun to publicly map the Internet's military-industrial legacy infrastructures. Publishing an online travelogue of her pilgrimages to data-centers across America, Burrington raises questions of labor conditions at retail distribution centers of Cloud-based services, such as Amazon Web Services, and the environmental impact of running their data centers.[27]

Burrington's practice is legible as a tentative lyrical call for infrastructural vigilance disguised as a joke. It is nonetheless legible as part of an American tradition, at least since Henry David Thoreau's accounts of Walden pond, that embrace a DIY approach to living well; consciously, ecologically and sustainably.[28] Burrington's *vision quest* or *pilgrimage* to find the Internet harnesses levity as a tool to pose discomforting questions of freedom, control, governance and education in an age increasingly defined by computerized automation and abstract protocols.[29] While Burrington's DIY approach is driven by a desire for self-awareness and understanding of being alive in a data-driven culture, the underlying imperative is to catalyze public discourse

Figure 6.1 Ingrid Burrington, Networks of New York: An Internet Infrastructure Field-Guide, 2014, image courtesy of the artist.

and turn attention toward the implications of the burgeoning data-industrial complex, and it's accountability in terms of environmental and social justice. Burrington's *Infrastructure Studies* is an open-ended *how-to* literature that seeks to bring "The Cloud" down to earth by asking questions of how the data-industry is folded into complicated relations of corporate and state power. Burrington's hope is that "learning more about the former might offer some insight into how we perceive—and potentially challenge—the latter."[30] Burrington's work frames a contemporary problem of visibility and attention on an increasingly consumer-based radio scene

HOW-TO . . . RECEIVE:

How to Use Fool's Gold (Pyrite Radio) is an artwork made by Sarah Browne, who describes it as a sculptural drawing; "a pragmatic and a poetic attempt to fashion something out of almost nothing."[31] Pyrite is a crystalline material that enables the reception of audible radio signals without any electrical input or external power source. The mineral's lustrous appearance meant that it was often mistaken for gold by prospectors, hence the colloquial name *Fool's Gold*. For Browne this raw material is "evocative of desire and naïveté in relation to the material resources that define wealth, as well as the less

Figure 6.2 Sarah Browne, How to Use Fool's Gold (Pyrite Radio), 2012. Pyrite, perspex, safety pin, Canadian penny, paperclip, bulldog clips, variable capacitor, plastic drainpipe, electrical wire, bakelite headphones: passive crystal radio set, dimensions variable. Detail view at Contemporary Art Gallery, Vancouver. Photo: Scott Massey. Courtesy the artist and CAG.

rational factors that underpin large-scale social and economic crises."[32] As the name suggests, *How to Use Fool's Gold (Pyrite Radio),* is basically a passive crystal radio set. Browne explains that the work always functions as such, but the way in which it functions varies with location. When the radio set was installed at the IKON gallery in Birmingham, England, its aerial was created "by threading electrical wire through and around the building to a height, and earthing it to the lightning rods outside."[33] In this way, the relatively small pyrite radio set became the catalyst of an "architectural-scale" drawing that was "practically invisible and unnoticed."[34] When installed at the Contemporary Art Gallery, Vancouver, Canada, an aerial needed to be constructed specifically around the radio set, and so a wooden frame was devised that could support the Pyrite Radio and accommodate the lengths of wire required to pick up radio signals through the crystal receiver.

Browne learned how to use fool's gold by seeking the support of amateur crystal radio artist Geoffrey Roberts, who gave advice on its construction and installation. Additionally, Browne sought to understand the way that radio waves are conceptualized in law, as a kind of mineral, by corresponding with telecommunications engineer Tim Forde. The DIY making of Browne's crystal radio has been understood by visual art curator Tessa Giblin as the development of a "radical resourcefulness" that acts as a subtle form of protest and resistance in "creative opposition to prevailing systems."[35] In the context of the contemporary art gallery the Pyrite Radio subtly calls into question prevailing power-relations of attention. The work explores the materiality of reception and transmission, and probes the edges of political freedom manifest through DIY radio practices. The aural and visual similarity between "pyrite radio" and "pirate radio" generates semantic ambivalence. This nudges attention toward the materiality of communication, agency and freedom as intra-active and co-constitutive. Through the crystal radio set, the quiet authority of geologic time imposes itself upon the listener, lyrically challenging the passivity of reception and the politics of art and technology. Browne's work frames a contemporary problem of reception and passivity on the radio scene.

HOW-TO . . . CONNECT

Air-Stream, a local Wi-Fi Community Network in Adelaide, Australia, is a do-it-together technology culture. According to ethnographer Katrina Jungnickel, its members adopt an approach that "marries a collaborative social engagement with a willingness to tinker predicated on an understanding of Wi-Fi as open, malleable and participatory."[36] The Air-Stream network was set up by a local community of gamers in the absence of adequate national broadband coverage in Adelaide. Many factors motivated this community to organize around Wi-Fi technology to support their gaming, including limited internet access, costly internet services, and frustration at asymmetrical bi-directional up/download speeds.

During her ethnographic fieldwork with this Wi-Fi community, Jungnickel attempts to get connected to the Air-Stream network. Jungnickel's research offers insight into the DIY tactics of the Wi-Fi community network. In order to ascertain whether a person's home is accessible to the network, a "line-of-sight" must be established between it and other antennae on the network. The "sight" is of course that of radio waves, invisible to the human eye, but detectable using various sensing equipment and software, such as *NetStumbler*.[37] The latter is a computer interface that can represent wireless signals in an area, thereby confirming whether or not that location is "visible" or "blocked" on the Air-Stream network. Checking whether a particular home or place is viable as part of the Air-Stream network is called *Stumbling*. This technique involves "sweeping" the air with an antenna that is connected to a laptop running a signal-detection programme. If Wi-Fi signals are detectable at a person's home then the likelihood is that an antenna can be erected

Figure 6.3 Katrina Jungnickel, DIY Wi-Fi, Chapter 6 Fig. 10, Stumbling, Image Courtesy of the Artist/Ethnographer.

there and a connection made to the Air-Stream community Wi-Fi network. *Stumbling* is a voluntary and generous choreography of communication that is carried out by an initiate of the Air-Stream network. It involves detecting possibilities, through the body and through computer technologies, for the transmission and reception of radio-signals between locals living in and around Adelaide. It is a political action that, according to one Air-Stream member, involves "getting out there and trying something which you don't necessarily know if it's going to work."[38] For Air-Stream members, "there is no such thing as *no way* of getting connected."[39]

Jungnickel teases out how observing this improvisational practice of *stumbling* around a backyard with a laptop and an antenna swinging through the air served to reconfigure a taken-for-granted idea of radio as a pay-plug-and-play communications infrastructure. Instead, radio became understood as part of "an uncertain digital landscape that relies as much on social cohesion and technological imagination as on hands-on technical skill."[40]

Jungnickel's ethnographic insight on Air-Streams DIY community Wi-Fi network is as fascinating as it is mundane. It draws attention to the strangeness of radio communication and yet how much it has become understood as a consumer commodity, determined primarily by property rights. Jungnickel shows that radio waves are imagined by the Air-Stream community in a way that does not align with traditional conceptions of the electromagnetic spectrum as property. Instead, as Jungnickel suggests, the DIY Wi-Fi radio practitioner "does not impose himself upon the wireless spectrum but lets it reveal what currently exists, imagines what might be possible and sets about weaving the potential of a new antenna into the social fabric of the digital landscape. The practice of stumbling . . . is less about mapping a landscape or diagnosing a problem and more about opening up a range of possibilities" for connection and communication.[41] Air-Stream's commitment to DIY Wi-Fi can thus be read as a utopian practice that re-defines connection not as commodity but as a collaborative process that constitutes a community through a complex ritual of giving, manifested in the act of *stumbling*.[42] Jungnickel's work frames a problem of the black-boxing and commodification of communication on the radio scene.

HOW-TO . . . OBFUSCATE

Allison Burtch has made a contract with herself to create *Liberation Technology* with the understanding that "discussions about technology are rarely about technology. They're about humans, money and power."[43] Drawing upon Gilles Deleuze's observation that "the problem is no longer getting people to express themselves, but providing little gaps of solitude and silence in which they might eventually find something to say,"[44] Burtch invents the *Log Jammer*. This is a radio device, at once literally functional and metaphorical, that challenges rhetoric's framing commercial connectivity as sociality and politics, rather than a proprietary transaction. Burtch's *Log Jammer* is designed to provide "a safe space in the woods, a right to be alone. What a relief to have the right to say nothing, because only then is there a chance of framing the rare, the thing that might be worth saying."[45] The *Log Jammer* incorporates hardware and software that literally allows users of Wi-Fi signals to disconnect. It does this by creating noise at a radio wavelength specific to cell phones with the effect that transmissions are blocked. By deliberately introducing wireless noise into the communications system, the *Log Jammer* interferes with the status quo of connectivity. This radio device deploys a tactic "both personal and political" and acts as a platform for reflection upon "problematic aspects of surveillance and resistance in an age of ubiquitous data capture."[46] Thus, Burtch's DIY radio practice can be framed as a mode of obfuscation.

The *how-to* of the radio making process is published through Github, so that technically literate others can reproduce the Log Jammer and, by way of facilitated radio solitude, presumably find something to say. While *Log Jammer* was a pragmatic satire developed as part of a postgraduate program at the NYU-ITP, the concept has since developed into another kind of DIY radio: *Mic Jammer*. This is a "privacy/anti-surveillance device" for mobile phone users. Described as the equivalent of "taping over your webcam," the *Mic*

Jammer is "an ultrasonic security system that gives people the confidence to know that their smart phone microphones are non-invasively muted."[47] The *Mic Jammer* works by means of "de-sensing the microphones of the cell phone by applying a very high level ultrasonic signal that is inaudible to humans by can be heard by microphones." Burtch wants to reproduce the *Mic Jammer* as an anti-surveillance commodity and is currently seeking "corporate or institutional support" or an "angel-investor" in order to do so. The *Mic Jammer* is a deadpan non-solutionist response to increasingly surveillance-based internet, information and communication technologies.[48] Burtch negotiates privacy through making ambivalent, obfuscatory DIY radio objects that reflect how "even in the freest environments, the new digital means of information and communication have important limits and costs. There are fine lines between pluralism and cacophony, between advocacy and intolerance, and between the expansion of the public sphere and its hopeless fragmentation."[49] Liberation Technology is defined by Larry Diamond as "any form of information and communication technology (ICT) that can expand political, social, and economic freedom." Diamond's work, corroborating Burtch's critical understanding of communications technology, highlights that the struggle for electronic connection *and* disconnection "is really just the timeless struggle for freedom by new means. It is not technology, but people, organizations, and governments that will determine who prevails."[50] Burtch's work frames a problem of surveillance and control on the radio scene.

In the simplest DIY radio terms, radio technology can be thought as an intra-action of *message*, *device* and *medium*. The *message* can be understood as both the content to be transceived and the way that it is encoded/decoded; the *device* can be understood as the physical technology that manipulates the *medium* (radio waves) to enable the transmission and reception of a message to take place. In the following sections, we summarize very briefly what we mean by these terms, bringing particular emphasis to the importance of the medium for DIY radio utopian practices.

RADIO DEVICE

Historically, radio devices are inventions that emerge from *ad hoc* processes over time, involving raw materials and industrial production, experiment, tinkering, imagination, curiosity, some more-or-less tangible questions and problems and a sense of adventure in responding to them. The term "radiowave" refers specifically to the band of waves within the electromagnetic spectrum ranging from 3 KHz to 300 GHz.[51] Radio devices are specifically designed to send and receive information at different frequencies within this range. A radio device transmits signals by manipulating the radio waves, embedding messages on them through a process called modulation. In this process, information is bundled onto the wave by using various techniques and is sent through electrical or optical pulses across the radio waves. On the other side a receiving device reverses the packing process, unbundling and de-modulating the information, recomposing the intended message (sound/image/vibration). Even though radio devices are more complicated than ever, with software and automation playing an increasingly important role in radio technology, it remains a possibility to build a receiving radio apparatus using relatively accessible materials, as Sarah Browne's pyrite radio demonstrates. Whatever the level of complexity, radio devices are always more than the sum of their parts.

Theatre maker Bertolt Brecht believed that "The public was not waiting for the radio, but rather the radio was waiting for the public."[52] His assessment of the advent of radio devices, echoing the motivation behind Allison Burtch's *Log Jammer*, was that "Suddenly there was the possibility to say everything to everyone, but upon reflection there was nothing to be said."[53] While radios can and do enable communication and currencies of distribution and exchange, as intra-active devices, they are constituted by society's ability to develop ways to articulate and organize ways of living and being alive with others through them.[54]

RADIO MESSAGE

Radio is an apparatus that enables the expression and circulation of commitments and values within a society. The message of radio is embedded at the level of the object and the gerund. For example, Sarah Browne's DIY radio practice has expanded from *How to Use Fool's Gold (Pyrite Radio)* across a series of works: *The Cognitive Radio*, *Scarcity Radio*, and *Remembering Grey*.[55] Browne's art practice develops ways of creating distance in order to respond to economic distress and disruption. This DIY radio utopian practice acknowledges radio as a crucial means of communication in times of crisis, particularly when language itself is at stake. Such practices speak to the difficulty of making a distinction between what radio technology is *saying* and what it is *doing*, acknowledging radio's complex material agency. The same can be said for Ingrid Burrington's bit-tourism of New York City's internet infrastructure. While Burrington draws attention to the hidden-in-plain sight signs and pock-marks of internet and communications technologies through artistic fieldwork, Browne's message is encoded in the DIY action of making a basic radio set and exhibiting it in a public gallery. Through making and exhibiting the Pyrite radio, Browne articulates a pervasive yet ambivalent problem of reception and passivity in contemporary information societies. In Browne's work the intra-action of device and message becomes tangible when, and *if*, visitors to the installation engage with the Pyrite radio.

RADIO MEDIUM

As mentioned earlier in this chapter, the electromagnetic spectrum is the collective term for all types of electromagnetic radiation. Radiation is energy that travels and spreads out as it propagates from its source. Though the term "electromagnetic spectrum" refers to all types of radiation and not just radio waves, in the field of wireless communications the phrase "spectrum" is often synonymous with the term radio waves or radio frequencies, and these terms are used interchangeably. There are different types of electromagnetic radiation (e.g., visible light, x-rays) but the type of electromagnetic radiation of interest in this chapter is the radio wave (ranging from 3 Hz to 3000 GHz in frequency), the medium over which radio devices communicate.

Fundamentally, radio devices would have no purpose without the radio wave, and messages would have no possibility of transmission and reception. The same applies the other way around: The communications channel that occurs between the transmitter and the receiver is contingent; it does not exist independently of the technical interactions involved between the devices and the medium.[56] Hence, spectrum can be understood as the lifeblood of radio infrastructure and the services and operations it supports; it is "the medium that enables us to communicate in the first place."[57]

In recent times, spectrum has become conceptualized as an *infrastructure space* comparable to a computer: "Like an operating system, the medium of infrastructure space makes certain things possible and other things impossible."[58] Keller Easterling understands infrastructure space as a "content manager" that dictates "the rules of the game." Drawing upon Marshall McLuhan's work, Easterling proposes that the *declared content* of infrastructure space is a kind of *distraction*; "in other words, what the medium is saying sometimes prevents us from seeing what the medium is doing."[59] This is a pervasive problem that DIY radio utopian practices engage with in various ways, as the vignettes above suggest. Arguably, the seamless protocols that delineate the medium of radio communications today further *distract* from the effects of spectrum allocation.[60] Under contemporary conditions of digitally networked communication it becomes more difficult for a lay (non-DIY or "black-box" radio) public to parse not only what the spectrum is "saying" or "doing," but to recognize *who* is controlling the medium and how accountability is distributed through the network. There is a need for DIY radio utopian practices that are capable of generating experiments that can transform conventional ways of appreciating, organizing and attending to natural resources like spectrum.

NEAR FUTURE—THE TRAGI-COMEDY OF DIY RADIO UTOPIA

The near future of radio continues to be anchored by its recent past. Nonetheless, there is a struggle for release and change. DIY radio utopian practices today are toggling historical conventions of infrastructure space. Attending to the genealogy of how radio space has been organized ad hoc throughout the twentieth century provides insight into the power of social imaginaries of control. Such imaginaries have been sustained by rhetorics of tragedy and scarcity, and continue to be countered by alter-imaginaries of comedy and abundance. The near future of DIY radio utopian practices operate according to tragi-comic logics of freedom and constraint.

A TRAGEDY OF CONTROL

In the beginning of radio, the medium (spectrum) was not regulated. Hence, alongside the development of commercial or military radio operations, a vibrant amateur radio community emerged. In the period prior to 1912, networks of amateur radio enthusiasts proliferated. These amateur radio operators built their own radio devices and they created their own messages with unfettered access to the medium. The DIY hobbyists of this era, in fact, contributed significantly to the growth of a radio apparatus. These amateur radio operators shared know-how and skills, extended understanding of radio as a broadcasting mechanism and not just a point-to-point communication system, and cultivated an appreciation of radio as technology for social interaction and cooperation.[61] In essence, early amateur or DIY radio was central to the development of mainstream radio. These DIY radio practices were instrumental in finding new directions for radio and establishing a broader horizon of possibility on the radio scene. At this time, pre-World War I and World War II, a de facto spectrum *commons* was in place. This meant that the different players in the radio space (commercial, military, and amateur), more-or-less cooperated and managed ways to coexist. However as the airwaves became busier, controlling the interference between different players became more challenging. The response to this growth of interference was the introduction of regulations, which ultimately led to the colonization of the medium by commercial and military interests and a significant reduction in access for amateurs.[62]

Since the 1960s, regulation has been partially informed, more-or-less directly, by rhetoric based upon an essay called *The Tragedy of the Commons*. The argument made by Garret Hardin in 1968 is based upon an essay written in 1833 by economist William Foster Lloyd of the same name. This polemical argument conceives of people as inherently self-interested creatures, where self-interest is equated to "rational" being. According to this argument, people will squander a resource to suit their individual needs over and above a common good or sense of material intra-actions: "As a rational being, each . . . seeks to maximize his gain," even at the expense of other's. This polemic has inadvertently served to cement a general view that the organizational principles and values of commons and commoning are irrational: "Freedom in a commons brings ruin to all." Hence, the teleology of tragedy. Since the 1960s, the "tragedy of the commons" argument has given permission to military and commercial incumbents to secure large parts of the infrastructure space of spectrum, while amateur radio operators have been cordoned off. This partitioning was part of a broader regulatory movement in which spectrum began to be divided up into different wavelengths or frequency bands and allocated for different uses.[63] Licensing regimes were introduced as part of the process to ensure orderly assignment of frequency bands to different interested parties. In the main, throughout the twentieth century, access to the radio medium remained dominated by the requirement for a license.[64] Thus, in addition to knowing *how-to* build and maintain a radio, all radio operators had now to acquire a license permitting one to use it. In its earliest manifestations, DIY radio utopia was constituted by a dialogic interplay between device, message, and medium. With the emergence of spectrum regulation possibilities for such practices became substantially curbed.

It is important to bear in mind, however, that Hardin's *tragedy of the commons* argument was devised to fuel a debate on the relationship between population growth and resource management. The purpose of the argument was perhaps more nuanced than the one-sided rhetoric its title suggests. Ultimately, the argument attempts to make a case for a better kind of education in relation to resource management, one that deals with the intra-acting concepts of freedom and necessity. Unfortunately, it seems as though "the tragedy" propounded by Hardin's article continues to be mapped onto regulatory mindsets, dominating the imaginary of spectrum as a natural resource like land or oil. Spectrum allocation is infused rhetorically by a political imaginary of radio waves as a scarce natural resource. Permeated by a pervasive mythology of the tragedy of the commons, attitudes toward spectrum regulation have in many ways become conditioned by a tragedy of control.

A COMEDY OF RESISTANCE

As regulation has developed over the years, the right to access the medium of radio has continually been protested. The most powerful examples of DIY radio practices that assume and protest this right to access are those of the pirate radio stations and free-radio movements that have emerged since the sixties. DIY radio operator and activist, Ron Sakolsky, provides insights on these practices at the turn of the twenty-first century: "Some of these pirate stations continue to exist, while others have been legalized and hence restratified, still others have disappeared. Yet new ones have been born all across the planet in the flames of the Nineties. Circling somewhere in the aether remains the vision of nomadic radio pirates whose transmitters navigate the airwaves liberating them on behalf of the voiceless, marginalized and downtrodden and viewing those waves as treasures in themselves which have unjustly been confiscated and debased by the rich and mighty; a touch stone image for current free radio activists throughout the world."[65]

Pirate radio operators build their DIY radio utopias through the creation and distribution of political, personal and/or social messages, both through the construction of radio devices and by accessing spectrum in defiance of regulations. Radio pirates operate for various reasons; from personal amusement and curiosity to political dissent and social experiment.[66] Traditionally, pirate radio operators, working individually or as part of a community, constructed homemade radio stations. These radio stations had no licenses and essentially they hijacked the airwaves in order to make transmissions. Famous pirate radio stations such as Radio Caroline and Radio London responded to staid commercial and/or state broadcasting by transmitting music for younger generations who wanted something new and more fulfilling. Pirate radio can be understood as a comedic and political mode of communication that draws attention to the ways in which radio wave regulation "misfires."[67] It does so by modeling ways of making radio otherwise, not just technically but socially and politically as well. The pirate has to take serious risks, whether by bending, inverting or breaking the rules.[68] She operates counter to oppressive regimes by enacting resistance through a logic of comedy and beginnings. The movements of free radio in the 1970s, across the world, inspired new thinking and anarchistic action on the radio scene that can be described as a comedy of resistance.

In the 1980s, policy makers in the United States took a disruptive step by reintroducing a *spectrum commons* and thereby establishing clearly delineated infrastructural spaces in which licenses were not needed. These *license-exempt bands* are officially called the Industrial, Scientific and Medical (ISM) bands. These license-exempt bands have served to support a *comedy of the commons* where radio users and operators can play by developing a shared etiquette, nonetheless governed within the rule of regulation.

The ISM license-exemption led to a widespread innovation delivering the highly successful Wi-Fi standards. These bands were allocated under the assumption that they were largely unusable, and would sometimes be referred to as "junk-bands." Though minor spaces on the electromagnetic spectrum, they afforded radio operators and experimenters access to the medium. The so-called "junk-bands" became a microcosm of the electromagnetic spectrum that reflected the earliest days of radio. Radio devices and messages were invented and shaped within this infrastructural space, and something like a DIY radio utopia began to emerge. The success of the Wi-Fi bands has, to an extent, punctures the myth of "the tragedy of the commons." Ironically, as the radio operators within the "junk-bands" began to demonstrate both invention and robustness (e.g., Wi-Fi devices and networks), mainstream licensed communication systems (e.g., the cellular networks) began to take advantage of these innovations, and have come to rely on Wi-Fi networks quite significantly. Up to 60 percent of mobile traffic from cellular/mobile networks is currently offloaded onto Wi-Fi networks. Licensed cellular networks would collapse under the weight of the traffic they pledge to serve were it not for the existence of other networks born out of the DIY radio utopia of the "junk-bands." The darker side of a comedy of resistance is its susceptibility to reterritorialization and exploitation by commercial incumbents.

"JUNK-BANDS": A TRAGI-COMEDY OF RESISTANCE

Despite the success of the ISM bands, and the emergence of pockets of DIY radio utopian activity, the electromagnetic spectrum has become largely controlled by powerful incumbents. There has been a pattern of colonization and decolonization of the radio medium by commercial mobile communications providers and military interests. Robert McChesney provides an apt example: "The major function of nonprofit broadcasting in the United States from 1920 to 1960 was, in fact, to pioneer new sections of the electromagnetic spectrum when the commercial interests did not yet view them as profitable. Thus it was educational broadcasting in the 1920s, and then FM radio and even UHF television in the 1940s and 1950s. In each case, once it became clear that money could be made, the educators were displaced and capitalists seized the reins."[69] Similar tendencies are taking place in the Wi-Fi space today and the struggle for different modes of access to spectrum continues.[70] In the past decade spectrum sharing, for example, has become a major topic of academic, regulatory, and industry focus. However, the ways of contesting normative practices which restrict access to the radio medium appear tamer today, revolving around advocating regulatory change on the basis of research evidence (e.g., PCAST, extension of Wi-Fi bands, LSA).[71] While such advocacy is encouraging, it sustains a *play-by-rule* approach that sustains rather than transforms the status quo.

Contemporary manifestations of pirate radio practices seem benign in comparison to the movements of the 1970s and 1980s. For example, the software-radio community has made partial challenges to the dominance of commercial mobile operator's/carrier's through the creation of open source versions of radio technology used in mobile/cellular networks.[72] One example is OPEN BTS—an open source version of a 2G mobile communication system.[73] Like all radio systems, it is designed to operate in specific frequency bands, licensed by various mobile operators around the world. The creation of the open source version is a rhetorical challenge to the dominance of mobile operator. However it remains illegal to switch on these radios, as they are not permitted to transmit in bands for which they do not have a license. This is why the intervention is "partial." OPEN BTS has been used as a "pop-up network" at Burning Man,[74] an event described as an experiment in community and art. Because of its isolated location at the Black Rock Desert in Nevada, Burning Man is not covered by mobile/cellular operators. Normally this location has no customers and therefore no commercial coverage is required. Therefore, at Burning Man an OPEN BTS system can function without causing interference to other official systems. While such applications as OPEN BTS at Burning Man cannot be said to constitute an act of piracy, they might be said to demonstrate a habit of *pyrite-cy*: a non-transgressive form of consumer culture primed and set to "receive-only," albeit creatively. Today, there is a pervasive understanding of *radio-as-commodity*.[75] It has become difficult to imagine radio as anything other than an item in currencies of consumerism. Contemporary DIY radio utopian practices (such as those touched upon in the vignettes) struggle to draw attention toward such habits of "Pyrite-cy," let alone to formulate and enact radical change through counter-cultures of communication on a distracted radio scene.

Access to the medium of radio remains a fundamental locus of trouble for all DIY radio utopian practices. Contemporary DIY radio utopian practices, whether professional or amateur, subsequently effuse a humor of tragi-comedy. This suggests a reluctance or inability to spontaneously enact transgressions that might actually transform the everyday of radio. Thus, an urgent question arises: can DIY radio utopian practices afford *not* to bend and break the rules?

ENACTING DIY RADIO UTOPIAN PRACTICES: A CALL TO ARMS!

In recent years, Ursula K. Le Guin has emphasized the urgency for a *how-to* literature that can help orient human civilization toward a better future: "We will be wanting the voices . . . who can see alternatives to how we live now and can see through our fear stricken society and its obsessive technologies, to other ways of being . . . we will need [voices] who can remember freedom; poets, visionaries . . . the realists of a larger reality."[76] The DIY radio utopian practices we have drawn upon have more or less manifested tensions of tragic and comic imaginaries and relations on the radio scene. These imaginaries become legible in the humor, or *humorlessness*, enacted through practice. For example, Allison Burtch's anti-3G/Wi-Fi device, *Log Jammer*, demonstrates a deadpan resistance toward the proliferation of radio devices and activity. Burtch trains her capacity to live alongside the ambivalence of infrastructural politics, all the while experimenting and imagining better ways of being alive with others. This is what Lauren Berlant refers to as "deadpan from below," a strategy that reflects the humorlessness of hegemonic authority as it seeks to transgress it's control.[77]

DIY radio utopian practices that experiment with, make and share infrastructural space challenge the hegemonic "situation tragedy" of radio spectrum. These practices help to frame and/or provide platforms for new and better ways of thinking about the role of radio spectrum, messages and devices in contemporary political, economic and social life. Berlant's concept of situation comedy resonates with DIY radio utopian practices in the way that they provide a contemporary *how-to* literature for political and social agency on the radio scene. In other words, DIY radio utopian practices (as per Jane Marcet, Michael Faraday and the 4 vignettes) provide various modes of training that can enable people to think affirmatively about being alive with others.[78] For example, the intrepid mapping practices of artist Ingrid Burrington demonstrates a desire and urgency to make infrastructural space recognizable, perceptible and accessible to nonexperts and radio professionals alike. This DIY radio utopian practice involves delineating that which is hidden-in-plain-sight by way of new adventures in piracy and smuggling.[79] Such work is committed to beginning and stewarding critical conversations on/through infrastructure space. This means talking about the interplay of money, ideology and power, while questioning who owns and/or controls the spectrum and manages how it is valued, and why. These minor movements resist and challenge the radio *pyrite-cy* of consumer culture by interrupting "regular broadcasts" in order to highlight the precariousness of radio freedoms and dependencies.

Contemporary DIY radio utopian practices might not be populated by *free-radio* pirates, but they continue to struggle, as Keller Easterling does, for better ways to address and actualize "what kind of infrastructure space might initiate a real paradigm shift, campaigning not on promises of freedom but on promises of interdependence, balances of freedom, or even obligation?"[80] In the near-present, DIY radio utopian practices urgently need to operate their *how-to* communications and tactics disruptively by toggling within the gray space of a tragi-comic radio hegemony. At the same time, they must seek out ways to transgress the status quo by proposing other possibilities and by generating platforms to think otherwise in places of power. This difficult work will necessitate attending to the formation of publics, counter-publics, temporary autonomous zones, and utopias that address and engage *others*. Transgressive DIY radio utopian practices can emerge through orthogonal methods of feminist experimentation and training, and in places where intra-actions of art, engineering and policy begin to catalyze each other to effect social change and transformation.

CONCLUSIONS

In this chapter we have drawn out an aspect of radio's near past, the comic and accidental relation between Michael Faraday and Jane Marcet, that demonstrate it as a distinctly utopian mode of DIY practice. Radio has always involved and depended upon a healthy interplay and interdependence between the medium, devices and message. Overtime, such interplay has become complicated by regulation and a technological politics informed by rhetorics which serve to frame the conception and management of natural resources (i.e., spectrum) as tragic. DIY radio utopian practices (as per the 4 vignettes) struggle to understand contemporary conditions of radio, and to imagine and enact transformational ways of being alive with others on the radio scene. In many ways, DIY radio utopian practices seek to evolve comic relations on the radio scene that can resist and potentially transgress the hegemony of tragedy and rhetorics of scarcity that serve the status quo politics of powerful interests and incumbents. DIY radio utopian practices both highlight and demonstrate the interplay and interdependence between the medium, devices and message. If the near-future of radio is to support and facilitate just ways of being alive with others (human and nonhuman) then a new idiom of radio piracy is called for.

NOTES

1. Tim Ingold, *Being Alive: Essays on Movement, Knowledge and Description* (London and New York: Routledge, 2011).

2. Ruth Levitas, *The Concept of Utopia* (Bern: Peter Lang, 2010), 207.

3. Lyman Tower Sargent, *Utopianism: A Very Short Introduction* (Oxford and New York: Oxford University Press, 2010), 6.

4. Anthropologist Paul Rabinow has defined "the contemporary" as "a moving ratio of modernity, moving through the recent past and near future in a (nonlinear) space that gauges modernity as an ethos already becoming historical." Paul Rabinow, *Marking Time: On the Anthropology of the Contemporary* (Princeton and Oxford: Princeton University Press, 2008), 2.

5. The writing process is asymmetrical; while the ideas in this essay have been developed over an extended period of time through dialogue and listening, the writing is developed principally through an artistic process structured by an engineering logic.

6. Sargent, *Utopianism*, 125.

7. Levitas, *The Concept of Utopia*, 231.

8. Michael Warner, *Publics and Counterpublics* (New York: Zone Books, 2005).

9. Laurens E. Whittemore, "The Development of Radio," *The Annals of the American Academy of Political and Social Sciences*, 142 (March 1929).

10. Graham Hall, "Maxwell's Electromagnetic Theory and Special Relativity," *Philosophical Transactions: Mathematical, Physical and Engineering Sciences*, 366, no. 1871 (2008).

11. Pearce L. Williams, "Michael Faraday's Education in Science," *Isis*, 51, no. 4 (1960).

12. Undoubtedly there is a genealogy in formation through the physical theories of Faraday and on through the later philosophical work of Gilles Deleuze and Felix Guattari, in their consideration of physical and social relations through the figures of rhizomes and lines-of-flight. Gilles Deleuze and Felix Guattari, *A Thousand Plateaus: Capitalism and Schizophrenia* (Minneapolis and London: University of Minnesota Press, 1987); ibid.

13. M. Susan Lindee, "The American Career of Jane Marcet's Conversations on Chemistry, 1806–1853," *Isis*, 82, no. 1 (1991): 9.

14. Williams, "Michael Faraday's Education in Science," *Isis*, 524; Lindee, "The American Career of Jane Marcet's Conversations on Chemistry," *Isis*.

15. Saba Bahar, "Jane Marcet and the Limits to Public Science," *The British Journal for the History of Science*, 34, no. 1 (2001): 29.

16. Bahar, "Jane Marcet and the Limits to Public Science," *The British Journal for the History of Science*, 29.

17. Glenn Adamson, ed. *The Craft Reader* (Oxford and New York: BERG, 2010), 9.

18 Faraday's later work sought out the possibility of producing electricity from magnetism, culminating in the discovery of the Law of Electromagnetic Induction in 1831 after years of experimentation. Michael C. Sexton, "Who Invented Radio? A Strange Controversy," *Studies: An Irish Quarterly Review*, 55, no. 220 (1966), 416.

19. Matt Ratto and Megan Boler, *DIY Citizenship: Critical Making and Social Media* (Cambridge, MA and London, UK: The MIT Press, 2014).

20. Anna Friz, "Transmission Art in the Present Tense," *PAJ: A Journal of Performance Art,* 31, no. 3 (2009): 47.

21. Toscano, *Marconi's Wireless*, xiii; Bruno Latour, *Science in Action: How to Follow Scientists and Engineers through Society* (Cambridge, MA: Harvard University Press, 1987), 2.

The word black box is used by cyberneticians whenever a piece of machinery or a set of commands is too complex. In its place they draw a little box about which they need to know nothing but its input and output . . . That is, no matter how controversial their history, how complex their inner workings, how large the commercial or academic networks that hold them in place, only their input and output count.

22. Al Brogdon, *Low Profile Amateur Radio: Operating a Ham Station from Almost Anywhere* (USA: ARRL Inc., The International Association for Amateur Radio, 2006); Ron Sakolsky and Stephen Dunifer, *Seizing the Airwaves: A Free Radio Handbook* (Edinburg and San Francisco: AK Press, 1998).

23. The philosophy of situated knowledge's is important to DIY radio utopian practices, therefore we recommend a reading of Donna Haraway's seminal 1988 text: Donna Haraway, "Situated Knowledge's: The Science Question in Feminism and the Privilege of Partial Perspective," *Feminist Studies,* 14, no. 3 (1988). Donna Haraway, "Situated Knowledges: The Science Question in Feminism and the Privilege of Partial Perspective," *Feminist Studies*, 14, no. 3 (1988).

24. Jessica Foley, "Like ;)—Maria O'Brien," *Exhibition Catalogue*, 2010.

25. Ingrid Burrington, Web Site, http://lifewinning.com/research/infrastructure-studies (accessed January 14, 2016).

26. Ibid.

27. Ingrid Burrington, Web Site, http://creativetimereports.org/author/ingrid-burrington/ (accessed January 19, 2016) and Ingrid Burrington, Web Site, http://www.theatlantic.com/author/ingrid-burrington/ (accessed January 19, 2016).

28. Thoreau, Henry David, *Walden; or, Life in the Woods* (New York: Dover Publications, Inc., 1995).

29. Alexander Galloway, *Protocol: How Control Exists after Decentralization* (Cambridge, MA and London, England: The MIT Press, 2004).

30. Ingrid Burrington, Web Site, http://creativetimereports.org/2014/05/20/ingrid-burrington-the-cloud is not the territory-wnv/ (accessed January 14, 2016)

31. Sarah Browne, Web Site, http://www.sarahbrowne.info/work/how-to-use-fools-gold-pyrite-radio/ (accessed January 19, 2016).

32. Ibid., (accessed January 15, 2016).

33. Sarah Browne, Email Correspondence with the Authors, January 18, 2016.

34. Ibid.

35. Sarah Browne, *How to Use Fool's Gold* (Dublin: Project Press, 2012), 3.

36. Katrina Jungnickel, *DiY Wi-Fi: Re-imagining Connectivity* (UK: Palgrave Macmillan, 2014), 24.

37. NetStumbler, Web Site, http://www.netstumbler.com/ (accessed February 13, 2016).

38. Jungnickel, *DiY Wi-Fi*, 80.

39. Ibid.

40. Ibid., 76.

41. Jungnickel, *DiY Wi-Fi*, 88.

42. Though the Air-Stream members, nor Katrina Jungnickel, do not frame the Air-Stream Wi-Fi network as art, it is intriguing to note how it resonates with certain modes of art practice since the 1960s that "attempt to install alternative models of exchange that counter, complicate or parody the dominant market— and profit-based system of exchange." Air-Stream engages with the logic of the gift economy and "functions as a mechanism to instigate social exchanges or interactions that specifically put into motion a circuit of obligation and reciprocity, typically involved in giving, receiving or accepting, and giving in return." Miwon Kwon, "Exchange Rate: On Obligation and Reciprocity in Some Art of the 1960s and After," in *The Market: Documents of Contemporary Art*, ed. Natasha Degen (London and Cambridge, MA: The MIT Press and Whitechapel Gallery, 2013), 135.

43. Allison Burtch, Web Site, http://blog.allisonburtch.net/ (accessed December 21, 2015).

44. Gilles Deleuze, *Negotiations* (New York and Chichester, West Sussex: Columbia University Press, 1995), 129.

45. Allison Burtch, Web Site, http://www.allisonburtch.net/log-jammer/ (accessed January 19, 2016).

46. Finn Brunton and Helen Nissenbaum, "Vernacular resistance to data collection and analysis: A political theory of obfuscation," *First Monday: Peer-reviewed Journal on the Internet,* 16, no. 5 (2011).

47. Allison Burtch, Web Site, http://www.allisonburtch.net/mic-jammer/ (accessed January 19, 2016).

48. Gilles Paquet describes "solutionism" as a way of interpreting "issues as puzzles to which there is a solution, rather than as problems to which there may be a response." cited p. 29; Evgeny Morozov, *To Save Everything, Click Here: The Folly of Technological Solutionism* (New York: Public Affairs, 2013).

49. Larry Diamond, "Liberation Technology," *Journal of Democracy,* 21, no. 3 (2010).

50. Diamond, "Liberation Technology," *Journal of Democracy*, 82.

51. Heinrich Hertz's name is attributed to the unit of measurement, (Hz), for radio waves on the electromagnetic spectrum. It was Hertz who first experimentally detected radio waves in 1887, based upon Maxwell's mathematical theories. Laurens E. Whittemore, "The Development of Radio," *The Annals of the American Academy of Political and Social Science,* 142, (1929).

52. Bertolt Brecht, "The Radio as Communications Apparatus," in *Bertolt Brecht on Film & Radio*, ed. Marc Silberman (UK: Bloomsbury, 2000).

53. Ibid.

54. Karen Barad, Web Site, https://www.academia.edu/1857617/_Intra-actions_Interview_of_Karen_Barad_by_Adam_Kleinmann_ (accessed January 19, 2016).

55. Sarah Browne, Web Site, http://www.sarahbrowne.info/work/the-cognitive-radio/ (accessed February 3, 2016).

56. Rachel O'Dwyer, "Spectre of the Commons: Spectrum Regulation in the Communism of Capital," (Trinity College University of Dublin, 2013).

57. J. Gabrys, "Atmospheres of Communication," in *The Wireless Spectrum: The Politics, Practices, and Poetics of Mobile Media* (Toronto, Buffalo & London: University of Toronto Press, 2010).

58. Keller Easterling, *Extrastatecraft: The Power of Infrastructure Space* (London & Brooklyn: Verso, 2014).

59. Ibid., 23.

60. It is worth keeping in mind that the word "distraction" means "to pull in different directions" or "to draw apart." In this sense, "distraction" is a tool that can be put to different purposes. A "distraction" might clarify or it might obfuscate.

61. O'Dwyer, "Spectre of the Commons: Spectrum Regulation in the Communism of Capital."

62. For a more in-depth history of spectrum allocation please refer to Hugh G. Aitken, "Allocating the Spectrum: The Origins of Radio Regulation," *Technology and Culture,* 35, no. 4 (1994).

63. US Frequency Allocations, Web Site, https://www.ntia.doc.gov/files/ntia/publications/2003-allochrt.pdf (accessed February 13, 2016).

64. Licenses are obtained in a variety of ways. They can be assigned to third parties by the state for free or for a specific fee or they can be bought through competitive processes such as auctions, for example. The amateur radio bands also have their own licensing regimes.

65. Ron Sakolsky and Stephen Dunifer, *Seizing the Airwaves: A Free Radio Handbook* (Edinburgh and San Francisco: AK Press, 1998).

66. A fascinating example of radio piracy in Ireland can be found in the story of Sean McQuillan. McQuillan's mundane and colloquial approach to radio piracy demonstrates a basic desire to experiment and share culture: Jackie Jarvis, "Sean Mcquillan - Engineer, Farmer, Pirate Radio Pioneer" (2014).

67. Noel Carroll, *Humour: A Very Short Introduction* (Oxford: Oxford University Press, 2014).

68. Leif Dahlberg, "Pirates, Partisans, and Politico-Juridical Space," *Law and Literature,* 23, no. 2 (2011).

69. Robert McChesney, "The Political Economy of Radio," in *Seizing the Airwaves: A Free Radio Handbook*, eds. Ron Sakolsky and Stephen Dunifer (Edinburgh and San Francisco: AK Press, 1998).

70. Web Site, https://www.freedompop.com/ (accessed January 20, 2016).

71. PCAST, "Realizing the Full Potential of Government-Held Spectrum to Spur Economic Growth" (Washington: The White House, 2012).

72. Software-radio is the practice of designing radios that either use a limited amount of hardware or use hardware that can be reprogrammed. Platforms such as GNU radio are examples of open source software that allows radios to be built from a modular set of radio components, for example, http://gnuradio.org/redmine/projects/gnuradio/wiki (accessed February 3, 2016).

73. http://openbts.org/ (accessed February 3, 2016). Mobile phone technologies are named according to generation, for example, 2G, 3G and 4G.

74. *Burning Man* is an annual gathering that takes place at Black Rock City—a temporary community erected in the Black Rock Desert in Nevada, USA.

75. Katrina Jungnickel, *Diy Wifi: Re-Imagining Connectivity* (New York: Palgrave MacMillan, 2014).

76. Highlights of the 65th National Book Awards, Web Site, https://www.youtube.com/watch?v=Et9Nf-rsALk (accessed January 20, 2016).

77. The idea of building "new capacities to be with ambivalence" was recorded in notes taken by the author during a lecture given by Lauren Berlant at Trinity College Dublin on the 7th September 2014, as part of the Unlearning Conference, http://www.unlearningconf.com/ (accessed February 3, 2016).

78. Walker Art Centre, "Opening-Day Talk: Pedro Reyes, Michael Hardt, and Lauren Berlant" (2011); ibid.

79. Ingrid Burrington, "The Cloud Is Not the Territory," *Creative Time Reports* 2014.

80. Keller Easterling, *Extrastatecraft*, 2014.

BIBLIOGRAPHY

Adamson, Glenn, ed. *The Craft Reader*. Oxford and New York: BERG, 2010.

Aitken, Hugh G. "Allocating the Spectrum: The Origins of Radio Regulation." *Technology and Culture* 35, no. 4 (1994): 686–716.

Bahar, Saba. "Jane Marcet and the Limits to Public Science." *The British Journal for the History of Science* 34, no. 1 (2001): 29–49.

Bauman, Zygmunt. *Culture in a Liquid Modern World*. Cambridge, UK and Malden, MA: Polity, 2011.

Brecht, Bertolt. "The Radio as Communications Apparatus (1932)." In *Bertolt Brecht on Film & Radio*, edited by Marc Silberman. UK: Bloomsbury, 2000.

Brogdon, Al. *Low Profile Amateur Radio: Operating a Ham Station from Almost Anywhere*. USA: The ARRL, Inc., 2006.

Browne, Sarah. *How to Use Fool's Gold*. Dublin: Project Arts Centre/IKON/CAG, 2012.

———. "How to Use Fool's Gold (Pyrite Radio) - Ikon Gallery." http://www.sarahbrowne.info/work/how-to-use-fools-gold-pyrite-radio/.

Burrington, Ingrid. "The Cloud Is Not the Territory." *Creative Time Reports*, 2014.

Carroll, Noel. *Humour: A Very Short Introduction*. Oxford: Oxford University Press, 2014.

Dahlberg, Leif. "Pirates, Partisans, and Politico-Juridical Space." *Law and Literature* 23, no. 2 (2011): 262–81.

Deleuze, Gilles and Felix Guattari. *A Thousand Plateaus: Capitalism and Schizophrenia*. Minneapolis and London: University of Minnesota Press, 1987.

Diamond, Larry. "Liberation Technology." *Journal of Democracy* 21, no. 3 (2010): 69–83.

Dunifer, Stephen and Ron Sakolsky. *Seizing the Airwaves: A Free Radio Handbook*. Edinburgh and San Francisco: AK Press, 1998.

Easterling, Keller. *Extrastatecraft: The Power of Infrastructure Space*. London and Brooklyn: Verso, 2014.

Friz, Anna. "Transmission Art in the Present Tense." *PAJ: A Journal of Performance and Art* 31, no. 3 (2009): 46–49.

Gabrys, Jennifer. "Atmospheres of Communication." In *The Wireless Spectrum: The Politics, Practices, and Poetics of Mobile Media*, edited by Barbara Crow, Michael Longford and Kim Sawchuk. Toronto, Buffalo, London: University of Toronto Press, 2010.

Galloway, Alexander R. *Protocol: How Control Exists after Decentralization*. Cambridge, Massachusetts and London, England: The MIT Press, 2004.

Hall, Graham. "Maxwell's Electromagnetic Theory and Special Relativity." *Philosophical Transactions: Mathematical, Physical and Engineering Sciences* 366, no. 1871 (2008).

Haraway, Donna. "Situated Knowledges: The Science Question in Feminism and the Privilege of Partial Perspective." *Feminist Studies* 14, no. 3 (1988): 575–99.

Hardin, Garrett. "The Tragedy of the Commons." *Science* 162, no. 3859 (1968).

Jarvis, Jackie. "Sean Mcquillan - Engineer, Farmer, Pirate Radio Pioneer." 2014.

Jungnickel, Katrina. *Diy Wifi: Re-Imagining Connectivity*. New York: Palgrave MacMillan, 2014.

Kwon, Miwon. "Exchange Rate: On Obligation and Reciprocity in Some Art of the 1960's and After." In *The Market: Documents of Contemporary Art*, edited by Natasha Degen. London and Cambridge, Massachusetts: Whitechapel Gallery and The MIT Press, 2013 (2003).

Lassinaro, Kaisa. "Kaisa Lassinaro Talks to Director Lizzie Borden About the Film 'Born in Flames' (1983)." *LABOUR*, 2011.

Levitas, Ruth. *The Concept of Utopia*. Ralahine Utopian Studies, edited by Raffaella Baccolini, Joachim Fishcer and Tom Moylan. Vol. 3, Bern: Peter Lang, 2010.

Lindee, M. Susan. "The American Career of Jane Marcet's Conversations on Chemistry, 1806–1853." *Isis* 82, no. 1 (1991): 8–23.

McChesney, Robert. "The Political Economy of Radio." In *Seizing the Airwaves: A Free Radio Handbook*, edited by Ron Sakolsky and Stephen Dunifer. Edinburgh and San Francisco: AK Press, 1998.

Morozov, Evgeny. *To Save Everything, Click Here: The Folly of Technological Solutionism*. New York: Public Affairs, 2013.

O'Dwyer, Rachel. "Spectre of the Commons: Spectrum Regulation in the Communism of Capital." Trinity College University of Dublin, 2013.

PCAST. "Realizing the Full Potential of Government-Held Spectrum to Spur Economic Growth." Washington: The White House, 2012.

Rabinow, Paul. *Marking Time: On the Anthropology of the Contemporary*. Princeton and Oxford: Princeton University Press, 2008.

Ratto, Matt and Megan Boler, eds. *Diy Citizenship: Critical Making and Social Media*. Cambridge, Massachusetts and London, England: The MIT Press, 2014.

Roberts, Geoffrey. "Crystal Receiver." http://crystalreceiver.co.uk/index.htm.

Sakolsky, Ron and Stephen Dunifer, eds. *Seizing the Airwaves: A Free Radio Handbook*. Edinburgh, Scotland and San Francisco, CA: AK Press, 1998.

Sargent, Lyman Tower. *Utopianism: A Very Short Introduction*. Oxford and New York: Oxford University Press, 2010.

Sexton, Michael C. "Who Invented Radio? A Strange Controversy." *Studies: An Irish Quarterly Review* 55, no. 220 (1966): 415–24.

The SWLing Post. "Where Radio History and Art Meet: An Interview with Geoffrey Roberts." http://swling.com/blog/2011/10/where-radio-history-and-art-meet-an-interview-with-geoffrey-roberts/.

Thoreau, Henry David. *Walden; or, Life in the Woods*. New York: Dover Publications, Inc., 1995 (1854).

Toscano, Aaron A. *Marconi's Wireless and the Rhetoric of a New Technology*. Dordrecht, Heidleberg, New York, London: Springer, 2012.

Tsing, Anna Lowenhaupt. *Friction: An Ethnography of Global Connection*. Princeton and Oxford: Princeton University Press, 2005.

Walker Art Centre. "Opening-Day Talk: Pedro Reyes, Michael Hardt, and Lauren Berlant." 2011.

Warner, Michael. *Publics and Counterpublics*. New York: Zone Books, 2005.

Whittemore, Laurens E. "The Development of Radio." *The Annals of the American Academy of Political and Social Sciences* 142 (March 1929): 1–7.

Williams, Pearce L. "Michael Faraday's Education in Science." *Isis* 51, no. 4 (1960): 515–30.

Part III

PROTESTS AND PERIPHERIES

Chapter 7

Remaking Street Corners as "Bureaux"

DIY Youth Spaces and Shifting Urban Ontologies in Guinea

Clovis Bergère

> If History IS "Time," as it claims to be, then the uprising is a moment that springs up and out of Time, violates the "law" of History. If the State IS History, as it claims to be, then the insurrection is the forbidden moment, an unforgivable denial of the dialectic—shimmying up the pole and out of the smokehole, a shaman's maneuver carried out at an "impossible angle" to the universe.[1]

Faced with decaying urban institutions, Guinean youth in cities such as Conakry or Labé have constructed a complex network of self-organized social spaces, locally known as "bureau," the French term for "office." These youth-created spaces have emerged as an alternative form of urbanism, a Do-It-Yourself or "DIY urbanism,"[2] for young Guineans caught in a double-bind: increasingly irrelevant or repressive traditional models and failed postcolonial urban institutions.[3] Given the bare-bones, dilapidated characteristics of most of these social spaces, often marked solely by the presence of "barada"—or makeshift charcoal burner for making tea—and a couple of improvised benches, it would clearly be misplaced or even dangerously naïve to idealize these DIY spaces. Yet, their ubiquity and the prominent place that they occupy in many Guinean youths' lives, who typically spend large amounts of time in these spaces and often feel the need to "check in" to their local base or "bureau" at least once a day, if not more, we are compelled to ask: what role do these self-organized spaces play in the social and economic lives of young Guinean urbanites? Why have they emerged as the center of young Guineans' social lives despites the existence of more formal spaces of socialization such as local youth centers or *maisons des jeunes* in French? What is more, as any observer of youth policy work in Guinea is forced to notice, these spaces exist in a kind of paradoxical urban political space: On the one hand they play a central role in the daily lives of young people who

Figure 7.1 Young Men Sitting in a "Bureau" in Simbaya, Conakry. Credit: Clovis Bergère.

invest a significant amount of time setting up, maintaining and using these spaces; on the other hand, "bureaux" are totally absent from any formal discussions on youth provision in Guinea, especially discussions and work done through official channels such as state agencies, international organizations or foreign donors. If this is the case, what explains this changing visibility of young Guineans' social spaces? And what are the collective and political implications of "bureaux" and other forms of DIY urbanism for young people's place in the Guinean city?

DIY YOUTH PROVISION

I first became acquainted with youth activities and particularly spontaneous forms of youth sociability in urban Guinea, in both Labé and Simbaya—a North-eastern suburb of Conakry—when I came to live in these places as a twenty year old. Between September 1996 and June 1997, I spent most afternoons in a place called the "bureau," a small vacant lot in a fairly central location in Labé shaded from the piercing winter sun, dusty Harmattan trade wind, and haunting presence of *charognards*—a particularly active and dreary brand of white-backed African vultures—by an apt combination of a mango tree and sheet of corrugated iron. Strategically located at a cross-road, a small wall provided a fortunate and useful mix of lookout and hiding opportunities, a back alley adding the safety of an available escape route. For a period of time, this informal meeting place became a *haut lieu*, or focal point of youth culture and activity in Labé, particularly under the hospices of a slightly older self-proclaimed and natural youth leader, an incredibly generous and complex disenfranchised thirty year old, known as the "inspector," who devoted a period of his life to running the "bureau." By their own accounts, most people who frequented the place around these times before it *de facto* dissolved itself around 2001, remained strongly attached to it, many noting how the experience had been a key defining moment of their youth, shifting their whole outlook on life in a lasting manner.[4]

In an effort to explore more systematically, the role of informal urban forms in the lives of young people in Guinea, I recently re-connected with these places. Improvised meeting places are highly mobile, and the younger generations had invested in other spaces. My more recent research there took place over a seven-month period between October 2010 and May 2011. My main aim was to initiate a dialogue with young people in Labé and Simbaya around the spontaneous activities they engage in in their daily lives and the notion of Temporary Autonomous Zones which I had come to know through my engagement with the squatters' movement in London. I sent four digital cameras[5] and worked with a Sociology student from the University of Conakry to coordinate the project in Guinea. To initiate the project, I sent a list of questions, which were quickly abandoned in favor of a more dialogic approach whereby I would send questions about the pictures I was receiving.[6] In no way, was this meant to be representative of more than a few very particular viewpoints; nevertheless I was surprised by the response I received and the enthusiasm young people showed in telling their stories both visually in photos and through email and telephone conversations. Very quickly I built up an impressive collection of photographs—over 400—and was able to converse at length with the young people involved. African cities are notoriously hard to pin point and have a tendency to constantly escape interpretations. Besides, the original notion of Temporary Autonomy Zones as developed by Hakim Bey was never intended to be anything more than an "an *essay* ('attempt'), a suggestion, almost a poetic fancy."[7] Therefore following Deleuze and Guattari, my aim was not so much to "represent, interpret or symbolize" but rather to delineate the practices and processes at stake, hopefully "marking their mixtures as well as their distinctions."[8]

Labé and Simbaya were chosen arbitrarily as a consequence of my own personal trajectory in Guinea. However in their differences, they capture something about the current phase of urban growth in the region, which is more concentrated in secondary centers and suburban agglomerations than at the heart of already overcapacity metropolitan centers and downtown areas of megacities,[9] thus challenging common understandings of what constitute the urban, especially as contrasted to the rural.[10]

With a population estimated at 107,000 inhabitants in 2007,[11] Labé is one of Guinea's most populous cities, and an important secondary urban center whose influence in the region has steadily risen since the 1980s.[12] The historic capital and cultural and religious center of the Foutah-Djallon—including the capital of the theocratic kingdom of the Foutah (1768–1898)—Labé is today a rapidly growing commercial and administrative center as well as a key regional transport hub. Lodged at the heart of a firmly rural region—the Foutah-Djallon is 85 percent rural—Labé in many ways embodies the current complexities surrounding firmly delineating what is urban and rural, constantly oscillating between dynamism—Labé's population has tripled between 1983 and 1996[13]—and stagnation, with 12 percent of its population engaged in agricultural activities in a sector that is still strongly organized along familial lines and highly localized.

Simbaya is a north-eastern suburb of Guinea's capital Conakry, split between the Matoto and Ratoma urban communes. Conakry is an ethnically diverse capital—the main groups are Susu, Fulani, Mandinka, Baga, Guerze and Kissi residents among others—whose population is today estimated at around 2 million. Conakry, and principally its suburbs have in recent decades grown dramatically and now reach the "Kilometer 36," an infamous crossroad that operates as a "check point" for all traffic entering and leaving the capital city, situated 36 km from the city center on "Route Nationale 1," the principal corridor out of the capital. Conakry's economic activities revolve around the port, through which raw materials and agricultural produce, mainly bauxite, bananas and palm oil are shipped. Service provision in Conakry is notoriously poor and its lack of reliable electricity and periodic power cuts have earned it a solid reputation as West Africa's darkest capital.

As became quickly apparent from my research, most "bureaux" do not follow formal planning procedures or legal prescriptions for setting up a youth center or social space in Guinea. They are not born out of a premeditated plan, have not gone through layers of a more or less meaningful public consultation and external funds were not raised from public or private funding streams. Their existence depends solely on the activities and willingness of its members to create it and keep it going, rather than on the availability of public or private funds, grants or profit-making opportunities as might be the case for an officially organized youth center. Most are born rather organically. Two youth—typically educated but unemployed young men—might meet regularly at the same location, not because of prior arrangements but simply because of where they live or where they do their daily errands, be it a trip to the market to help out a sister, mother, or aunt or purposeless wander to the center or an improvised football game. As they meet, they start talking in the same spot on a regular basis. A third youth who lives close-by notices them, and joining the conversation, offers to pull out a wooden bench, and here a "bureau" is born. On good days, the young men, whose numbers will typically rise as they engage in conversation with more youth passing by, will pull together a few hundred Guinean francs to buy a few sugar cubes, a small sample bag of gunpowder tea to make "ataya," the local green tea brewed over a small coal-burner or get a few cigarettes sold individually or if they are in that kind of mood a little wrap of marijuana, locally grown and sold everywhere. Over days, weeks and months this will become an established spot, a "bureau" with its own identity, its own deals and arrangements to scrape a few francs here and there, its own temporality. As the "bureau" grows the youth will start to feel like they have to stop there every day, as it will start to play a key role in their social and economic lives. The use of the term "bureau" is here revelatory. It is their "bureau" or "office" in French and they have to go to "work" so to speak. The activities that typically take place there include talking about "politics, women, the problems of society, and linked to these, the problems regarding the future of the country" (male respondent, photoelicitation notes). Within them, a number of activities such as drinking, smoking—both cigarettes and marijuana—or kissing take place and become permitted, tolerated. An FM radio is often heard, with the youth listening to both local radio in vernacular languages and international radios in French such as Radio France International (RFI) or BBC Afrique. Increasingly, a laptop computer or an Internet-ready smartphone provides the sources of entertainment, be it music, sports results, or news from friends and relatives across the world (photoelicitation notes). The practice of young people remaking empty lots and street corners into sites of sociability in Guinea can be inscribed in a broader West African urban context. "Bureaux" in Guinea for instance resonate strongly with "bases" and "junctions" in Lagos, which Olawale Ismail defines as "a neighborhood recreational or meeting place where youths gather, typically after work to relax, argue and debate sports and politics."[14] Susann Baller's work also comes to mind; she explores the different ways in which vacant lots in the suburbs of Dakar are remade into soccer grounds by locals, who thereby invest them with their own alternative historical meanings.[15] Indeed, the practice of reinvesting vacant urban space has long been a key feature of unofficial sociability in West Africa. For instance, the Malian writer Amadou Hampâté Bâ recalls not without humor the importance of two such spontaneous meeting places in Diagaramba at the turn of the twentieth century in his tongue-in-cheek ode:

Come to Diagaramba.
Come in the morning and chew kola at Eldika,

And join the evening celebrations at Telerke,
Then return to your country and die. You may
Be certain that the angels in heaven will say to
The Lord: Show clemency and compassion to
That man. For he has "done" Eldika and Telerke.
He has been purified.[16]

Young people in Labé and Simbaya favor the term "bureau" or office to refer to these places, which in some ways is perhaps closer to the self-depreciating humor of Hampâté Bâ than the more military image of the "base" allows for. The term "bureau" in Guinea also acts as a way to somehow atone for the prominent lack of jobs through humor, as well as account for the large amounts of time many disenfranchised young people end up spending in these places. The term "bureau" which connotes a site for non-manual, service-based and literate work, also acts as a marker for complex changes at play in urban Guinea where young men from traditionally dominant casts are not allowed to work manually in what is still often seen by elders as demeaning trades. As a consequence, these young educated men find themselves largely unemployed, and, as one research participant pointed out often find themselves with less money in their pockets than their peers who work as apprentices and other manual occupations. The gender politics of "bureaux" also reveal the extent to which they exist and interact with existing forms of domination, whether class, cast or gender-based. What the research revealed was not that young women did not create DIY meeting spaces of their own, but rather that these tended to center around much more domestic spaces, typically within the confines of the household compound. Young women did create informal social spaces that afforded them opportunities to look out onto the street and other public spaces within the city space. However, these tended to be situated away from the city center, within more residential neighborhoods. This reflects gendered spatial arrangements and power inequalities within many West African cities, as famously documented by Schildkrout in Kano, Nigeria.[17] Although most "bureaux" in Labé and Simbaya are not street corners, but rather a diverse mix of more or less exposed stretch of street, walls or shade under a tree, they also operate in much the same way as the widely documented investment of street corners across the continent which Eileen Moyer notes, "serve as centers of economic and social activity for young people."[18] In Conakry and Labé, as in Dar es Salaam—the site of Moyer's research—it is primarily young men who turn street corners into bases for their social and economic operations.

In making sense of "bureaux" as an urban form, Donavan Finn's notion of DIY urbanism is particularly helpful. For Finn, DIY urbanism solutions

Figure 7.2 Young Women Position Themselves in the Street to Observe Local Activity. Credit: Clovis Bergère.

typically take on three major characteristics. First, DIY solutions are "instigated, designed, created, paid for and implemented by single users or small voluntary groups and not municipalities or corporations" and they emerge "from citizens seeing and responding to some unmet need in urban space."[19] As described above, "bureaux" in Guinea are set up sometimes by one, two, or a small group of individual youth. These tend to be unorganized, or very loosely organized groups of youth perhaps identified as the youth from a particular neighborhood or area. They are responding to an unmet need for spaces where young people can talk, socialize, and exchange information, in particular spaces where they can do this on a regular basis, close to their homes. The need for places of exchange in not only something that the youth themselves recognize but something that is much more widely acknowledged. For instance, on a recent visit to Labé, the then youth minister addressed a group of youth workers (*animateurs*) and community activists on a seven-day seminar and training—organized by the French cooperation effort—exploring ways of "re-vitalizing" (*re-dynamisation*) youth centers (*Maisons des Jeunes)* in the region. Loosely referring to the recent political turmoil as well as the more generalized issues of rampant inflation, and unaffordability of even basic goods such as rice and electricity, he explained:

> If we had *animateurs* everywhere, if we had *Maisons des Jeunes* everywhere, if we had spaces of exchanges everywhere, if we had places where young people could talk about themselves, talk about their experiences, talk about their difficulties, I swear that it would have attenuated what we have lived through here. This is why to me this particular training is important. It will enable you to obtain skills, and, within *Maisons des Jeunes* to be able to improve not only skills but also to offer more opportunities to young people so that they can exchange but also so that they can acquire positive behaviors.[20]

Reading this quote, it is striking how much similarity there is between young people's need for spaces of exchanges, spaces where they can discuss personal, local and societal problems, and the minister's definition of what young people need. Yet, thinking about need in the context of DIY urbanism it is also key to teasing out the highly unequal relations of power that underlie discussions of need in the Guinean city. Although young Guineans rarely spell out their needs in such clear terms as the minister does in this quote, their actions do reveal a desire for spaces of exchange and discussion. However, the need seems to be for spaces where they can do this on their own terms, away from the necessary control and pressures that come from adult youth workers' insistence on positive outcomes and the acquisition of so-called "positive" behaviors. This is highly significant in a notoriously gerontocratic society, where most key aspects of one's life as a youth need the assent and consent of older members of society.[21] In many ways, the attraction of informal "bureaux" comes from this subversive possibility of at least temporarily reversing the terms of the gerontocratic order, thus gaining relief from the pressures of moral and social reforms imposed by an increasingly compromised and irrelevant older class, who sometimes find refuge in idealized versions of traditional models. My contention here is that in the space of a "bureau," Guinean youth can at least potentially meet on their own terms and collectively envisage alternatives to the gerontocratic—traditional or nationalist—order that defines Guinean cities. In these moments of temporary autonomy, young Guineans cannot simply be conceptualized as socially determined, or moreover as victims. As authors working in other contexts in Africa such as Henrik Erdman Vigh (2006), Joshka Philipps (2013), or Jennifer Cole (2004, 2010) have clearly shown, even in situations of war, extreme poverty or political violence, young Africans also retain, and hold dearly onto, an albeit compromised, ambiguous or overly limited, ability to steer or navigate their shifting social terrains. However, celebrating the freedom of tone and flow of discussions that take place in the space of a "bureau," a space at least potentially shielded or turned away from strict norms of social interactions that dictate much exchange in Guinea, also comes at a price. There is also a risk to sometimes be moved by our ethical and moral commitments to the young lives we research and re-constitute youth as essentially agentic. However, as the gendered and classist nature of "bureaux" show, young people in creating DIY youth spaces in Guinea operate within clearly defined and highly unequal gender and class roles within the urban public sphere. The more visible and strategically placed "bureaux" in Labé or Simbaya were frequented almost exclusively by men, whereas women's social spaces tended to be shielded from the public gaze, typically centered around the domestic sphere of the household compound or in more suburban or "out-of-the-way" locations. As such, "bureaux" actively contributed to the perpetuation of gender-based forms of domination in urban Guinea. Agency here cannot be thought of as an individual property that youth possess, a capacity to change *per se*, but rather it is what David Oswell calls "distributed," it exists as a capacity supported or hindered but particular arrangements. As he explains:

> In this sense, agency is always relational and never a property; it is always in-between and interstitial; and the capacity to do and to make a difference is necessarily dispersed across an arrangement. Moreover, [it] constitutes a problem space, which is composed of questions, investigations and methods of analysis, but which also invites further questions, investigations and analyses. It is not constituted as a solution.[22]

Thinking about youth agency as distributed, clearly highlights the importance of spaces such as "bureaux" and their roles in supporting or hindering collective agency, and sociohistorical movement and change. Or, as AbdouMaliq Simone puts it:

> Given the difficulties most African urban households face in "making do," the contexts which provide the sites of rehearsals must also be available to being objects of that very rehearsal. They must serve as affirmations that change is possible, that it is worth being engaged in efforts to try and change things.[23]

THE AMBIVALENCE OF EMULATION

I now turn to the second characteristic of DIY urbanism as presented by Finn, namely that DIY efforts "emulate or augment official municipal infrastructure."[24] As he explains:

> As opposed to traditional painted graffiti, political poster "sniping" and other tactics, DIY efforts included here are generally more functional as opposed to merely aesthetic or political. Some [. . .] may persist for months without city officials even noticing their presence. Others may fill such an obvious need that

they are left in place and given tacit official sanction, or even become so integrated into the urban fabric that they are replaced by official versions.[25]

Discussions of DIY solutions and emulation become particularly interesting in the context of the African city, predominantly defined by decrepit or dysfunctional municipal infrastructure. As Ismail for instance notes in Lagos, groups of marginalized youths have been recruited by incapacitated municipal agents in order to perform local governmental functions such as collecting taxes from taxis at various transport hubs in Lagos. In this case, intimidation tactics and muscle power honed in the streets and at "junctions" are put to work by Lagosian street youth and "area boys" in order to perform municipal functions in return for a fee, a new form of "securo-commerce" for Ismail.[26] In Labé and Conakry, emulation of municipal provision takes on several forms, clearly placing "bureaux" in the context of DIY urbanism, at least as defined by Finn. Firstly, as we have seen, "bureaux" end up performing the function of "spaces of exchange," spaces where youth can discuss their problems and difficulties, a strategic long-term goal of municipal youth services as stated, for instance, by the Youth minister in the excerpt quoted above. It is striking that at precisely the same time when the Youth minister was pronouncing this speech in Labé, a few blocks down the road, local youth were meeting in their DIY social space, their local "bureau" doing precisely what the Youth minister was claiming was missing in Labé's infrastructure, meeting in a "space of exchange" where they could "talk about their experiences, talk about their difficulties."[27] What is more, as we have seen above, youth in Guinea are in their DIY efforts not only responding to a need identified by municipal powers, thus emulating these otherwise defunct services, but they are also augmenting these services by responding to a more precise need, not just for "spaces of exchange" but for spaces of exchange on youth's own terms.

The role of "bureaux" in the constitution of a municipal infrastructure for youth in Guinea is not limited to spontaneous efforts by local youth. In Labé and Conakry, local "bureaux" are often approached by local municipal agents or political interests in order to perform tasks which would in other contexts be incumbent on local governments or other formally organized youth services, such as cultural events, concerts or sporting tournaments. I, for instance, remember sitting in a local "bureau" in Labe, in the Spring 1997, when a local political figure approached its members to organize a football tournament in the honor of the much-hated and disgraced Parti de l'Unité et du Progrès (PUP), the then authoritarian ruler of Guinea, Lansana Conté's party. Despite some reticence from a number of youth, the "bureau" quickly put together a soccer tournament, a well-understood masquerade of an event, took the money from the political player and spent the summer enjoying the proceeds. In the face of increasingly under-funded and dysfunctional municipal services in Guinea, these kinds of direct solicitations from municipal and political powers for organizing events and performing a range of tasks that fall more typically under the purview of municipal services or other formally constituted nongovernmental organizations have rapidly increased.[28] A parallel is here found with youth gangs in Conakry, who as Philipps has recently noted, "represent exceptionally stable and manipulable vehicles with which politicians may organize rallies, plot political riots, or threaten political competitors, gangs have become deeply enmeshed in the business of street politics."[29]

DIY PRACTICES AND THE POLITICS OF ASSEMBLAGE

The third characteristic of DIY interventions for Finn is that they exist away from direct financial benefits, to create a "more user-friendly urban environment,"[30] as such they are also an ontological statement on what the city is or at least could be. "Bureaux" do not provide its members with any direct financial benefits or returns, they are free to attend, do not require funds to keep running, and although there may be occasions, such as the one described above, when members of a "bureau" perform a service—such as organizing a cultural event or attending a demonstration—for a fee, these not to constitute the primary motive of the DIY youth spaces, only an occasional side benefit. They do, however, contribute in making the Guinean city more user-friendly for youth. As was made clear to me by the youth participants, "bureaux" are often the first place youth visit when arriving in town after spending time elsewhere. As such, "bureaux" in Guinea have long operated as a kind of network. Young people in Guinea spend a lot of time moving back and forth between relatives in various cities across the country and region mainly as a way to relieve some of the strain that has come to characterize familial and social relations under increased strain to provide food, shelter, etc. for each other.[31] Most young people I have spoken to in Guinea spend extended periods of time between Conakry and their home town typically a secondary urban center to which they are somehow related. In this context of high mobility, "bureaux" operate as key sites, enclaves where youth trade information, goods, news from relatives or friends abroad or opportunities for making money, etc. They are usually the first place that young travelers visit, and as such help in a relatively direct way make the city user-friendly to the newcomer.

However, in thinking about the ways in which DIY social spaces such as "bureaux" contribute to make the Guinean city more youth-friendly, I would argue that it is crucial to go further than Finn's somewhat practical or pragmatic definition allows. Specifically, I think it is key to understand these DIY spaces in the context of urban political power in Guinea. My argument here is that "bureaux" help create a particularly ambiguous political space for urban youth in Guinea, one that rests on a shifting visibility. As is evident in the quote from the Youth Minister above, as well as from most other policies aiming to improve outcomes for youth in Guinea,[32] informal social spaces are absent from any official discussions on youth provision of the type conducted through official channels such as youth services, policies and national and international organization work. They are in a sense invisible to dominant urban administrative orders that rely on a transparency of process, an adherence to protocol and readability that "bureaux" simply cannot offer. As we have seen, most are born organically, outside of formal plans and they can be dismantled as easily as they are put together. This is part of their attraction in the Guinean context where being able to circulate and if need be, to disappear can be a strength, as I will explore.[33] The kind of "readability" formally expected of organized youth social spaces is, for Lefebvre, part of a typically modern ordering of urban space, one that relies on strategic plans, bureaucratic process, competent programming and best outcomes.[34] However, for Lefebvre, this increased ordering of urban space rests on an illusion, a systematic opacity, which allows the social relations of labor that underpin the construction of urban space to be erased, rendered invisible.[35] In the chronically under-funded Guinean city, the illusion also doubles as an illusiveness, with most plans for well-funded youth centers remaining just that, plans. Nonetheless, Lefebvre's point remains: youth infrastructure perhaps also needs to be read as an attempt to control a potentially dangerous youth "class."

Yet, although "bureaux" might be invisible from a certain bureaucratic standpoint, they also provide youth with a clear visibility in the Guinean city. As noted above, local political powers, including the very same that omit the existence of these spaces in strategic planning, go precisely to these informal spaces when they need the help and support of youth. As Philipps' research on youth gangs in Conakry shows, this shifting visibility forms the basis of a highly complex and ambivalent political agency for Guinean youth, one that is based on navigating clientelistic and often highly compromised political relations and patronages.[36] Going back to Oswell's notion of agency as distributed, it is clear that "bureaux" which provide a physical anchorage in the city, a place to be seen and found for Guinean youth, are part and parcel of this complex assemblage. At the heart of this physical anchorage, however, lies an ability to maneuver the terms of that visibility. As Simone demonstrates, in his study of youth in the New Bell quarter of Douala, Cameroon's largest city, the ability to hide, to play with appearance is for many urban youth in Africa a resource, and means of survival. As he notes, with regard to the importance of managing appearances:

> While the trappings of wealth may be incessantly hidden, "finds" of all kinds—t-shirts with obscure insignias, computer parts, packaging, wires and even body parts—are displayed. They are displayed not simply in the event that, for example, another person needs something to fix a car or a radio or make a pirate electrical connection. More importantly, that are displayed in order to demonstrate that something took place, something out of the ordinary, something on which a story can be based, and where these stories can lead to a specific introduction to new actors, new stories.[37]

In Guinea, "bureaux" can disappear at the drop of a hat, providing a necessarily narrow escape when military might or oppressive forces take youth as their blind target, as is often the case when demonstrations turn sour, for instance. Hiding, and the ability to disappear into thin air is often the best strategy in these cases. Yet, "bureaux" can also become incredibly loud, raucous, visible, and "in your face" when being seen provides a means of inserting oneself into someone else's business. "Bureaux" then become spaces to be reckoned with. As organizations, "bureaux" tend to be incredibly loose and fluid formations with no membership requirements, fees, or rites of passage. Yet, they can also in an instant be reinvented as reliably constituted formations with clear lines of accountability, roles and responsibility if that kind of formality is necessary in order to benefit from institutional opportunities, such as delivering a contract job for a local nongovernmental organization or organizing a cultural event for a local politician or municipal branch. Within this context, circulation becomes the mode of operating within the city space. As Simone notes:

> As youth in Douala frequently remark, the ability to "become someone" is directly linked to the ability to "move around," and so circulation is also about acquiring a facility to operate everywhere, and to not be known as a specific son or daughter of a specific family coming from a specific place with specific ethnic origins and professions.[38]

"Bureaux" as urban spaces, as specific orderings of the urban fabric, have an ability to circulate. Thinking back theoretically about the city, these kinds of practices on the part of youth that emphasize circulation and an ability to navigate and insert oneself across different social fields challenge Lefebvrian notions of space as necessarily embedded within historically determined relations of labor. In many ways, Simone's depiction of the everyday practices of urban youth in Douala relates much more closely to recent conceptions of the urban as assemblage[39]). "Bureaux" in a sense express an ontological commitment to urban space as assemblage, which Deleuze defines as a "co-functioning: it is a symbiosis, a 'sympathy'. It is never filiations which are important but alliances, alloys; these are not successions, lines of descent, but contagions, epidemics, the wind."[40]

Figure 7.3 Young Men Gather in a Bureau in Labé. Credit: Clovis Bergère.

For Colin McFarlane, this points to the fact that urban actors are defined less in terms of their specific attributes—for instance, youth being defined as a group with certain visible presences in the public realm—but rather by the kinds of alliance they enter into, the assemblages they form. In other words, it is the interactions between various components, actors, technologies, policies, or historical constructions that form the assemblage.[41]

My argument here is that although these spontaneous DIY social spaces have a long history as illustrated by Hampâté Bâ's poem above, it is really within a context increasingly characterized by crumbling urban institutions which began under structural adjustments in the 1990s, a legacy that continues today, that current political dimensions of "bureaux"-based activities began to surface. The change is particularly dramatic in Guinea. Indeed, for all of its authoritarian, strong-armed and dictatorial qualities, Sékou Touré's post-independence socialist regime, which lasted from 1958 to his death in 1984, did invest in youth provision to a rarely seen level. As Jay Straker, in his sociohistorical study of youth and nationalism under Sékou Touré notes, "[no] postcolonial regime took matters of youthful cultural development and authenticity more seriously than the one led by Sékou Touré from 1958 to 1984."[42] As Straker clearly shows, the re-envisioning of youth that was necessary for Sekou Toure's socialist nation-building effort was mediated by, took expression in, and was ultimately contested through a variety of platforms such as political tracts, newspaper articles, revolutionary poems and novels, photography and perhaps most importantly "militant" theater, which became compulsory practice for all young Guineans. What is key here in understanding the political dimensions of Do-It-Yourself social spaces is that their significance needs to be approached relationally rather than in essentializing terms. In other words, it is really from the late 1980s and early 1990s, when drastic reductions in public spending under the impetus of structural adjustment policies or neo-liberal ideologies led to the incredibly rapid dismantling of youth provisions in urban Guinea, that the ordinary activities within "bureaux," the DIY forms of sociability they embodied started to acquire a deeply political dimension, to represent a "quiet encroachment of the ordinary" to borrow Asef Bayat's apt phrase.[43] Just as DIY forms of land occupation or economic activities such as street vending that Bayat describes in Iran conferred poor Iranians with real social power at the time of the Islamic Revolution, the practice of setting up DIY social spaces in urban Guinea are part of an assemblage of distributed agency that establishes young people as a force to be reckoned with in the city. Within the context of disappearing urban institutions that started in the 1990s, these "bureaux" gesture toward the continued need for youth social spaces and against the prescribed dismantlement of collective social investment in youth provision, one of the first victims of structural adjustment policies. "Bureaux" are also "micro-political" formations in that they constitute circulation as opposed to "readability" as key principals for ordering urban space. In that sense, they become sites where ontological alternatives to the "modern" city—in the Lefebvrian sense of the term—can be rehearsed, where new possibilities can be temporarily glimpsed. As Simone noted above, such contexts where maps can be opened become incredibly important in cities where "making do" and getting by are often the only daily aspirations. Clearly, "bureaux" as spaces of youth sociability do not hold any inherent qualities that would make then necessarily more just. Quite the opposite, they are in fact often the very sites where gender, class or ethnic inequalities become reproduced. As we have seen, in Labé and Simbaya, for instance, young men are the most ready and able to make these insurgent spatial claims on the city, therefore reinforcing gender as well as class inequalities, as not all young people have access to the best spots. Yet, they do also gesture toward an alternative relationship to urban space to the modern planned city, one that makes social as well as spatial circulation a constituent principal of space-making. How to build on this, rather than suppress it, in order to build a more just Guinean city, then becomes a key question in moving toward a truly post-colonial city in Guinea.

CONCLUSION

"Bureaux" operate within the particularly strained social, material and economic conditions of contemporary Guinean cities and give rise to specific forms of urban practices in Guinea, both highly ordinary and extraordinary, bringing new meaning to the notions of temporary and autonomous. For many disenfranchised Guinean urban youth who occupy and appropriate urban space and time, they become key sites of sociability that operate as a heuristic, a means of testing and charting out possibilities. In the context of Guinea, thinking about the relationship with what are in effect highly dysfunctional local and municipal authorities and the everyday practices of youth might seem pointless. As Edgar Pieterse rightly notes:

> Under certain circumstances the forces of conservatism may be so strong that there is little point in working with and through mainstream discourses; instead one should confine one's activism almost exclusively to a politics of opposition, resistance and militant refusal.[44]

Militant refusal is in many ways what we have witnessed in recent years in Guinea and young people have played a key role in the strikes, protest and demonstrations that have brought about the country's first general election that can be described as democratic.
However, as Pieterse further goes on to note:

> Even in those cases, if a politics of opposition eventually succeeds in shifting the terrain of decision-making and power, a moment arrives when certain profound institutional and formal decisions need to be made about consolidating within the practices of the state particular orientations and practices that will systematically shift the weight of exploitation in the city off the shoulders of the poor and disenfranchised.[45]

In the context of the Guinean, and African city more broadly, all options and alternatives need to be explored. As Achille Mbembé notes:

> Against those theoretical approaches that would reduce the range of historical choices gestating in Africa to a stark alternative of either "transition" to democracy and the shift to a market economy, or descent into the shadows of war, we must stress again the role of contingency, and reassert the hypothesis that the organizations likely to emerge from the current developments will be anything but the result of coherent premeditated plans.[46]

In this context, "bureaux," rather than anomalies on the way toward the modern city, become key sites of rehearsal where alternative ontologies can be tested and tried. As DIY urban forms they erect circulation as constituent principal, rather than readability and predictability. In action, the central role of "bureaux" in young Guineans' lives highlights how important spaces that facilitate rather than hinder movement might be. The question remains, however, of how urban institutions can build on those synergies and signals no matter how faint they might be. Self-organized youth spaces are a profound reminder of not only the need of policy to engage with everyday processes but that they also challenge the current approach to local governance on a deep level.[47] Ultimately local authorities in Africa should probably start asking themselves not how do we control these practices but rather how do we let go without retreating but rather finding a facilitating role.[48] As Simone puts it, "perhaps in the near future, local development will require ways of imagining how better to go with the flows."[49] Guinean youth have already set up networks of "bureaux" or offices throughout urban Guinea where alternative urban ontologies are being worked on and worked out.

All photos taken as part of the engagement project coordinated by Amadou Oury Diallo (University of Conakry).

NOTES

1. Hakim Bey, *T.A.Z.: The Temporary Autonomous Zone, Ontological Anarchy, Poetic Terrorism* (Brooklyn NY: Autonomedia, 1991), 98.
2. Donovan Finn, "DIY urbanism: Implications for Cities." *Journal of Urbanism: International Research on Placemaking and Urban Sustainability* 7, no. 4 (2014): 381–398.
3. Mamadou Diouf, "Engaging Postcolonial Cultures: African Youth and Public Space." *African Studies Review* 46, no. 2 (2003): 1–12.
4 This is based on numerous discussions with the original "bureau" members many of whom have remained close friends, and with whom I have been in regular contact since. Key elements of that lasting influence included the philosophical insights and -often all-night -discussions which the "Inspector" regularly tried to pass on to his younger fellow members.
5. Mike Crang, "Qualitative methods (part 3): There is nothing outside the text?" *Progress in Human Geography* (2005). Accessed June 3, 2014: http://eprints.dur.ac.uk/archive/00000069/01/Crang_qualitative_3.pdf
6. See Les Back, *The Art of Listening* (English ed., Oxford: Berg, 2007) and Howard Becker, *Telling About Society* (Chicago: University of Chicago Press, 2007) for a detailed discussion of photoelicitation research methods.
7. Bey, *T.A.Z.: The Temporary Autonomous Zone*, 1.
8. Gilles Deleuze and Felix Guattari, *Anti-Oedipus: Capitalism and schizophrenia* (2nd ed., London: Continuum, 2004), 250.

9. See Barney Cohen, et al., *Cities Transformed: Demographic Change and Its Implications in the Developing World* (National Academies Press, 2003) and Saskia Sassen, *The Global City* (Princeton, NJ: Princeton University Press, 1993) and Saskia Sassen, *Globalization and its Discontents: Essays on the New Mobility of People and Money* (New York: New Press, 1998) for detailed discussions of the growth of mega-cities in Africa.

10. Ibrahima Diallo, « Rôle d'une ville secondaire dans l'organisation de son espace: le cas de Labé dans la région du Fouta-Djalon » in *Les Cahiers D'Outre-Mer*, Vol. 217 (January 2002), Guinea.

11. For population data, see www.sicoval.fr.

12. Diallo, "Rôle d'une ville secondaire," 5.

13. Ibid., 4.

14. Olawale Ismail, "The Dialectic of 'Junctions' and 'Bases': Youth, 'Securo-Commerce' and the Crises of Order in Downtown Lagos." *Security Dialogue* 40, no. 4–5 (2009): 464.

15. Susann Baller, "Transforming Urban Landscapes: Soccer Fields As Sites of Urban Sociability in the Agglomeration of Dakar." *African Identities* 5, no. 2 (2007): 217–230.

16. Amadou Hampâté Bâ, *The Fortunes of Wangrin* (Bloomington: Indiana University Press, 1999), 10.

17. Enid Schildkrout, "Roles of Children in Urban Kano," in *Sex and Age as Principles of Social Differentiation,* ed. Jean La Fontaine (New York: Academic Press, 1978), 110.

18. Eileen Moyer, "Street-Corner Justice in the Name of Jah: Imperatives for Peace among Dar es Salaam Street Youth." *Africa Today* 51, no. 3 (2005): 32.

19. Finn, "DIY Urbanism."

20. Radio Television Guinéenne, 30/11/2010. The translation from French is mine.

21. Joschka Philipps, *Ambivalent Rage: Youth Gangs and Urban Protest in Conakry, Guinea* (Paris: L'Harmattan, 2013), 60.

22. David Oswell, *The Agency of Children* (Cambridge, UK: Cambridge University Press, 2010), 270–271.

23. AbdouMaliq Simone, "Straddling the Divides: Remaking Associational Life in the Informal African City." *International Journal of Urban and Regional Research*, 25, no. 1, (2001): 112.

24. Finn, "DIY Urbanism."

25. Ibid., 383.

26. Olawale Ismail, "The Dialectic of 'Junctions' and 'Bases': Youth, 'Securo-Commerce' and the Crises of Order in Downtown Lagos." *Security Dialogue* 40, no. 4–5 (2009): 463–487.

27. Radio Television Guinéenne, 30/11/2010. The translation from French is mine.

28. Joshka Philipps, "Gang Politics: The Instrumentalization of Urban Counterculture in Conakry, Guinea," *Paper Presented at ECAS 4 Conference*, Uppsala, Sweden (July 2011).

29. Philipps, *Ambivalent Rage,* 101.

30. Finn, "DIY Urbanism," 383.

31. Simone, "Straddling the Divides," 104.

32. See for instance: Ministère de la Jeunesse et de l'Emploi des Jeunes « Grands Axes et Synthèses des Projets » (Gouvernement de la République de Guinée, 2014) or Mignon, Jean-Pierre « Contribution à l'Elaboration d'une Politique de Jeunesse et d'un Programme de Formation des Cadres et des Animateurs de Jeunesse en République de Guinée, » (Paris: Unesco Press, 1988).

33. AbdouMaliq Simone, *City life from Jakarta to Dakar* (New York, London: Routledge, 2010), 111.

34. Henri Lefebvre, *The Production of Space* (Malden, MA: Blackwell Publishing, 1991).

35. Ibid., 80.

36. Amadou Bano Barry, *Les Violences Collectives en Afrique: le Cas Guinéen* (Paris: L'Harmattan, 2000).

37. AbdouMaliq Simone, "Urban Circulation and the Everyday Politics of African Urban Youth: The Case of Douala, Cameroon." *International Journal of Urban and Regional Research* 29, no. 3 (2005): 516–532.

38. Ibid., 520.

39. See for instance Colin McFarlane, "The City as Assemblage: Dwelling and Urban Space." *Environment and Planning-Part D* 29, no. 4, (2011): 649 or Ash Amin and Nigel Thrift, *Cities: Reimagining the Urban* (Cambridge, UK: Polity Press, 2002).

40. Gilles Deleuze and Claire Parnet, *Dialogues II* (New York, NY: Columbia University Press, 2007 [1977]).

41. McFarlane, *City as Assemblage*, 653.

42. Jay Straker, *Youth, Nationalism, and the Guinean Revolution* (Bloomington, IN: Indiana University Press, 2009), 2.

43. Asaf Bayat, *Street politics: Poor People's Movements in Iran* (New York, NY: Columbia University Press, 1997).

44. Edgar Pieterse, *City Futures: Confronting the Crisis of Urban Development* (London, UK: Zed Books, 2008), 131.

45. Ibid.

46. Achille Mbembé, *On the Postcolony* (Berkeley, CA: University of California Press, 2001), 77.

47. Arjun Appadurai, "Spectral Housing and Urban Cleansing: Notes on Millennial Mumbai." *Public Culture* 12, no. 3 (2000): 627–651.

48. John Bennington and Mark Moore, *Public Value: Theory and Practice* (Palgrave MacMillan, 2010).

49. Simone, *For the City Yet to Come*, 111.

BIBLIOGRAPHY

Appadurai, Arjun. "Spectral Housing and Urban Cleansing: Notes on Millennial Mumbai." *Public Culture* 12, no. 3 (2000): 627–651.

Amin, Ash and Nigel Thrift. *Cities: Reimagining the Urban*. Cambridge, UK: Polity Press, 2002.

Bâ, Amadou Hampâté. *The Fortunes of Wangrin*. Bloomington, IN: Indiana University Press, 1999.

Back, Les. *The Art of Listening*. New York, NY: Berg, 2007.
Baller, Susann. "Transforming urban landscapes: Soccer fields as sites of urban sociability in the agglomeration of Dakar." *African Identities* 5, no. 2 (2007): 217–230.
Barry, Amadou Bano. *Les Violences Collectives en Afrique: le Cas Guinéen*. Paris: L'Harmattan, 2000.
Bayat, Asef. *Street Politics: Poor People's Movements in Iran*. New York: Columbia University Press, 1997.
Becker, Howard. *Telling about society*. Chicago: University of Chicago Press, 2007.
Bennington, John and Michael Moore. *Public Value: Theory and Practice*. London, UK: Palgrave MacMillan, 2010.
Bey, Hakim. *T.A.Z. : The Temporary Autonomous Zone, Ontological Anarchy, Poetic Terrorism*. Brooklyn, NY: Autonomedia, 1991.
Cohen, Barney, et al. *Cities Transformed: Demographic Change and Its Implications in the Developing World*. Washington, DC: National Academies Press, 2003.
Cole, Jennifer. "Fresh Contact in Tamatave, Madagascar: Sex, Money and Intergenerational Transformation." *American Ethnologist* 31, no. 4 (2004): 571–586. Reprinted in *Generations and Globalization: Youth, Age, and Family in the New World Economy*, eds. Jennifer Cole and Deborah Durham, 74–101. Bloomington: Indiana University Press.
———. *Sex and Salvation: Imagining the Future in Madagascar*. Chicago: University of Chicago Press, 2010.
Crang, Mike. "Qualitative methods (part 3): There is nothing outside the text?" *Progress in Human Geography* (2005). Accessed June 3, 2014: http://eprints.dur.ac.uk/archive/00000069/01/Crang_qualitative_3.pdf
Deleuze, Gilles and Parnet. Claire *Dialogues II*. New York, NY: Columbia University Press, 2007 [1977].
Deleuze, Gilles and Felix Guattari. *Anti-Oedipus: Capitalism and Schizophrenia (Second edition)*. London: Continuum, 2004.
Diallo, Ibrahima. « Rôle d'une ville secondaire dans l'organisation de son espace: le cas de Labé dans la région du Fouta-Djalon. » *Les Cahiers D'Outre-Mer*, no. 217 (2002), Guinea.
Diouf, Mamadou. "Engaging Postcolonial Cultures: African Youth and Public Space." *African Studies Review* 46, no. 2 (2003): 1–12.
Durham, Deborah. "Disappearing youth: Youth as a social shifter in Botswana." *American Ethnologist* 31, no. 4 (2004): 589–605.
Finn, Donovan. "DIY urbanism: implications for cities." *Journal of Urbanism: International Research on Placemaking and Urban Sustainability* 7, no. 4 (2014): 381–398.
Ismail, Olawale. "The Dialectic of 'Junctions' and 'Bases': Youth, 'Securo-Commerce' and the Crises of Order in Downtown Lagos." *Security Dialogue* 40, no. 4–5 (2009): 463–487.
Lefebvre, Henri. *The Production of Space*. Malden, MA: Blackwell Publishing, 1991.
Mbembé, Achille. *On the Postcolony*. Berkeley, CA: University of California Press, 2001.
———. "African modes of self-writing." *Public Culture* 14, no. 1 (2002): 239–273.

McFarlane, Colin. "The City as Assemblage: Dwelling and Urban Space." *Environment and Planning-Part D* 29, no. 4 (2011): 649.

Mignon, Jean-Pierre. « Contribution à l'Elaboration d'une Politique de Jeunesse et d'un Programme de Formation des Cadres et des Animateurs de Jeunesse en République de Guinée ». Paris: Unesco, 1988.

Ministère de la Jeunesse et de l'Emploi des Jeunes. « Grands Axes et Synthèses des Projets. » Conakry : Gouvernement de la République de Guinée, 2014.

Moyer, Eileen. "Street-Corner Justice in the Name of Jah: Imperatives for Peace among Dar es Salaam Street Youth." *Africa Today* 51, no. 3 (2005): 31–58.

Opondo, Sam. "The Wound of the Other: Diplomatic Time, Encounters and Humanitarianism" *Paper presented at the annual meeting of the International Studies Association Annual Conference "Global Governance: Political Authority in Transition," Le Centre Sheraton Montreal Hotel,* Montreal, Quebec, Canada, March 16, 2011.

Oswell, David. *The Agency of Children.* Cambridge, UK: Cambridge University Press, 2010.

Philipps, Joschka. *Ambivalent Rage: Youth Gangs and Urban Protest in Conakry, Guinea.* Paris: L'Harmattan, 2013.

———. "Gang Politics: The instrumentalization of urban counterculture in Conakry, Guinea." *Paper presented at ECAS 4 conference,* Uppsala, Sweden, July 2011.

Pieterse, Edgar. *City Futures: Confronting the Crisis of Urban Development.* London: Zed Book, 2008.

Sassen, Saskia. *The Global City.* Princeton, NJ: Princeton University Press, 1993.

———. *Globalization and its Discontents. Essays on the New Mobility of People and Money.* New York: New Press, 1998.

Schildkrout, Enid. "Roles of Children in Urban Kano." In *Sex and Age as Principles of Social Differentiation,* edited by Jean La Fontaine, Jean (New York: Academic Press, 1978), 110.

Simone, AbdouMaliq. *In Whose Image? Political Islam and Urban Practices in Sudan.* Chicago, IL: University of Chicago Press, 1994.

———. "Straddling the Divides: Remaking Associational Life in the Informal African City." *International Journal of Urban and Regional Research* 25, no. 1 (2001): 102–117.

———. *For the City Yet to Come: Changing African Life in Four Cities.* Durham and London: Duke University Press, 2004.

———. *City Life from Jakarta to Dakar.* New York; London: Routledge: 2010.

———. "The Social Infrastructure of City Life in Contemporary Africa." Discussion Paper 51, Uppsala: Nordiska Afrikastitutet, 2010.

Straker, Jay. *Youth, Nationalism, and the Guinean Revolution.* Bloomington IN: Indiana University Press, 2009.

Vigh, H. *Navigating Terrains of War: Youth and Soldiering in Guinea-Bissau.* Berghahn Books, 2006.

Chapter 8

Whose City? Art and Public Space in Providence

Martha Kuhlman

In 2006, the year that my family moved from the relatively affluent East Side of Providence, where we were renters, to the West Side, where we became owners, the headline of the local paper read "Class Warfare in Olneyville," referring to a neighborhood just a few blocks from our new home. Anti-gentrification posters with slogans such as "Do not Destroy Neighbors for Profit" and "We Live in this Neighborhood, it Belongs to Us" began to appear on West side streetlamps, signs, and electric boxes.[1] This eruption of street art exposed the cracks between the interests of the real estate developers, who are transforming the landscape in the name of revitalization, and the DIY ethic of local artists, who engage in artistic interventions and exchanges that defy capitalist interests in the name of free expression. Between these separate contingents is the city of Providence, which tries to preserve a balance between these sometimes conflicting sides of development and artistic expression.

In what follows, I will consider how a number of related artistic projects based in Providence—Provflux (2004–2008), New Your City/Magic City Repairs/And We Built a City Together (Ian Cozzens, Andrew Oesch, Meg Turner, 2006, 2007, 2009), and the Apartment at the Mall (2003–2007) (Townshend and Yoto) have tried to lay claim to the city in the name of the community.[2] What unites these projects is a common desire to transform the urban environment from a place dominated by consumer images and interests to a space where creative interactions and oppositional tactics are set in motion. In a city that promotes its image as welcoming to the arts, rebranding itself in 2009 as a "Creative Capital" to attract tourism and rejuvenate its tax base,[3] these projects constitute a form of resistance, a utopian micropolitics of everyday life that test the limits of what constitutes public art.

THE RIGHT TO THE CITY

To appreciate the unique contribution of these projects to a dialogue about the city and public space, I will return to some of the philosophical assumptions associated with the Situationist movement and the writings of Henri Lefebvre in order to consider how these ideas are altered and adapted in their more contemporary incarnations. In some cases, the interventions I describe are explicitly inspired by Situationism, and others—while perhaps not directly rooted in Situationist practice and Lefebvre's writings, raise similar questions about art, community, and public space.

From 1958 until it dissolved in 1972, the Situationists proposed that cities should be the site of invention and play in opposition to the hegemony of consumer culture. Through the practices of the "derive," "détournement" and "psychogeography," terms which still retain popular currency although in different contexts, the Situationists sought to shake urban dwellers out of their routine and awaken a sense of wonder and conscience about their environment. Through the practice of détournement, which can be translated as a "diversion" or "detour" from the expected, but also as "hijacking" and "embezzlement," texts such as advertisements, street signs, or comics could be playfully appropriated to subversive ends.[4] A "dérive" is a form of wandering or walking in a city with no other aim than creating an aesthetic experience; according to the first issue of *Situationist International* (1958), it is defined as "a mode of experimental behavior linked to the conditions of urban society. A technique of transient passage through varied ambiences."[5] Related to this is the concept of psychogeography, which is "the study of the specific effects of the geographical environment, consciously organized or not, on the emotions and behavior of individuals."[6] These experiments resembled the leisurely strolls of the Baudelairean flâneur, and the surrealist wanderings through Paris depicted in André Breton's *Nadja* (1928) and Louis Aragon's *Paris Peasant* (1926). Another generation of artists, inspired by Situationism, Fluxus, and psychogeography, reinvent how we perceive and move through the metropolis, and offer access to an alternative city that reclaims public space from the monotony of commercialization.

Henri Lefebvre initially inspired the Situationists by validating everyday life as a form of political critique outside the sphere of conventional politics in *The Critique of Everyday Life* (1947). In his later work *The Right to the City* (1967), Lefebvre offers a utopian vision of shared public space in the city that is not dominated by commercialism, what Guy Debord termed *The Society of Spectacle*. Lefebvre laments that city planners and commercial interests have overlooked the importance of creativity and play in the urban context, activities that would elude the demands of "exchange value, commerce, and profit."[7] Moreover, he abhors the idea that the city would be "an object of cultural consumption for tourists, for aestheticism, avid for spectacles and the picturesque," and instead imagines a future in which the working class urban dweller would be able enjoy the city as an integral part of their daily lives.[8] Although Situationism eventually fizzled out, finding its logical culmination in the 1968 Paris demonstrations, the notion that ordinary people have a right to the city remains strikingly relevant in contemporary analyses of urban space.

FROM THE RENAISSANCE CITY TO THE SITUATIONIST CITY

The central concerns that come out of the writings of Lefebvre and the Situationists—pursuing a tactical approach against the strategic plans of city planners and developers, finding spaces for creativity and invention, inverting the relationship between artist and spectator, and reimagining everyday life—have assumed a sense of urgency in Providence at the turn of the twenty-first century. After suffering for decades under corruption scandals and mismanagement, Providence rebranded itself first as a "Renaissance" city under Mayor "Buddy" Cianci, and more recently again as a "Creative Capital" under David Cicilline. The waterfront renovation of the 1990s uncovered waterways that had been buried beneath the streets and created inviting promenades along the two rivers that converge where the downtown meets the East Side.[9] On summer nights, gondolas glide down the Woonasquatucket past one hundred floating braziers as part of an ongoing art installation designed by Barnaby Evans called "Waterfire." Given the presence of a nationally renowned art school, the Rhode Island School of Design, gallery night events, theaters and a number of active arts nonprofits, one might conclude that the relationship between the arts and the city supports a mutually beneficial "creative economy" lauded by Richard Florida. To describe the qualities that make a city attractive to the "Creative Class," Florida cites a "thirty-something professional" from Providence in 2001, "My friends and I came to Providence because it already has the authenticity that we like—its established neighborhoods, historic architecture and ethnic mix."[10] What Florida apparently fails to appreciate, despite his passing acknowledgment of gentrification, is the extent to which the influx of these creative professionals might endanger the very "authenticity" that they seek.

Perspectives on city development change drastically if one follows the Woonasquatucket upstream under the quaint European-inspired bridges, past the braziers, and under the mall back to the West Side and Olneyville, where local artists and low-income Hispanic residents live. Fort Thunder, an artist colony in a dilapidated nineteenth-century mill building, became legendary for its punk music, noise, and artistic rebellion since the mid-1990s. When the Long Island developer Feldco wanted to transform the surrounding area called Eagle Square into a big box-style shopping center, community members, artists, and preservationists were galvanized by what they perceived as an intrusion in their neighborhood, and forced Feldco to revise their plans to preserve four of the original fourteen mill buildings.[11] Despite these concessions, however, the demolition of the building that housed Fort Thunder in January 2002 was a defining moment for the Providence counter culture.[12] Feldco had tried to argue that the artists were in part responsible for the redevelopment of the neighborhood given the familiar and well-documented pattern of gentrification in American and Canadian cities.[13] Understandably, local artists rejected this charge as grossly unfair, and saw themselves as victims of the process; for them, the destruction of Fort Thunder epitomized the contradiction between the city's commitment to the arts and the simultaneous desire to promote real estate development.[14]

Influenced by the legacy of Fort Thunder, a number of Providence artists adopted a playful approach to claiming public space by using celebration, performance art, and alternative uses of the city. John J. McGurk, RISD '04, initially had the idea of applying psychogeography to Providence, and with a number of his friends–PIPS, the Providence Initiative for Psychogeographic Studies–became the meeting ground for local artists who wanted to stage DIY events that would challenge the city's consumerist agenda. Modeled after the Situationists, their stated purpose is quasi-utopian:

> In order to create understanding and transformation of the world we must create adventures. Society's emancipation will not be found in the existing structure of the world, but in the cracks and lost spaces. PIPS works to facilitate and create actions and adventures that exercise human potential in new and inventive ways. Our intention is the creation of a better world through community and action.[15]

In one of their early actions from 2003, they stole some of the burning embers from the tourist spectacle of Waterfire, and encouraged curious onlookers to follow as they relocated to a bridge behind the Providence Place Mall where they could tour a PIPS outdoor art gallery. The following spring, a group of PIPsters wearing clothes from recycled materials paraded through the mall, prompting more signage and regulations regarding prohibited behaviors.[16] But their most sustained endeavor was a gathering of local and international artists in an annual festival called Provflux from 2004 to 2008.[17]

Inspired by Conflux 2003 in New York City, Provflux launched "investigations of contemporary psychogeography and experimental forms of public art" in the hopes of creating "a space for imaginative and innovative solutions to a sometimes homogeneous and uninspiring urban landscape."[18] The Providence version of psychogeography was considerably more DIY than

Figures 8.1 and 8.2 Postcards from Provflux 2006, a Free Festival with Situationist Tendencies. Reproduced with permission from Meredith Younger.

its New York predecessor; there was no admittance fee, and all entries were accepted. As Meredith Younger, one of the key organizers explained, as long as the people proposing the project could get themselves and their materials to Providence, PIPS would supply free lodging with friends, communal food, and perhaps even a repaired yellow bicycle.[19] All of this was accomplished with minimal funding, although they did receive a grant from Providence Arts, Culture and Tourism in 2005, and a grant from the LEF foundation another year.

For a few days over the summer, Provflux transformed the streets of Providence with dérives, bike tours, ecological exhibits, map making, lectures, and parties. Interventions over the years have included "selling Virgin Mary grilled cheese sandwiches to the public as edible art objects," the "Taste of Providence" (whose goal it was to lick every building in the city), the "Virtual Flaneur Project," which used cell phones and text messaging to engage in "locative electronic writing," and a kickball game between New Urbanists and the psychogeographers. Recycling was another common Provflux theme, leading to several iterations of "Art Riot," a foray into the city led by a group who would transform garbage into art, and the Progressive Runway project, an extension of the earlier Providence Place Mall action in which people would wear clothing constructed from trash and discarded materials. Although Provflux was more dedicated to play than to politics, their zine *Crosswalk III* (2006), was their most ambitious contribution to anti-gentrification debates given that the festival was planned to coincide with a meeting of the New Urbanists in Providence.[20] Reprints of Paolo Soleri's utopian plans for "Solare 1" and Ivan Chtcheglov's 1953 "A Formulary for a New Urbanism" appear alongside articles on low-income housing, critiques of New Urbanism, and "Civics 101" primers.

Eventually it became too difficult to sustain the level of energy and organization needed to hold a festival every year, and people involved in Provflux gravitated to other events such as the annual Foo Fest (organized by AS220, Providence's most famous local arts nonprofit) and Woolly Fair, a festival for alternative art held at the Steel Yard (an arts nonprofit in Olneyville that offers courses in blacksmithing, welding, and ceramics). Many Provflux participants remain in Providence and continue their artistic practice at various local nonprofits such as AS220, New Urban Arts, the Steel Yard, the RISD Museum, and Firehouse 13.[21] But the central inspiration of Provflux—viewing the city as a utopian site of possibility and play—was continued in another form through the successive installations "New Your City" (2006), "Magic City Repairs" (2007), and "We Built a City Together" (2008, 2009).

PROVIDENCE: DIY CITY

"New Your City" was the product of a collaboration between Ian Cozzens and Anne Shattle, a librarian in charge of children's programming at the Fox Point branch of the public library in 2006. Starting with a supply of recycled materials, anyone visiting the library over the course of one month was invited to "build" whatever they wanted to contribute to a collective version of the city. The resulting landscape included "a defense robot, a tunnel, a house of terror, a court, a public restroom, an ice obelisk, a junk food/candy store, a half pipe for skateboarding, trees, murals, a beautiful library, and much much more."[22] Oddly mimicking real neighborhoods, the city included "Happy Town" (the East Side), the West Side, and "Falldown" community, "where everything falls down." Toddlers, children, parents, grandparents—all people from the neighborhood—added their small piece to the conglomeration; none of them were "artists" in the conventional sense. Probably the most valuable part of project was the resulting discussions about private property, the police, graffiti, laws, and who wields power in the community. Participants could reflect on their own positions and collaborate with others. Rather than accept the status quo, the project invited library visitors to realize their own visions of the city.

"Magic City Repairs" (2007) was a similar project, but was situated in the Stairwell Gallery on Broadway on the West Side of Providence, and thus drew in a different group of pedestrians. In this iteration, Cozzens teamed up with Andrew Oesch to create screen-printed designs of bricks and wood to add to the recycled cardboard. Oesch and Cozzens, both graduates of RISD, had participated in Provflux, and had served as artist-mentors at New Urban Arts, an after school program for high school students from disadvantaged backgrounds.[23] Their time with NUA significantly contributed to their passionate advocacy for community involvement in the arts, and informs their statements about the project. "We're modeling a way we want to exist in the world," stated Oesch, "which is this subtle democratic vision." Cozzens emphasized that "order and organization don't have to come from above; it can be mutually created and shared."[24] The project was somewhat altered and brought to New Urban Arts in 2008 when high school students were invited to add stickers, drawings, and buildings to a map posted on the wall of the NUA studio.

A final version of the DIY city called "And We Built a City Together," designed by Meg Turner and Andrew Oesch, was a one-day interactive installation in the RISD museum in September 26, 2009. Strategically organized to complement the "Providence Initiative," a yearlong process of meetings with leaders in the arts community which culminated in the publication of "Creative Providence: A Cultural Plan for the Creative Sector" (June 2009), the installation asked Providence museum visitors to "consider their role as authors of the city and how we dictate our environment through individual desire and group effort."[25] Each visitor received a letter-pressed card with instructions inviting them to color, alter, and augment a collection of building stickers, and then place them on a map posted on the wall. The card addresses museum visitors:

> This is now based upon your ideal of the city. There is no final goal. Keep in mind that you are allowed and encouraged to co-opt, build upon, or cover the decisions of a previous author. In this one moment, you may freely re-write past decisions, but beware that someone might soon re-write yours!

Although the exercise is playful, the illustrations at the top of the card resemble mill buildings, thus referencing Providence's industrial past but also potentially alluding to the Fort Thunder demolition, a touchstone for Providence underground artists.

APARTMENT AT THE MALL

For the most dramatic example of Situationist-style détournement and appropriation of "undeveloped" space, we will consider what came to be known as "the apartment at the mall." Michel Townshend and Adriana Yoto, who were part of the Fort Thunder scene, observed the construction of Providence Place Mall between 1997 and 1999 from their Olneyville studios in mill buildings that were eventually torn down.[26] Like many other artists and community members, they attended the public hearings when Struever Brothers was making its case for converting mills into condos, and they were struck by the way that Olneyville was dismissed as an "underutilized space" with "no community." In this context, they perceived the mall as inverse of the neighborhood, and saw themselves as "the bastard children of development." To alleviate their acute sense of frustration, they decided to turn the tables on the developers by viewing the mall as rich in "microdevelopment potential," and in 2003 they occupied a 750 sq. foot "underutilized" space in the mall parking garage. Yoto, Townshend and six friends patiently assembled cinder blocks, hoisted in a couch, a table, and a china cabinet, and succeeded in creating a kind of ersatz bourgeois living room complete with a PlayStation. In his website statement, Townshend writes: "I cannot emphasize enough that the entire endeavor was done out of a compassion to understand the mall more and life as a shopper." After inhabiting the apartment intermittently with his friends for four years, security guards finally noticed and arrested Townshend in 2007 as he was showing the apartment to a visiting artist from Hong Kong, which inconveniently interrupted his "plans to finish the kitchen, install the wood flooring, add a second bedroom and replace the outdated cutlery."[27] While the mall spokesperson characterized the project as a "violation," their blatant poaching on enemy territory, as it were, and their reversal of the passive consumer role into an act of playful creation earned the respect and admiration of the general public. As a consequence of his trespassing, Townshend was banned from the mall, but otherwise suffered no penalty.[28]

Although their original apartment was dismantled, the couple recreated the space in a downtown gallery.[29] Their "microdevelopment" efforts entered a new phase when they concocted their own ad campaign for a luxury condominium that they simply called "The One." Noting that a local street had been renamed for the mall, they exposed this reversal by restoring the name—Kinsley Ave—and using this as the address for their exclusive new condo which is glowingly described as "The first intellectual resort residence inside a regional shopping mall" (in fact, an architectural drawing of a space in the parking garage). Even though the apartment was gone, Townshend and Yoto continued the experiment in another form over the month that the gallery was open, inviting visitors to discuss how the apartment at the mall challenges our notions of public space.

WHOSE CITY IS IT?

What unites the projects I have outlined here is a common desire to stake a claim for an alternative city—not the "object of cultural consumption for tourists, for aestheticism, avid for spectacles and the picturesque" as Lefebvre states—but the inversion and critique of cycles of consumption and gentrification that are naturalized and valorized in city hall's eager embrace of the "creative economy." The fact that these particular works reject conventional networks of economic exchange is especially significant given that artists are frequently cited as the catalyst that transforms a low income community into "trendy" or "upscale" neighborhood that the artists themselves can no longer afford.[30]

On the other hand, it is worth asking what part of the Providence community was free to engage in these playful experiments. Were they as inclusive as they pretended to be, or were these art interventions only tolerated by authorities because they were staged by white college graduates, mostly former RISD students? Although it is impossible to measure who participated and what the impact was given the ephemeral, DIY nature of these projects, one can compare the reaction of authorities to these projects with other incursions into public space by those outside of the elite, white, college-educated community. The artists I interviewed for this chapter, Ian Cozzens, Meredith Younger, and Joan Wyand, openly acknowledged that as white college graduates, they were not subject to the same scrutiny as minorities.

As one counter-example, consider Devin Costa, also known as the "lonely tagger," who was convicted of vandalism for his graffiti and fined over $12,000 in the fall of 2015.[31] Costa, 19 years old and Hispanic, grew up in East Providence, and has been using a paint roller to scrawl phrases such as "Lonely as I've ever been," and "I love you even when you don't notice" on walls in public spaces in downtown Providence. Bereft by the suicide of two friends from different towns, and isolated in a new high school where he was one of the only minorities, Costa wanted to express a different kind of message. "I guess what I did was the opposite of advertisement," he explained, "Advertisement is meant to entice you to buy something, to look a certain way, to want something. What I did was advertise something that you don't want to feel, you don't want to see."[32] Business owners and the police condemned his acts as vandalism that's "bad for business," and expensive to remedy.[33] The irony of his punishment in light of the city's ostensible support of the arts was not lost on Costa, "I think art is being exploited in this city. They take who they want to take and they use it as a way to brand the city as a place where people that want an urban feeling would want to go."[34] Vida Mia Ruiz, organizer of Costa's online crowdfunding campaign, sees the justice system as inherently biased against poor and minority youth, and laments that the city "chose to make one kind of example of Lonely while blissfully ignoring their own branding as a 'creative capital.'"[35]

Inspired by artists such as Shepard Fairey, who got his start in Providence, and the British artist Banksy, Costa points to the contradiction in accepting "street" art as a commodity when it's on a gallery wall but not when it's actually on the street. In his exhibit at the Columbus Theater on the West Side of Providence, he asked viewers to consider "if you saw the Lonely tags in a museum would you consider it a more valid form of art?"[36] Unfortunately, Providence is part of a larger trend that welcomes some forms of street art that is a "'brandable' creative practice for middle-class, white consumers," while rejecting less palatable art by racialized subjects who are excluded from this category.[37] The Providence underground arts community, however, has been supportive of Costa, contributing to the online fund, holding a fundraising event at AS220 through the Providence Comics Consortium, and enlisting the help and mentorship of artists Brian Chippendale of Fort Thunder fame and William Schaff from the local What Cheer brigade marching band. As of the writing of this chapter, about one-third of the money needed for Costa's fines has been raised, in addition to the money Costa has earned through printing T-shirts, stickers, and posters.[38]

While the city of Providence recognizes that cultural inequities exist, it seems necessarily limited to institutional remedies. When asked for comment on Costa's plight, the Providence Department of Art, Culture and Tourism referred to the number of "nationally recognized youth arts organizations" in Providence, and stated that "we work closely with the arts community to support their innovative ideas."[39] And it is true that Providence boasts a wealth of arts nonprofits and takes freedom of expression as a form of social justice seriously. In fact, the topic of the Claiborne Pell lecture in the fall of 2015, an annual event sponsored through foundation support, was "Advancing cultural equity in the arts." Patrice Walker Powell, former Deputy Director of the National Endowment for the Arts, led a panel discussion of local and national arts organizations to discuss the challenges of making connections between marginalized communities and arts nonprofits.[40] As well-intentioned as these statements and efforts are, however, they remain somewhat distant and abstract to DIY artists like Costa who want to find their own way regardless of whether their work fits within the boundaries of expression legally sanctioned by the city. In this sense, Providence as a DIY utopia will always be an ideal rather than a reality—but it is a vision for which the arts community must continue to strive.

NOTES

1. Ian Donnis, "Class Warfare in Olneyville," *The Boston Phoenix*, May 24, 2006, accessed January 28, 2016.
2. This is only a subset of the numerous Providence arts projects that have taken place in this time period, but I have chosen to focus on these because they overtly represent or engage with the city. I thank Ian Cozzens, Andrew Oesch, Meredith Younger, Joan Wyand, and Anna Shapiro for their invaluable help with this chapter.
3. See David Cicilline, *Creative Providence: A Cultural Plan for the Creative Sector*, June 2009, accessed January 28, 2016, https://www.providenceri.com/efile/47
4. Simon Sadler, *The Situationist City* (Cambridge: MIT Press, 1999), 17.

5. Ken Knabb, *Situationist International Anthology*, Trans. Ken Knabb (Berkeley: the Bureau of Public Secrets, 1981), 45.

6. Ibid., 45.

7. Henri Lefebvre, "The Right to the City," in *Blackwell City Reader*, eds. Gray Bridge and Sophie Watson (Malden, MA: Blackwell, 2002), 365.

8. Ibid., 365.

9. Rich Lang, "Rejuvenating Waters," *Preservation* (Sept/Oct 2001), 57.

10. Richard Florida, *The Rise of the Creative Class* (New York: Basic Books, 2002), 232.

11. Lang, "Rejuvenating Waters," 62.

12. The irony of the situation was dramatically illustrated when an installation by the group "Forcefield," which consisted of former Fort Thunder residents Matt Brinkman, Jim Drain, Leif Goldberg, and Ara Peterson, was featured as part of the Whitney Biennial exhibition that opened in March of the same year. See Judith Tannenbaum, "Thirty, but still dirty . . . Providence's freewheeling art scene," 21.

13. David Ley, "Artists, Aestheticisation and the Field of Gentrification," *Urban Studies* 40, no. 12. (November 2003). Ley argues that "to blame artists for the gentrification that so often follows their residency in a district is a misplaced charge; it is the societal valorization of the cultural competencies of the artist that brings followers richer in economic capital" (2540–1). The radio documentary "Reconstructing Providence" by Robin Amer records many of the first person accounts of this clash between artists and developers at this time.

14. On the other hand, Olneyville property owners were eager to have any kind of economic development in the neighborhood, including a big-box style grocery store. See Micah Salkind's detailed account in "Scale, Sociality and Serendipity in Providence, RI's Post-Industrial Renaissance," in *Creative Economies in Post-Industrial Cities* (Surrey, UK: Ashgate, 2013), 47.

15. Mission statement for PIPS, supplied by Meredith Younger.

16. Dana Goldstein, "The City We Bought," *College Hill Independent* (April 15, 2005): 14, 18.

17. In 2005, Provflux included 200 participants from the United States and nine foreign countries. From Provflux meeting notes supplied by Meredith Younger.

18. *Crosswalk III*, ed. Meredith Younger, Providence, 2006.

19. Conversation with Meredith Younger, November 22, 2015.

20. Bryan Rourke, "Provflux Encourages community collaboration," *The Providence Journal* (May 30, 2006): E1–2.

21. Conversation with Meredith Younger and Joan Wyand, November 22, 2015.

22. "New Your City," *The Agenda*, Issue 18 (April 2006): 12.

23. In fact, ideas from Provflux were included in the 2006 New Urban Arts Art Inquiry theme, Creative Cartography.

24. Greg Cook, "Dreaming a Better World," *The Boston Phoenix*, June 5, 2007.

25. Press release from the RI State Council on the Arts, September 26, 2009, accessed January 28, 2016, http://www.arts.ri.gov/blogs/?p=5625.

26. Townshend and Yoto gave a presentation on their clandestine apartment as part of Provflux 2007.

27. See their website, Trummerkind, for quotes and documentation regarding Townshend and Yoto's occupation of the mall. www.trummerkind.com

28. Lisa Selin Davis, "The Couple who Lived at the Mall," *Salon*, August 15, 2008, accessed January 28, 2016.

29. "The One" was featured in a gallery space at 70 Eddy St. from December 8–31, 2007, accessed January 28, 2016, http://heragallery.blogspot.com/2007/12/following-is-repost-from-todays.html

30. Ley, "Artists, Aestheticisation and the Field of Gentrification," 2534.

31. Emma Jerzyk, "After fines, 'lonely' tagger sparks debate about public art," *Brown Daily Herald*, September 16, 2015.

32. Ben Williams, "If These Walls Could Talk," *College Independent*, November 2015, accessed January 28, 2016, http://www.theindy.org/744.

33. Katie Mulvaney, "Lonely graffiti sparks conversation on depression," *Providence Journal*, September 2, 2015.

34. Costa qtd. in Williams.

35. Vida Mia Ruiz, Facebook post on "Lonely as I've Ever Been—Providence." December 2, 2015.

36. Ibid.

37. Sarah Banet-Weiser, *Authentic: The Politics of Ambivalence in a Brand Culture* (New York: NYU Press, 2012), 106.

38. Williams, "If These Walls Could Talk."

39. Jerzyk, "After fines, 'lonely' tagger sparks debate about public art."

40. Inside the Foundation, blog post, Rhode Island Foundation, November 2, 2015, accessed January 28, 2016, http://www.rifoundation.org/InsidetheFoundation/OurBlog/TabId/106/PostId/328/advancing-cultural-equity-in-the-arts.aspx.

BIBLIOGRAPHY

"Advancing Cultural Equity in the Arts." Inside the Foundation (blog). *Rhode Island Foundation.* November 2, 2015. Accessed January 28, 2016. http://www.rifoundation.org/InsidetheFoundation/OurBlog/TabId/106/PostId/328/advancing-cultural-equity-in-the-arts.aspx.

Agniel, Sara. "Only in Lonelyville." *Wunderground: Providence 1990 to the Present.* Corte Madera, CA: Ginko Press and the RISD Museum, 2006, 75–84.

Amer, Robin. *Reconstructing Providence*, edited by Paul McCarthy and Jim Moses. 2004. Audio CD. Originally performed before a live audience at AS220 May 10, 2004.

Banet-Weiser, Janet. "Branding Creativity: Creative Cities, Street Art, and 'Making your Name Sing.'" In *Authentic: The Politics of Ambivalence in a Brand Culture.* New York: New York University Press, 2012, 91–124.

Cicilline, David. *Creative Providence: A Cultural Plan for the Creative Sector.* June 2009. Accessed January 28, 2016. https://www.providenceri.com/efile/47

Cook, David. "Dreaming a Better World." *Boston Phoenix.* June 5, 2007. Accessed January 28, 2016. http://thephoenix.com/Boston/arts/41235-magic-city-repairs/

Davis, Lisa Selin. "The Couple who Lived at the Mall." *Salon*. August 15, 2008. Accessed January 28, 2016. http://www.salon.com/mwt/feature/2008/08/15/living_in_mall/

De Certeau, Michel. *The Practice of Everyday Life*. Trans. Steven Rendall. Berkeley: University of California Press, 1984.

Donnis, Ian. "Class Warfare in Olneyville." *The Boston Phoenix*. May 24, 2006. Accessed January 28, 2016. http://thephoenix.com/boston/news/13331-class-warfare-in-olneyville/?page=7#TOPCONTENT

Florida, Richard. *The Rise of the Creative Class: How it's Transforming Work, Leisure, and Everyday Life*. New York: Basic Books, 2002.

Goldstein, Dana. "The City We Bought: Providence's Psychogeographic Revolution." *The College Hill Independent*. April 14, 2005, 14–18.

Hocking, Peter. "I wish I had a place like this when I was growing up: New Urban Arts and the Cultivation of Creative Practice." *Radical Teacher*, no. 89 (Winter 2010): 47–56.

Jerzyk, Emma. "After fines, 'lonely' tagger sparks debate about public art." *The Brown Daily Herald*. September 16, 2015. Accessed January 28, 2016. http://www.browndailyherald.com/2015/09/16/after-fines-lonely-tagger-sparks-debate-about-public-art/

Knabb, Ken. *Situationist International Anthology*. Trans. Ken Knabb. Berkeley: The Bureau of Public Secrets, 1981.

Lang, Rich. "Rejuvenating Waters." *Preservation* (Sept/Oct 2001): 56–63.

Lefebvre, Henri. "The Right to the City." *Blackwell City Reader*, edited by Gray Bridge and Sophie Watson. Malden, MA: Blackwell, 2002.

———. *Writings on Cities*. Translated and edited by Eleonore Kofman and Elizabeth Lebas. Cambridge: Blackwell Publishers, 1996.

Ley, David. "Artists, Aestheticisation and the Field of Gentrification." *Urban Studies* 40, no. 12 (November 2003): 2527–2544.

Rourke, Brian. "Proflux encourages community collaboration." *The Providence Journal* (May 30, 2006): E1–E2.

Sadler, Simon. *The Situationist City*. Cambridge: MIT Press, 1999.

Salkind, Micah. "Scale, Sociality and Serendipity in Providence, RI's Post-Industrial Renaissance." *Creative Economies in Post-Industrial Cities*. Surrey, UK: Ashgate, 2013, 33–57.

Schwartzapfel, Beth. "Psychoactive Providence." *The Boston Phoenix*. May 24, 2006. Accessed January 28, 2016. http://thephoenix.com/boston/news/13317-psychoactive-providence/

Tannenbaum, Judith. "Thirty, but still dirty…Providence's freewheeling art scene" *Wunderground: Providence 1990 to the Present*. Corte Madera, CA: Ginko Press and the RISD Museum, 2006, 19–30.

Townshend, Michael and Adriana Yoto. "Trummerkind" (Apartment at the Mall). Accessed January 28, 2016. http://www.trummerkind.com/theone/Home.html

Younger, Meredith. ed. *Crosswalk III*. Providence, 2006.

Chapter 9

Livestreaming in the Black Lives Matter Network

Chenjerai Kumanyika

Shortly after 9 pm on July 6, 2016, Diamond Reynolds and her 4-year-old daughter sat in their car at gunpoint. Officer Jeronimo Yanez stood aiming the gun at her through the passenger side window. Minutes earlier Yanez had shot her boyfriend Philando Castile, who now lay in the chair next to her with his white T-shirt soaked in his own blood.[1] Reynolds feared for her own life and knew that the narrative of these events would come down "his word against my word." So she made the best choice she could think of. She opened up the Facebook live app on her phone and started livestreaming. "Had I not started livestreaming that video, who is to say I wouldn't have been executed the way my boyfriend was?"[2]

Within an hour the video—now archived on Facebook—had hundreds of thousands of views and shares. When the announcement came later that evening that Castile had died the hashtag #PhilandoCastile flooded corporate media networks and the story appeared on television news. Castile's shooting merged with the momentum of the still fresh videos of the killing of Alton Sterling who had been shot roughly 44 hours earlier in Baton Rouge, Louisiana. What's clear is that Reynold's harrowing livestream was a key component in the nationwide protests in the weeks following these incidents. Reynold's broadcast and subsequent streams documented instances of overwrought and violent police response to peaceful protest, highlighted the impact of this form of media production in decentralized, dynamic movement networks like Black Lives Matter.

In recent years, both citizens and social justice organizers have grasped for more urgent and potent logics of resistance, against an intensification of social insecurity, militarization, and corporate hegemony. This dovetails with other developments in media economics and production that have propelled "liveness" and spontaneity to increasingly dominant media aesthetics.

I was thinking about this on the afternoon of November 25, 2014—otherwise known as Black Friday—as my wife and I sat in the food court of a shopping Mall on the outskirts of St. Louis, Missouri. As I gobbled down a falafel too quickly, I compulsively checked to make sure that the smartphone in my left pocket was still plugged in via a USB cord to a heavy portable battery in my right pocket. Heat from the battery was seeping into my leg. I took another bite of my falafel, and then I heard what I had been waiting for. A young dreadlocked African-American woman yelled at the top of her lungs: "If we don't get it!?" Instantly, a chorus of voices thundered back in unison "Shut it down!" Jumping to my feet, I frantically fumbled around in my pocket for my phone. By the time the young woman chanted "If we don't get it?" the second time, about 100 people—a large number of them young African-Americans in the mall—were standing and chanting with her. By the third time, there were 200 people chanting with the diversity of the protesters becoming more visible. People of various ethnicities, genders, ages, and political aesthetics flowed toward the young woman and followed her as she marched through the mall. I was here to support these protests and also to livestream them.

These Black Friday mall protests had been planned by a small group of protesters in St. Louis less than a week after a grand jury determined that officer Darren Wilson would not be indicted for the killing of Michael Brown. Similar protests occurred in other cities.[3]

They represented a shift in tactics at a time when the St. Louis police, and National Guard were becoming accustomed to protests in front of the police department headquarters. Protesters interrupted shopping in at least five malls between Friday November 25, and Saturday November 26, 2014. Due to the planned unpredictability of this tactic, the opportunities for mainstream media coverage during the protests were limited, but several independent media producers documented these events.

While walking fast to catch up with the protesters, I wrestled my phone out of my pocket and opened my Ustream application.[4] Trying to keep up and not drop my phone, I hastily typed a name for the stream with my thumbs. "#BlackFridayMallShutdown" and hit the large red button that said "Go Live." Not surprisingly, the number of viewers read "0." I clicked the Twitter icon in the corner of the screen to let my followers know that I was live. Then I pointed the phone's camera in the direction of chanting and looked at what was happening around me through the application's visual interface. Frightened customers ran out of a Zales jewelry store and brushed past, jostling me as they did so. The sound of metal roared in the hallway as storeowners quickly pulled down the gates. Speaking to the screen, I cleared my throat and said. "What's up ya'll thank you for watching! We're here live in Ferguson at the 'Black friday shut down' protest. Please share the stream." The number of viewers went up slowly to one hundred views and then to one hundred fifty. By this time, a manager at Footlocker had already pulled down the gate with confused and curious customers temporarily stuck inside. As we walked past, a young black male employee with a red and white striped footlocker shirt put his fist up and nodded his head. I steadily moved the phone around to capture as much of this as I could. Holding the camera straight ahead, I swiveled my head to look around for police and mall security. I spotted three panting obese officers about thirty feet to my right lumbering up the hallway to the front of the mall and radioing to their colleagues. As protesters began to mount an escalator, I was startled by a voice behind me exclaiming in loud tones. Heather Di Man—a St. Louis-based streamer who is one of the most consistent protest streamers in the country—pushed past me in her wheelchair. She explained that it was inconsiderate when some people just decide to do things like that. By the time we were halfway down the hallway, the chant had changed: protesters now shouted "Black Lives Matter! Black Lives Matter" I looked down at my screen. A viewer had posted "Black Lives Matter!" in the chat.

Livestream broadcasts (like the one I was haphazardly producing) provided key footage and a unique televisual experience early on in the Ferguson uprisings. For example, less then four months earlier in August of 2014, unpaid local livestream journalists had broadcast the initial video footage of the Ferguson police department shooting unarmed citizens with rubber bullets and teargas. A *Time* magazine article, published the day after this incident, featured a link to fuzzy green images of these incidents filmed by streamer Mustafa Hussein.[5] Another moment that underscored the importance of livestream journalists to the emerging movement occurred shortly before midnight on Tuesday, August 19, 2014.[6] According to St. Louis County Police spokesman Brian Schellman: "a St. Ann police officer pointed a semi-automatic

Figures 9.1 Protesters Use Their Smartphones to Stream and Produce Media during the Shutdown at the Saint Louis Galleria.

assault rifle at a peaceful protester after a verbal exchange." The peaceful protester was streamer Jon Ziegler (Rebelutionary_Z) who was broadcasting to his Ustream channel at the time. The verbal exchange consisted of the officer (Ray Albers) telling Ziegler "I'll fucking kill you. Get back! Get back!" When Ziegler asked the officer's name, the officer replied " Go Fuck Yourself." The video footage went viral. In addition to providing an instructive anecdote regarding the training and temperament of police in St. Louis, Ziegler's footage became a part of the evidence leading to Albers' firing.

Streamers like Ziegler, Heather Di Man, Hussein, Baseem Masri, and Leigh Maibes who streamed in Ferguson comprised an informal network of protesters and citizen journalists. Their broadcasts connected both regular audiences and mainstream media to a number of demonstrations, rallies, gatherings, interviews, and other protests focused mostly on individual police use of force incidents and systematic problems in law enforcement and criminal justice. These livestream journalists also took on significant personal risks and challenges in order to produce their streams. Masri, another consistent and outspoken streamer, had his camera robbed twice and was arrested numerous times during 2014. All of the consistent streamers in Missouri had been tear gassed. These sacrifices obviate the complicated position that streamers occupy as both independent journalists embedded in social movements and as a precarious front line of corporate media platforms and broader mainstream news coverage.

This chapter will explore the aspects of streaming that might be understood as DIY media-making practice, and some examples of how these practices helped to construct Black Lives Matter as a networked community of protesters with an ethics of solidarity and support. While I attempt to highlight what streaming contributes to this movement, and how streamers see our own roles, I also remain deeply concerned about problems of precarity, exploitation and even some of the aesthetics of livestreaming as a citizen-journalist practice. Using both narrative and description, I provide some empirical data that can help readers to see how both the potentials and problems of this practice take shape in lived experience.

I focus heavily on my participation Ferguson and St. Louis protests but I also draw on my participation in over twenty-one protests as a livestream producer and over fifty protests as a viewer/participant between August 20, 2014, and December 2015. Sites that I 'streamed' and conducted research in included Ferguson and St. Louis Missouri; New York City; Philadelphia, Pennsylvania; Cleveland, Ohio; and Charleston, South Carolina. While I did not always join these protests with the intention of conducting participatory-action research, I ultimately became quite embedded in "in-person" protest groups, networks of streamers, and online viewers, thereby gaining a strong sense of the lived experience of production and community in these contexts.

The ethics of studying and writing about media making in these protests are complicated and I've done my best job of navigating those. As a streamer, I observed protests from a unique and somewhat embedded perspective, but all of the events that I discuss took place in public and can generally be cross-referenced using other sources. Some of my decisions about what to include and to omit were made in consideration of the fact that as of this writing, BLM protests are ongoing. I've had frank discussions with some of the streamers and activists that I worked with about my position as a scholar/activist/streamer and many of these conversations happened via livestream and are publicly available.

BLACK LIVES MATTER: DIY BLACK LIBERATION POLITICS

In their important work on critical making and DIY citizenship, Ratto et al. argue that "increasingly, the DIY ethos has seismically reshaped the international political sphere, as can be seen in ongoing global uprisings and the uses of media and communications within a 'logic of connective action.'"[7] A logic of connective action is a useful way to think about the network of DIY resistance that is called Black Lives Matter. By most accounts, Black Lives Matter began when Alicia Garza wrote the phrase in a Facebook post as a reminder, a lament, and a "call to action."[8] Joining a variety of other organizations that had been protesting police brutality for many years, Garza and two other queer activists, Patrice Cullors and Opal Tometi, began organizing protests. Following Michael Brown's death on August of 2014, Cullors and Tometi organized buses to bring activists to support the already in progress Ferguson uprisings. This effectively constituted St. Louis as a central node of the movement. New York, Ohio, Milwaukee, and many other cities emerged as other important nodes as protests and protest communities developed in response to subsequent non-indictments. In locations across the world other organizers, activists, and outraged community members took it among themselves to make signs and T-shirts, and banners that displayed the phrase "BlackLivesMatter." They gathered in person for direction action efforts, and to share imagery on networked corporate media outlets. The phrase Black Lives Matter also became an analytical lens and a statement of political priorities, foregrounding the racial dimensions of other political problems.

A basic DIY sensibility permeates the highly decentralized and inclusive approach to resistance in this network. Local residents, college students, and other supporters create their own tactics, provide their own transportation and funding, acquire the materials for their own signs and spontaneously plan direct actions in solidarity with the motivating cause or related issues. Protest actions associated with this phrase are frequently organized without the consent or involvement of traditional organizations such as the NAACP, the ACLU, or Al Sharpton's National Action Network. It is true that Black Lives Matter has organized a formal structure with regional chapters, but this structure was only formalized after protests in the Fall of 2014. Local grassroots groups like Justice for Akai Gurley, Take Back the Bronx, Baltimore Bloc, and other organizations such as Organization for Black Struggle in Missouri, the National Lawyers Guild, Millennials United, The Stop Mass Incarceration Network, the Revolutionary Communist Party, the Gathering for Justice, Street Medics, the NYC Justice League, and many others seemed to have played key supportive roles in actions that were called Black Lives Matter protests. Both Ferguson and Baltimore, however provide instances where institutionalized efforts supported or imposed upon an original wave of "organic" uprising initiated and sustained by community members that were not necessarily affiliated with formal organizational structures.

STREAMING AND DIY PRACTICE

Streaming in the Black Lives Matter network involves the successful execution of video production techniques, and the building and maintenance of a viewing audience. But it also requires the coordination and management of knowledge about protest logistics, relationships with the protest community and participants, and the maintenance of physical limitations and safety, equipment and software. In practice, the challenges of these working conditions reflect a broader set of neoliberal socioeconomic arrangements.

Due to the expectation that streamers will broadcast for longer periods than other forms of media production, streamers in the Black Lives Matter network tended to be among the hardest working producers while also being poorly and sporadically funded and precarious. Most streamers use smartphones that are mass produced by technology corporations and they stream on advertising funded corporate platforms such as livestream, Ustream, Bambuser, Facebook, and Periscope. Given that David Gauntlett describes DIY practices as rejecting "the idea that you overcome problems by paying somebody else to provide a solution," it wouldn't be accurate to describe streaming as a DIY practice in any strict anti-consumerist sense.[9] In a sense, streamers could be considered neoliberalism's version of community-based media although they intend quite the opposite.

However streamers also reached for a kind of ethics and aesthetics of citizen-produced community journalism. Scholars such as Gauntlett[10] (2013a), Matt Ratto and Megan Boler[11] have expanded the concept of DIY to include a range of processes that aim at various forms of belonging, utopian values and semiotic self-determination. Many of the livestream broadcasters that

Figures 9.2 Activist Saadiqa Kumanyika Livestreams during Black Friday Mall Shutdowns in Saint Louis, Missouri.

I met at various Black Lives Matter protests, see themselves as citizen journalists that are providing an important service. Some streamers function as though inspired by a "be the media" ethic that gathered momentum as a result of indymedia.[12] Streamers forge their own vocational identities precisely within the commitment to physical presence at protests, the commitment to endurance, the ability to adapt to dynamic and sometimes dangerous circumstances, the creativity to work within and around the limitations of technology and the ongoing contextual analysis of events. During racially tense protests that focus on institutions of law enforcement and criminal justice and their employees who would generally not like to be filmed, all of these factors are intensified.

Physical Presence and Transportation

Livestreaming involves a variety of concerns that have to do with physical presence and the body of the streamer. The first concern in that regard is identifying and traveling to protest sites. This is not as simple as it might sound and informal membership in the regional activist communities, social media groups, can be a crucial element of this. In the context of St. Louis and in New York, many police brutality protests took place in a predictable well-promoted (often online) fashion in front of identifiable centrally located police stations, government buildings businesses, etc. But there were also many instances where the element of surprise was part of the protest strategy and these events could be difficult to learn about.

As a streamer, I experienced these challenges first hand. Once I became sure about where the protests would start, I had to think through acquiring transportation to and from the event, where I would park if we drove etc. Each of these factors affected what and how long I would be able to stream and they added a sense of uncertainty. In late St. Louis, in November 2014, I made the mistake of broadcasting and offering editorial commentary as I drove around searching for a protest site. I made this choice thinking that this would make for a compelling stream and that stream viewers might even help me find the protest by using their comments in the chat dialogue. They did, but shortly thereafter, other streamers pointed out that my stream was indeed compelling and likely being watched by law enforcement. My stream would then expedite the police shutdown of these protests and they asked that I refrain from filming until the protest had begun.[13]

Once I had arrived at the protests location there were additional physical challenges. Frequently walking long distances with marching protesters can be demanding. These challenges include the physical work of holding the phone—often with arms raised for several hours. The Millions March NYC attended by over 50,000 people was an example of a fairly long protest. By some accounts this march covered 15 miles. Since eating or drinking would require interrupting my broadcast this was another concern. I carried water with me but this could weigh me down, making long marches tedious. Although I carried protein bars with me and became rather good and opening them with one hand, I also developed a certain discipline about eating before and after protests and accepting a certain amount of hunger-fueled discomfort. Jon Ziegler, the streamer who took me on as an apprentice in August of 2014, also took advantage of my apprentice status in this regard. I was happy to try my hand at taking control of his broadcast and he seemed relieved to have a few moments to grab a sandwich from a local food truck.

There was also a sense of sacrifice and community shared by protesters and streamers as we endured challenging weather conditions such as extreme heat and humidity (which I experienced in Ferguson in August of 2014, and in Columbia and Charleston South Carolina during the Summer of 2015) and biting cold, wind, and snow (which I experienced in both November 2014 in Missouri and Ohio in January 2016).

Physical safety was another important matter. The fear, pain and chaos of police deploying tear gas and rubber bullets on protesters and streamers is very alive in the memory of both protesters and streamers like Mustafa Hussein, Jon Ziegler, Baseem Masri. As a result, law enforcement officers presented a clear threat to physical safety and autonomy through the force of arrest and assault with nightsticks, tasers, tear gas, rubber bullets, real bullets, and guns.

Equipment

Livestreaming requires at least one camera that is capable of capturing both video and audio and sending a signal to the Internet in real time. In the protests that I traveled to, most streamers used their smartphones for the purpose of broadcasting, although a few used more dedicated devices such as GoPro cameras. For example in Ferguson, streamers such as Rebelutionary_Z, Heather Di Man, Baseem Masri, and News Revo all used their phones to livestream. It is possible to stream from many different kinds of phones, but most streamers seemed to use higher end smartphones, capable of running multiple applications, and of shooting high definition video.

As a streamer, when I learn of a protest that I may attend, the first thing that I do is plug in my external battery. Since streaming drains smartphones rapidly, and it was not uncommon for Black Lives Matter protests to last for over 3 hours, the limitations of phone battery life were a major threat to uninterrupted streaming. Streamers like Jon Ziegler taught me to "hack" this problem by attaching my phone to powerful USB battery packs that could allow smartphones to stream for as long as 5 or 6 hours with little to no loss of battery life. These devices can be bulky and they add small amounts of weight to coat or pants pockets, causing these outfits to sag. When connected to easily tangled USB, this can make walking more cumbersome and slowly add to fatigue and physical discomfort when marching and broadcasting for several hours. Battery maintenance also adds another level of planning and preparation to streaming production. These devices often require many hours of charging and so streamers must commit to a fairly disciplined practice of charging both batteries and phones, and keeping track of charges etc. both before and after events. This also means that streamers are likely to have additional battery power and I have shared my battery power with protesters.

As an artifact and a commodity, the phone battery acquired a variety of connotations in the context of protest. Despite my own critical sensibilities, I experienced a sense of efficacy related to having found a way extend the phone's battery. (This consumption friendly version of hacking was of course not lost on the rapidly growing list of phone battery producers.) On several occasions other streamers displayed a similar sense of enthusiasm as they exchanged information about their batteries with each other.

In the fall of 2014, a clergy member in a location that I will not name who had been leading protests asked me if he could borrow my battery pack to charge his phone. As he asked, he looked directly in my eyes in a rather deliberate manner. Several regular streamers in that location lived in the city; however there were also many others like myself whose ethics and politics were unclear to local organizers. In addition to the practical matter of replenishing his phone's charge, I sensed that this was a test as to whether he could trust me. I lent him my pack for several hours both because I was genuinely supportive of his efforts and also because I hoped to be accepted as an supporter that would be respectful of boundaries.

This kind of community building between streamers and protesters could understandably be seen as a way that the objectivity of streamers is compromised. However it is also true that streamers intentionally challenge mainstream journalism's pretense of objectivity, producing their work through an intimacy and consubstantiality with protesters and a foregrounding of transparency. Finally, it underscores the ongoing necessity of reestablishing familiarity in a context where citizen journalists associated with protest are often not community members.

Technique

Despite the celebration of streaming as a "raw" and "unedited" and fully transparent genre, this form of video production requires a variety of choices. Streamers are often guided by a sense of best practices that are softly emphasized by other broadcasters and formed and negotiated in response to specific problems that are encountered in the field. These skills include the ability to choose and film camera shots, keeping the camera as stable as possible while moving, catching the right moments on video, spontaneous interviewing skills, narration- in order to describe things to viewers and interaction with the online community.

An influential and popular streamer, Ziegler also known as Rebelutionary_Z talks about the importance of making citizen journalism frequently in the narration of his streams. Ziegler began streaming during Occupy and then moved to Ferguson in the wake of the Ferguson Uprisings. He later traveled to Baltimore and a variety of other locations for police brutality related protests. In August 2014, it was Ziegler who encouraged me to begin streaming in Ferguson, provided my first lessons, and shared his own hard won followers with me. In this process, he would critique mainstream media on and off camera and emphasize what in his view was stronger authenticity and autonomy made possible by his kind of journalism. Ziegler also expressed and displayed a commitment to a vocational code that combined elements of experimental amateurism, interviewing a wide variety of participants, and a commitment to his own process of rigorous investigation of facts. As a facilitator of the chat feature of his streams, Ziegler was vigilant about moderating "trolls" but he also spoke about the importance of tolerating viewpoints that conflicted with his own. For Ziegler, this was one of the elements that made his livestream journalism more authentic than highly scripted and censored mainstream media.

LIVENESS, PARTICIPATION, AND COMMUNITY BUILDING

Patrice Cullors is broadly recognized as one of the three founders of the Black Lives Matter movement. The title of her 2016 Medium article asserts "We didn't start a movement we started a network."[14] As a livestream journalist and livestream watcher, I had a particularly strong sense of what she meant. A key way that Streamers contribute to a sense of community among protesters is by offering compelling real-time, and visual connection points to a movement that has been hard to capture within traditional definitions. Alicia Garza, Patrice Cullors, and Opal Tometi created the #BlackLivesMatter!!! Hashtag thus hyperlinking both sympathetic and severely critical audiences to each other on the Internet.[15] Eventually, Black Lives Matter became a formal organization with chapters, but even the leaders of the movement are clear that these chapters don't really encapsulate or define the larger network. By adding live and archived visual updates, livestreams from various protests of police brutality and murder, streamers helped to constitute Black Lives Matter as an imagined and networked community.

The streaming that took place during protests of Eric Garner's 2014 killing by the NYPD illustrates the important role that livestreaming played. In July of 2014, Ramsey Orta distributed a phone-recorded video (not streamed) that showed the arrest of Eric Garner by six NYPD officers.[16] During the video, Garner—who is unarmed—is subdued by six police officers, and placed in a chokehold by former officer Daniel Pantaleo. While restrained, Garner pleads eleven times that he cannot breathe. Shortly thereafter, Garner is pronounced dead at the hospital. On December 3, 2014, a grand jury announced that no officer would be indicted for Garner's death.

Orta was not livestreaming, but as part of the larger ecology of media production Orta's video and his personal fate illustrate the janus-faced nature of this kind of citizen journalism. The extremely compelling and damning Garner video stood in as a grotesque example of the daily realities of law enforcement for Black men in US urban areas. It became the basis for protests and some calls for reforms of police use of force policies. But its immediacy also threatened to colonize viewers attention within the witnessing of direct violence. Other kinds of journalism were needed to support a fuller analysis of the complex of economic, juridical, tactical and racial forces at work in this moment. After documentating this event, Orta was followed by the NYPD who seemed to press on his already vulnerable legal situation. One might easily argue that while Pantaleo remains unconvicted and corporate outlets continue to monetize his smartphone footage in a variety of ways, Orta mostly experienced the teeth of his risk. It is also precisely these kinds of challenges that more institutionalized forms of community media can work to anticipate and challenge.

Later that evening and over the next 48 hours, thousands of people took to the streets and protested. Protests took place in Manhattan, Boston, Oakland, California, Chicago, Minneapolis, Baltimore, and several in Washington, DC. At one point on December 4, 2014, Streamers in New York, Boston, Chicago, and Oakland broadcasted compelling footage from these demonstrations.

As always, streamers straddled a line between documenting resistance and fetishizing a politics and aesthetics of endless spectacle and reaction. A popular livestream account called "globalrevolution.tv" posted a split screen stream that combined some of these livestreams protests in New York, Boston, and Chicago all happening simultaneously. People in each of those cities marched through the chilly nights repeating chants of "I can't breathe" and "Black Lives Matter." The protests involved various local organizations and as well as non-organization-affiliated people who felt moved to take to the streets in protest and anger.

WATCHING STREAMS AS PARTICIPATION

The streams of the Black Lives Matter protests that I watched on December 4 and 5 were on the Ustream, or Livestream online web apps and I connected to them primarily through Twitter ("Justice for All Protests March WATCH LIVESTREAM VIDEO," 2014). I found these through hashtags such as #BlackLivesMatter #EricGarner, #I Can'tBreathe. Other viewers may have found them by following Twitter accounts such as or @OpFerguson, @Deray @Netaaaaaaaa, @GlobalRevLive, @StopMotionSolo, or eventually the Twitter accounts of local and mainstream news networks.

However, watching these protests as livestreams for several hours was a fundamentally different televisual experience than watching looping snippets of cable news footage of these events with pundits offering commentary. In the livestream there was no studio, and no orgy of animated brand graphics. There was the annoying experience of periodic ad-interruptions that forced a consistent 30-second acknowledgment of the various forces that were monetizing these events, but there were no cuts back and forth between pundits. Instead, what we saw was hundreds of people together in the street, blocking traffic, confronting traffic, publicly mourning, and interrupting the unreflective and acquiescent march forward of everyday life. What I saw activated memories of my own experiences of physically being at protests. Comments in the stream thanked the streamer for being there. After watching 45 minutes of this kind of "slow media," those who had watched had a shared sense of virtual presence with the streamer and with the protesters.

Like many viewers, I watched these streams to connect to a community of people who shared my sense of outrage and urgency regarding this verdict.

I first heard about the grand jury decision not to indict Pantaleo when a colleague informed me of this at work. An acute feeling of panic seized my insides and I felt disoriented. I sat down in my office to regain my own breath, as CNN broadcasted Garner being placed in a chokehold repeatedly. At that moment, the vast majority of colleagues and students on my floor and on my campus were carrying on the daily business of academic life, unaware of this. I wasn't sure what to do with these emotions or how to contribute. Tuning into the streams of these Black Lives Matter protests was therefore part of my individual process of emotionally coming to terms with the implications of this verdict, but it was also a collective mode of activist inspiration, activist networking, and political education. The video of Garner's death, the decision not to indict, and my subsequent feeling of isolation had all felt like alienating, dystopic indicators of the current state of social justice. But *seeing* the diverse group of thousands of citizens taking to the streets in response in several cities across the United States created a more empowering kind of shared experience.

These shared experiences related to viewing and broadcasting also contributed to movement community building by creating a context for certain kinds of interpersonal relationships. One such experience happened during an organizing meeting in Columbia, South Carolina. The meeting was held in response to the assault by officer Ben Fields of an African American student at Spring Valley High School. While the meeting brought together a variety of different individual citizens and actors, one group there had been protesting under the Black Lives Matter banner. After the meeting was over, a man and woman approached me and asked if I ran the unrulysubjects Ustream channel. I confirmed that that was indeed my stream. Both the man and woman told me that they had watched my streaming of the KKK rally at the statehouse and some of my other streams and found them compelling and eye-opening. I had never met these people and now meeting them for the first time I felt that we shared something. The connection that we had was not the same connection that I had to other people that were physically at the protest. In some ways it was a closer kind of connection because they had experienced the protest through my camera, my narration and my broadcast choices. This sense of connection made the work of organizing easier in the new context.

Another moment that demonstrated the "networkness" of Black Lives Matter/Livestream relationships happened during a general protest of police brutality in New York on December 24, 2014. We were on 5th avenue listening to a young dreadlocked African-American woman wearing black clothing as we prepared to March. As a key organizer and leader of the March, she confidently and loudly gave instructions to the crowd through a bullhorn. I had begun my livestream and was holding my camera up recording this woman, the crowd around us, and the shopping that the protest would soon aim to interrupt. A gentleman who appeared to be in his late twenties who was also apparently streaming moved directly next me. He tapped me on the shoulder and said "are you catchatweetdown?" Yes I said nodding. He was referring to my Twitter hashtag. I didn't recognize him. Looking around, I asked "How did you know that? "I'm @Stopmotionsolo and I follow your streams sometimes. Nice to meet you. I recognized his handle and had watched his streams many times as well. Once again we didn't know each other and this was a relatively rare instance of streaming in NY (since I live in South Carolina). But because I had seen his streams I felt that we shared something. One reason that he took note of me was because he, as a person of color streamer, was making efforts to keep track of and help promote other streamers who were people of color since there were relatively few of us who streamed on a regular basis. I saw him at many other New York-based protests and continue to watch his streams periodically.

COUNTER-SURVEILLANCE AND COMMUNITY

The idea that human beings can and should organize collectively to protect the most vulnerable members of society is central in the language and ethos of the Black Lives Matter network. It is also enacted as a tactical obligation for protesters at specific events. Many of the dedicated streamers that I worked with accepted some version of this obligation as part of our vocational code.

During a protest that took place in June 2015 after Dylan Roof's shooting of nine African-Americans at Emmanuel A.M.E church, I stood at a gathering of 300+ people in a park in downtown Charleston, preparing to livestream the Black Lives Matter march. The first person to speak was a young African American woman. Opening with a Yoruba prayer ritual that involved pouring of libations for the deceased, including the Charleston nine victims Despayne Middleton Doctor, Cynthia Hurd, Susie Jackson, Ethel Lance, Reverend Clementa Pinckney, Tywanza Sanders, The Rev Dr. Daniel Simmons Sr. Sharonda Coleman Singleton, Myra Thompson, and others killed by various kinds of violence, the activists then lead the crowd in the chanting of a phrase by Assata Shakur that has become a ritualistic within Black Lives Matter.

We have a duty to fight for our freedom.
We have a duty to win.
We must love each other and protect each other.
We have nothing to lose but our chains.

The crowd repeated this phrase several times, each time more loudly and with more conviction. I couldn't help but notice that the crowd—in attendance at an event that ~~was~~ explicitly bore the Black Lives Matter band, was at least 50 percent white. This was noteworthy in Charleston, South Carolina whose history of radical progressive organizing has never been a dominant cultural trend. Looking around the crowd as people of various ethnicities, genders, ages, political ideologies etc. spoke these words, it was clear that there was an effort to enact a utopian value of solidarity in the act of protest itself. (Of course, this uncharacteristic response also risked communicating the unfortunate implication that it is Black death rather than Black life that finally matters. Reverend William Barber of North Carolina's NAACP would point this out several months later at a different march in Charleston.)

As we prepared to march through the streets of Charleston, the phrase "we must love each other and protect each other" seemed to function as a tactical reminder as well as a broader ethic. As a streamer, the phrase "we must love each other and protect each other" meant some specific things to me. Since protesters are frequently accused of being violent, and law enforcement often used that violence—real or imagined—to justify arrest, use of force, and denial of the right to protest, I thought about the various ways that I might use my citizen journalism to protect the human and civil rights of all involved. This included a particular kind of vigilance about documenting policing practices and use of force incidents that might occur during the protest as well as providing a sense of the broader context.

This obligation had also been clear to me one evening during my first days in Ferguson. Various groups were marching up in the area of West Florrisant. One small group of about twenty protesters decided to walk from our current location at West Florrissant to 222 South Florrisant which was few miles away. Jon Ziegler and another streamer had a brief conversation about which one of us would walk with the streamers. It is quite possible that some layers of this decision making involved competitive negotiation based in their desire to carve out their own exclusive sites of coverage. However, this wasn't the language that was used, and it didn't seem to be the guiding ethic. Instead, the streamers that were present discussed factors like the lighting of the streets, the density of police presence and the location of their cars. The small community of dedicated streamers didn't work according to any formal organizational commitments. But there was a mutual understanding that it was best to have a streamer with every group of protesters where possible.

Ziegler and I chose to walk with the group while other streamers stayed on West Florrisant. The group marched on the right hand side of West Florissant close to the curb. About 10 to 15 minutes later, our group walked through a rather dark section of West Florrisant, with no lights for businesses and no street lights. We were now separate from the other protesters. Suddenly, blue and red police lights bathed the area as police pulled up and through bullhorn staccato, static drenched voices barked orders for us to move off the street

Figures 9.3 The Author Livestreams in Front of a Target in Ferguson During Protests in Saint Louis, Missouri.

and on to the sidewalk. Given that West Florrisant was a fairly wide avenue and that most protesters were already on the sidewalk, this seemed like an odd occasion for police intervention. Three police cars pulled up and six police officers got out of their cars. Two of them kept one hand on their weapons while others radioed for more back up. At that time, I was highly conscious of our isolation.

Jon walked in front of the police officers holding his camera up conspicuously. He attempted to put officers' faces and badges on camera. He narrated the scene for his viewers and then calmly asked why the police were harassing these protesters. He also filmed debates between protesters and the police that might potentially precede an arrest or use of excessive force. The protesters tolerated Jon's surveillance and in some cases seemed emboldened by the presence of cameras, becoming more vocal and defiant. Eventually, we continued walking with the police driving along side of us for five more minutes or so before moving on.

It would be naïve and reductionist to say that streaming was the only reason that no one was arrested or hurt during that incident. However, the presence of a camera also seemed to be one of several interacting factors in play. If nothing else, the camera gave the protesters a feeling that their act of resistance was visible to a broader audience, that there would be an accessible record of any violations of their rights.

Because streamers often blur the line between journalism and activism, the rules can be less clear when they face situations that are common in journalism. In the protection of civil rights or human rights when is the time to stop documenting and intervene in more direct ways?

I faced this dilemma during the Black Friday protests that I described in the beginning of this chapter.

Before entering the mall protest leaders warned that police in this county were particularly intolerant and prone to quickly engage use of force tactics. An hour or so of protest in the mall led to the gates being drawn on every store in the mall and shoppers being asked to leave. When the protest started, there had been few police present. As more police arrived, they delivered an ultimatum to the protesters that they/we could leave or be arrested. As we backed toward the mall exit, I continued to stream. The crowd was startled as a small black quadcopter surveillance drone appeared and flew erratically in the air above us. Backing up, I raised my phone to capture this. A police chief clearly frustrated with the deliberately slow pace of our retreat, explained that we had 2 minutes to leave or we would be arrested. The number of viewers of my stream began to climb rapidly from 150 to 200.

Roughly thirty seconds later, as we backed out of the first set of glass doors, a sweaty, muscle-bound, white police officer grabbed the arm of an African-American female protester. This officer's face had become increasingly wrinkled with anger at the situation throughout the protest and he seemed eager for an excuse to reassert his authority. I moved instinctively toward the woman, but then caught myself feeling torn between two conflicting instincts.

My first instinct was to physically prevent the officer from touching or arresting the woman. I feared for her safety and due process if she was arrested alone. I thought that perhaps if enough of us intervened, they would have to arrest all of us. But then I caught myself as I instinctively moved forward. I was also conscious that they were hundreds of people watching my stream and I recognized that this moment might illustrate the clear pattern of censorship of democratic protest by St. Louis area police. Ziegler's video evidence of an officer telling journalists "to go fuck yourself" had led to that officer's firing and become part of the Department of Justice investigation. I moved closer to the officer and held my camera up.

Letting go of the woman's arm the officer yelled "Get out now or you're going to be arrested!" Seeing this, a legal observer looked directly at the officer making sure to catch his eye. When the officer failed to respond, the legal observer became vocal. "Earlier, I heard you give them two minutes to leave. That's contradictory orders. Are you seriously going to do that right in front of me?" The woman looked at me in what I interpreted as a signal to keep filming even if she was arrested. Even if my phone was confiscated,

I was confident that viewers of the stream would share what they were seeing. I filmed even more conspicuously now making it clear to the officer that I was broadcasting all of this. Several other protesters held up their phones as well. I later found out that my stream had frozen about 6 minutes earlier. The officer let the woman go and the protesters exited the mall and then blocked the highway for another half hour.

CONCLUSIONS

Streamers provide a service that has been essential to the particular nature of movement and community building within the Black Lives Matter Network. Journalists that are willing to make these sacrifices are easily able to find their place in a movement driven by direct action and efforts to make ongoing resistance visible, attending events on short notice, without the consent of a larger corporate media organizations, and distribute fairly clear, archivable, shareable, live video. Additionally, streaming creates experiences of decentralized, synchronous being together in moments of resistance, counter-surveillance, and solidarity. It is difficult to quantify the full impact of this in terms of network building, awareness building, and morale.

But the practice poses a challenge for thinking about what constitutes a democratic, sustainable, form of media production that is responsive to the needs of social justice advocates. I Identify three primary concerns in this regard (in no particular order)

1. Streamers provide labor, media production talents, and absorb risks to personal safety while large technology and media companies, and advertisers profit from this sacrifice. The worry here is the way that the rhetoric of DIY and technology deployed by both technology corporations and protesters help to rationalize and continue a system where the most resourced actors profit from the unsustainable labor of the most vulnerable.
2. Closely related to this are problems of access related to production and viewership of streams. While streaming technology is now a built-in feature on Twitter, Facebook, YouTube, and the operating systems of many phones, one must still have a high end phone and an expensive data plan to produce or view streams. These economic barriers to accessibility should be considered alongside media ethics that want to create sustainable solutions to media production for the least resourced.
3. In contrast to the forms of liveness that one might find in more increasingly common quotidian uses of streaming in corporate network platforms, Black Lives Matter streamers frequently amplify both spectacles of protest, police use of force, and voices protest participants.

> This approach to documentation cuts many ways in a movement that is struggling to articulate a long-term political vision. Streaming can be complicit in compelling organizers into a seductive politics of reaction, and endless awareness raising. The pleasures of watching a stream in real time are partially related to the uncertainty and indeterminacy of how events will unfold. That uncertainty and anticipation includes the possibility that the viewer might witness a violation of human rights. In this context we can and should ask how we are being trained to look, analyze, and challenge complicated social problems as the camera tethers our attention to the relentless pace of the unfolding present. But it is also true that the aesthetics of streaming in the Black Lives Matter networks create the potential for diegetic political analysis onscreen and that prefigures similar instincts in analogous dimensions of our own subjective experience.

Given these concerns, social justice advocates should not consider streaming a replacement for the ideal of community-based institutions that can provide and argue for the funding, security, training of journalists and sustainable and equitable community access to content and production.

NOTES

1. Pheifer and Peck, "Aftermath of Fatal Falcon Heights Officer-Involved Shooting Captured on Video."
2. Dickinson, "Diamond Reynolds."
3. CBS/AP, "Ferguson, Missouri, Protests Seek Black Friday Shoppers' Attention."
4. At this point streaming applications such as Facebook, Periscope, or various phone-based applications were not yet available.
5. Trianni, "Protesters Hit With Tear Gas."
6. Patrick, "St. Ann Officer Removed after Pointing Gun, Threatening Ferguson Protesters."
7. *DIY Citizenship: Critical Making and Social Media.*
8. Garza, "A Herstory of the #BlackLivesMatter Movement by Alicia Garza."
9. David Gauntlett, *Making is Connecting*. John Wiley & Sons, 2013. p. 56.
10. Ibid.
11. Matt Ratto and Megan Boler, *DIY Citizenship: Critical Making and Social Media*. MIT Press, 2014.
12. Wolfson, *Digital Rebellion: The Birth of the Cyber Left.*
13. This issue of police using livestream as a surveillance mechanism is an important issue that deserves fuller treatment.
14. Cullors, "We Started A Network."

15. McLaughlin, "The Dynamic History Of #BlackLivesMatter Explained."
16. Sanburn, "Behind the Video of Eric Garner's Deadly Confrontation With New York Police."

WORKS CITED

CBS/AP. "Ferguson, Missouri, Protests Seek Black Friday Shoppers' Attention." News. *Cbsnews.com*, November 28, 2014. http://www.cbsnews.com/news/ferguson-missouri-protests-seek-black-friday-shoppers-attention/.

Cullors, Patrice. "Medium." Blog. *We Didn't Start a Movement, We Started A Network*, February 22, 2016. https://medium.com/@patrissemariecullorsbrignac/we-didn-t-start-a-movement-we-started-a-network-90f9b5717668#.76icsnrb5.

Dickinson, Caitlyn. "Diamond Reynolds: Castile's Gun Was 'Absolutely Not Visible' before Shooting Video." *Yahoo News*, July 11, 2016. https://www.yahoo.com/news/diamond-reynolds-castiles-gun-absolutely-000000446.html.

Garza, Alicia. "A Herstory of the #BlackLivesMatter Movement by Alicia Garza." *The Feminist Wire*, October 7, 2014. http://www.thefeministwire.com/2014/10/blacklivesmatter-2/.

Gauntlett, David. *Making Is Connecting*. John Wiley & Sons, 2013.

———. In *Making Is Connecting*, 56. John Wiley & Sons, 2013.

McLaughlin, Michael. "The Dynamic History Of #BlackLivesMatter Explained." News Blog. *The Huffington Post*, February 29, 2016. http://www.huffingtonpost.com/entry/history-black-lives-matter_us_56d0a3b0e4b0871f60eb4af5.

Patrick, Robert. "St. Ann Officer Removed after Pointing Gun, Threatening Ferguson Protesters." *Stltoday.com*, August 20, 2014. http://www.stltoday.com/news/local/metro/st-ann-officer-removed-after-pointing-gun-threatening-ferguson-protesters/article_3854ed72-a14c-5b8e-b32f-ddb35de94803.html.

Pheifer, Pat, and Claude Peck. "Aftermath of Fatal Falcon Heights Officer-Involved Shooting Captured on Video." *Star Tribune*, July 7, 2016. http://www.startribune.com/aftermath-of-officer-involved-shooting-captured-on-phone-video/385789251/.

Ratto, Matt and Megan Boler. *DIY Citizenship: Critical Making and Social Media*. MIT Press, 2014.

Sanburn, Josh. "Behind the Video of Eric Garner's Deadly Confrontation With New York Police." *Time*, July 22, 2014. http://time.com/3016326/eric-garner-video-police-chokehold-death/.

Trianni, Francesca. "Watch: Protesters Hit With Tear Gas and Rubber Bullets During Ferguson Unrest Francesca Trianni @frantrianni Aug. 14, 2014." *Time*, August 14, 2014. http://time.com/3111829/ferguson-tear-gas-rubber-bullets-protests/.

Wolfson, Todd. *Digital Rebellion: The Birth of the Cyber Left*. University of Illinois Press, 2014.

Part IV

POPULAR CULTURE AND UTOPIA

Chapter 10

Making Do and Mending—Domestic Television in the Age of Austerity

Kirstie Allsopp's Kirstie's Homemade Homes

Deborah Philips

The 'Make Do and Mend' movement was a literal 'home front' campaign in Britain, organised by the British Board of Trade from 1941 as a response to the need for rationing during the Second World War. In his foreword to the *Make Do and Mend* booklet, the Chair of the Board of Trade thanked its readers 'for the way in which you have accepted clothes rationing. You know how it has saved much-needed shipping space, manpower and materials, and so assisted our war effort'.[1] The Make Do and Mend campaign was overseen by the Board of Trade with a 'Make Do and Mend' Advisory Panel. It was supported by sewing classes across the nation; a Board of Trade leaflet exhorted 'housewives' to 'Make the most of your sewing time—by taking your work along to your nearest Make-do and Mend class. . . . Your local Evening Institute, Technical College or Woman's Organisation is probably running a class now'. The advice offered in their booklet included sections on 'To Make Clothes Last Longer', 'Turn Out and Renovate' and 'Unpick and Knit Again'. The instructions on darning stockings and tea towels, reinforcing trousers and sheets, were given from a sense of national emergency rather than from any sense of sewing or knitting as craft activities. Silk and nylon were now required for military purposes, and from 1941 until 1949 clothing was rationed. The Board of Trade advice was supplemented by items in women's magazines and on BBC radio. *Woman's Hour* featured regular slots on making do and mending, where 'Mrs Sew and Sew' encouraged households to save clothing coupons with 'Patriotic Patches' and to 'Try and make do for the present with the clothes you have'. The BBC developed two programmes in support of the campaign, *Beating the Coupon* and *New Clothes for Old*.[2] This was a campaign that was not about renovation as a lifestyle choice, it was a government led programme that required the nation to desist from consumption.

'Make Do and Mend' references a period in British history in which the nation triumphantly united in austerity measures against a common enemy. The British Conservative led coalition government of 2010 ushered in a new 'age of austerity' as a response to the financial crash of 2008. Both the then Prime Minister David Cameron and Chancellor George Osborne invoked the term in their pre-election speeches, promising that they would bring 'Progressive reform in an age of austerity'.[3] George Osborne's statement to the Conservative Party conference, 'we're all in this together',[4] along with the choice of the term of 'austerity', referenced the years of rationing that continued after the Second World War, and appealed to a national interest in the face of a global recession.

The Channel 4 day time series *Make Do and Mend* was first broadcast in 2010, and appeared in the context of this new austerity. It directly referenced the war time Make Do and Mend campaign in its title, and addressed its audience as a national body that could learn to be frugal from television 'experts' who would advise on how 'thrift' could be fun, as the Channel 4 online publicity put it:

> We all want to save money, but just how much penny pinching can you go in for without missing out? Brand new weekday series Make Do & Mend follows three money-saving experts proving that being thrifty can also be fun. . . . the Make Do & Mend gurus give hands-on practical moneysaving advice to people across the UK.[5]

An episode of the Channel 4 fashion programme *How to Look Good Naked* and a new programme on the same channel, *Kirstie's Homemade Home,* both referred to the Make Do and Mend campaign in their sub-titles. In the wake of the financial crisis, television turned to austerity measures; if this was not explicit, popular television programming had to recognise that unalloyed consumption could no longer be celebrated without some qualification. In 2012 the UK government annual Family Spending Survey reported that household spending on clothes and furniture had fallen as the price of fuel and heating had risen.[6] Making do and mending was not, in this new 'age of austerity' a life style choice, but for many an economic necessity.

In popular culture, 'Thrift' was now in vogue; in 2013, a festival of thrift was held in Darlington and attracted 25,000 visitors. The festival's curator, designer Wayne Hemingway explained its appeal:

> The generation coming through now is the first that is worse off than their parents and yet we continue with a culture of mass consumption . . . Thrift isn't just a flash in the pan, it's a genuine response to the economy and the state of the world that is creaking under mass-consumption.[7]

Programmes such as *Location, Location, Location,* and *Property Ladder,* which had once advocated investment in rental properties and which had dominated primetime slots on television for a decade, now came to seem inappropriate as a response to the economic situation. The global financial crisis had been bound up in subprime mortgage lending, and exhorting television audiences to invest in property no longer seemed judicious. A generation of property programmes had once been very positive about the investment potential of housing, but now their presenters turned their skills to new kinds of television. *Property Ladder,* which first appeared in Britain in 2001, had followed subjects who were investing in buy to let property, but saw its final episode in 2009. The presenter, Sarah Beeny, is currently on television advising on repairs to broken down homes in *Country House Rescue* and *Help! My House is Falling Down.*

Location, Location, Location began in 2001, and has run ever since on Channel 4; (the series was initially accompanied by a book[8]) which advocated property as a secure investment. In 2002, the confidence of television property programmes was evident in the introduction's certainty that property was then a prudent and profitable financial venture:

> Every property bought should represent a long-term investment. . . . Putting money into property is increasingly being seen as a real alternative to investing in the stock market. It is possible not only to increase your capital growth but also to achieve high returns in rental income . . .
>
> Buy to Let . . . has been an area that has experienced extraordinary growth in both cities and less prosperous areas. Mortgage lenders have schemes that, thanks to low interest rates, have enabled many people to invest in this way.[9]

As the housing market slumped in the credit crisis of 2009, the 'plethora of mortgages'[10] that *Location, Location, Location* had once promised in its handbook were no longer so available to ordinary people, as house prices went on to balloon to unaffordable levels for many.

Kirstie's Homemade Home, first broadcast in 2009, was presented by Kirstie Allsopp, best known as a presenter of *Location, Location, Location,* who now repositioned herself as a champion of home crafts. *Kirstie's Homemade Home* was recognised at the time as a 'credit crunch makeover show' and as a response to the new austerity; a columnist in *The Times* noted:

> This recession has been all about resourcefulness. Writers have turned from diet manuals to thrift books with beautiful sepia covers, festooned with ribbons and pins. iPods have been swapped for sewing machines and tonight Kirstie's new programme on knitting your own home begins on Channel 4. (Kirstie's Homemade Home, 8pm.) Craftiness is back in style.[11]

In an interview in the *Times* newspaper, Allsopp herself claimed that her move to craft and homespun interiors was in part inspired by public reaction to the financial crisis:

> Everyone started blaming me for being one of the people who had helped the housing market get out of control and I thought that I had to do something to help people with their houses on the downturn. So this programme will show you how to decorate on a budget.[12]

This was a somewhat disingenuous claim; Allsopp had already published a series of craft books in 2006, well before the financial crash, *Moving Sense*, a collection of craft kits and manuals which was accompanied by a range of home accessories. *Kirstie's Homemade Home* was not a new programming idea either, *Home Front* which ran from 1992 to 2000 on the BBC (a precursor to *Changing Rooms*), had regularly featured sequences with craftspeople demonstrating their skills, as does *Kirstie's Homemade Home*.

The first series of *Kirstie's Homemade Home* featured the renovation of Allsopp's own second home, 'Meadowgate' (bought with her partner, a property developer); a Christmas series devoted to craft, *Homemade Christmas* was also set in the house. In the book of the series Allsopp describes Meadowgate as a derelict house that she has painstakingly restored herself:

> . . . what really excited me about Meadowgate was that it presented the ultimate blank canvas. With five bedrooms, two bathrooms, a grown-up sitting room, a playroom for the kids, and a fantastic family kitchen that works as the hub of the home, it was the perfect house form to create my own dream interior.[13]

This is a considerably larger and grander house than most of her readers and viewers will ever inhabit, and its renovation was achieved with considerable backing from Channel 4. There is no mention in the book or television series of the support (financial and otherwise) given by Channel 4, nor was there any acknowledgement that this was a house being prepared for the rental market. The house is available for rent thorough the agency 'Classic Cottages', which advises on its website that: 'Meadowgate is enchanting and inspired Kirstie to fill it with love, and she feels confident that guests will enjoy this unique and delightful Devonshire bolthole' (www. classic.co.uk). Set within 'its own enclosed grounds', and able to accommodate fourteen people, this is not a family holiday home, but a business investment.

In the second series, Allsopp brought the experience of restoring Meadowgate together with her considerable cultural capital to bear on the more modest homes of 'ordinary' people featured in the programme. As the *Radio Times* put it: 'After her success in transforming her Devon cottage, Kirstie

Allsopp . . . helps a Wolverhampton couple sprinkle vintage magic on their shabby Victorian house'.[14]

This series of *Kirstie's Homemade Home* (first broadcast in November 2010) regularly featured a traditional artisanal trade or a 'feminine' craft skill (the crafts are strictly gendered on the programme, it is invariably women who sew and knit). The use of blacksmiths, glassblowers, quilters, and seamstresses conjured up a nostalgic world of preindustrial production—and one that chimed neatly with the prelapsarian tendencies of the then new coalition government. It also validated the ambitions of the Conservative Big Society advocated by Phillip Blond, in which community work is seen as voluntary rather than financially rewarded. In his role of reinventing the Conservatives as the party of the Big Society, Phillip Blond described a long list of Britain's woes:

> Something is seriously wrong with Britain. . . . We all know the symptoms: increasing fear, lack of trust and abundance of suspicion, long-term increase in violent crime, loneliness, recession, depression, private and public debt, family break-up, divorce . . .[15]

In its championing of the 'vintage' and craft against the modernity of mass production *Kirstie's Homemade Home* offers a fantasy retreat from a contemporary world of the global and the urban in which these 'symptoms' are all too apparent. The sepia and the sewing machine invoked by the *Radio Times* are signifiers of a nostalgia that repudiates the metropolitan and the technological. The taste for nostalgic commodities has been recognised as a marketing phenomenon; in 2013, the marketing officer for Asda[16] pointed to an observed connection between the recession and consumer demand for traditional products:

> We see people coming back to old favourites. A lot of the big bets that we are investing in . . . are very traditional. Whenever you go through a tough economic time, customers generally pull back to how things used to be when they were growing up.[17]

Kirstie Allsopp presents television viewers with such 'old favourites', and takes them back to a childhood of hand crafting. Meadowfield is apparently situated in a world that is constructed as an English organic community, in which craft traditions are unbroken and handed down from generation to generation. An idealized rural community is evoked in the refashioning of the house in each programme, the home represented as a refuge against the assaults of late capitalism. This imagined rural retreat was also a regular trope in the spin off property programme *Relocation, Relocation, Relocation* (also presented by Allsopp), in which families took refuge from the strain of urban living by finding a dream house in the country. Diane Negra has pointed out that:

> The intense domesticity of postfeminism is not a historic or economic coincidence. Rather, it appears as a manifestation of anxieties about atomization and dislocation at a time when social connections are thin on the ground, where long haul moves for corporate careers are rather common and where . . . fantasies of being safely situated at home and in a hometown community proliferate widely.[18]

In her book, published in 2010 as an accompaniment to the Channel 4 series, Allsopp describes the world of craft in terms of that fantasy:

> It is about a journey into a world full of dedicated and talented people who make beautiful things, both traditional and modern. Their commitment to the wonderful crafting heritage we have in the UK is proof that handmade British things are here to stay . . .[19]

This is a United Kingdom in which the blacksmith, the pewter caster, and the cabinet maker all appear to be within easy reach, a view of England which refuses to acknowledge that the majority of the population live in cities and that most people do not work with their hands. The domestic front is here seen to represent a cocoon against the hard winds of recession and global economics. Richard Sennett warned in *The Fall of Public Man* that: 'Intimate vision is induced in proportion as the public domain is abandoned as empty'.[20] The 'intimate vision' of the vintage home appeared in Britain precisely at the moment when the public domain was being abandoned for a conservative vision of the Big Society.

Eliane Glaser has also identified the rise of 'craft' and the fashion for 'vintage' as a defence against the sweeping developments of global capital and corporate culture. She cites the promotion of handcrafted goods and 'shabby chic' as symptomatic of a search for 'authenticity' in an increasingly alienated world:

> Authenticity is . . . contemporary culture's preferred style. Supermarkets sell fruit and veg in rustic wooden baskets. High street shops hand you your purchases in brown paper bags . . . Digitisation and mass production are shielded by this artfully distressed trend . . . The onward march of global capitalism is obscured by the ramshackle parade of knit-your own and grow-your-own. The cupcake is hegemony's new best friend.
>
> So it does a lot of political work, the shabby-chic retrospection. As well as lending an alibi to the corporatisation of our culture, it bolsters the social inequalities created by Austerity Britain.[21]

In its championing of 'vintage', its celebration of the local and of craft ornaments and furniture, *Kirstie's Homemade Home* represents such a retreat from mass production and from the world of alienated urbanism. There is a constant tension throughout the series between the championing of craft skills and the promotion of craft work as a bargain for the consumer. Allsopp writes of a rug maker who appeared in the series:

> She's the real deal, an artisan who adores her craft and has been developing for more than 27 years. And you have to love it, because like so many of the crafts I've tried for *Kirstie's Homemade Home*, these artists aren't in it for the money. Hilary makes absolutely beautiful rugs that she sells from as little as £150. I know that's not peanuts, but when you consider that it takes her a week to make one rug, you soon realise that she's working well below the minimum wage . . . If you're looking for a new rug, remember the Hilarys of the UK (the few that are left, that is).[22]

There is an inability here to make the connection between the low cost of the rugs with the loss of such artisanal work; that the maker is working 'below the minimum wage' is not Allsopp's concern, for Hilary is an artist, and so 'not in it for the money'.

For Kirstie Allsopp, her own 'passion' (her term) for craft and home making is not understood in any way as a commercial enterprise, but as an expression of family love:

> Sewing is the ultimate in 'make do and mend', and there's no better way to make savings than by learning how to stitch. But it's not all about saving money. Taking the time to sew something can be an expression of love and care, and can also be a refuge from the crazy world.[23]

Richard Sennett has argued that such retrenchment into the personal and the domestic, the 'refuge from the crazy world', cannot offer any real critique of contemporary problems:

> All too often, what is 'self-evidently wrong' about a social system is self-evident precisely because the critique fits nicely into, and does little damage to the system as a whole . . . the celebration of territorial community against the evils of impersonal, capitalist urbanism quite comfortably fits into the larger system, because it leads to a logic of local defence against the outside world, rather than a challenge to the workings of that world.[24]

A popular television programme such as *Kirstie's Homemade Home* is clearly not what Sennett has in mind here, but nonetheless it can be understood as a contribution to a discourse of 'the celebration of territorial community';

it shares the logic of a local defence, an insistence on the personal and the rural, that does not in any way challenge the current political formation.

Kirstie Allsopp's series and her book exude an authority and confidence in her own taste, while she does acknowledge that she belongs to a world of cultural capital, she considerably underplays her own privileges:

> I don't profess to be an expert on interior design, but more than a decade of looking at houses while working on *Location, Location, Location* and *Relocation, Relocation, Relocation*, plus my time at *Country Living* magazine, as well as growing up surrounded by people who work in the worlds of antiques and interiors has definitely had its effects on me . . . Most importantly, I've learned to be confident about my taste . . .[25]

In an interview with the *Radio Times* to promote the second series, Allsopp was keen to stress her own focus on thrift: 'Buying second-hand is incredibly important . . . I mean, my father . . . spent a lifetime flogging second hand goods. And heirlooms are wonderful'.[26] Allsopp neglects to say (although the interviewer reminds us) that her father is Lord Allsopp, a former chairman of Christie's antique auction house (where she was first employed in interior design), and that the second hand goods that he was 'flogging' were hardly the stuff of car boot and jumble sales. Kirstie Allsopp is the daughter of a Baronet, she was public school educated, her partner is a property developer, she owns houses in London, East Devon, and Cornwall. These facts are not her fault, but while she claims to understand and share in the privations of the new austerity, she is herself from an immensely privileged background. Kirstie Allsopp can take for granted a heritage of both economic and cultural capital, in which antique (rather than 'vintage') furniture and pictures are part of family tradition. Angela McRobbie has identified the phenomenon of a privileged woman sharing her knowledge on popular television as a post-feminist trend[27]:

> . . . it is not without irony that we now see so many upper middle-class women trying to earn their own living by drawing from their own store of cultural capital, by in effect flogging it on the market-place of populist television. (It is surely a bit like selling off the family silver.)[28]

In 2011, a newspaper report noted the fashion for craft across the United Kingdom: '. . . a trend that has seen craft centres spring up across the UK, offering an ever-widening variety of courses from quilting to lampshade making, Fair Isle knitting to linocut printing'.[29] These courses were invariably run by women, and those responsible had all once been professionals who had held careers as lawyers and journalists. Kirstie Allsopp is only one among many contemporary career women who have, in the context of austerity Britain, reinvented themselves as professional homemakers. Tania Lewis has identified the:

> . . . popular culture turn to domesticity and in particular the 'domestic nostalgia' associated with figures such as Martha Stewart and Nigella Lawson, such trends . . . dovetail with calls by US cultural conservatives for a return to family values . . . reality television offers a plethora of contradictory images of home and personal life, where the complexity of shifting gender roles often tends to be reduced to questions of personal responsibility and lifestyle 'choice' and where the realities of domestic labor and the socioeconomic factors underpinning people's lifestyles are glossed over.[30]

That 'glossing over' is very evident in the representation of Kirstie Allsopp as a television presenter, she is yet another figure of 'domestic nostalgia', her considerable cultural capital and commercial interests are resolutely underplayed in the programme, in a mystification of professional and commercial interests masked by an emphasis on domesticity and nostalgia.

It is easy to berate Allsopp for her poshness, but she is one among (and a supporter of[31]) a breed of the new 'toffs' who present themselves as 'just like us'; with George Osborne, then the British Chancellor, she claims that 'we are all in this together'. Like a contemporary Lady Bountiful, Allsopp denies her own class and professional status, but instead presents herself as an amateur who is sharing her largesse and 'confidence' with the subjects in her programme. For the participants in her programme who do not come from such privilege, such as the Wolverhampton couple whose home she transformed, she can 'sprinkle vintage magic' and distribute her taste and cultural capital.

While repudiating her own professional expertise, Allsopp displays all the qualities of the contemporary entrepreneur; she is a successful business woman, with a line in home furnishings, gift-ware and books, while also operating a rental business, a property finding service, and acting as an after dinner speaker.[32] She is seen on television as spending time and effort for family and friends, but she has a significant financial stake in promoting craft work; she has produced a series of books and commercial craft making kits, the Kirstie Allsopp Craft Kits Range.

Allsopp belongs to the group of feminised 'cultural intermediaries' identified by McRobbie:

> The new cultural intermediaries are no longer so predominantly 'gentlemen and scholars', as Bourdieu described . . . They are now likely to be a 'society girls' and 'educated girls', with the former imparting advice and guidance, sometimes with a sneer and always with casual elegance, and in unhurried ways . . .[33]

McRobbie is here invoking the 'society girls' Trinny and Susannah of *What Not to Wear*, which ran on the BBC between 2001 and 2007. Allsopp is another 'society girl' with an aristocratic background, (by her own admission) she is not an 'educated girl', but she does impart advice and guidance derived from her experience as an upmarket estate agent. While the programme claims to vaunt the intrinsic value of the handmade and of craft, Kirsty Allsopp herself has used these domestic skills, combined with her considerable cultural capital, to develop an empire in property and consumer goods. *Kirstie's Homemade Home* promotes craft work as an entertaining hobby and family centred activity, but elides the fact that this is a lifestyle that requires considerable work, and expense.

Kirstie Allsopp's television persona reconciles the contradictions of two opposing ideas of contemporary femininity, she is a professional entrepreneur while simultaneously she manifests all the attributes of traditional femininity, a phenomenon that Janice Winship has termed 'The Domestic Face of Enterprise'.[34] Allsopp has reconfigured the 'domestic goddess' (a term popularised by Nigella Lawson's 2000 book *How to be a Domestic Goddess*), in a new formation for the age of austerity. While she presents craft and homemade artefacts to her audience as manifestations of familial love and homemaking, she herself has turned domesticity into a business enterprise. Allsopp can be understood as one of the 'corporate housewives' that Brunsdon and Spiegel identified in 2008:

> The lifestyle shows have . . . spawned a new contradictory figure - the corporate housewife exemplified by media mavens Martha Stewart, Delia Smith, Rachel Ray and more. With huge fandoms, these women wield power across media platforms and turn homemaking skills into media empires, making them in some critics' views postfeminist figures *par excellence*[35]

It is significant that these 'media empires' are (with the possible exception of Martha Stewart, whose empire was very publically embroiled in an insider trading scandal for which she was jailed in 2004) invisible on television. Kirsty, Nigella, Delia, Trinny, and Susannah, popularly known and recognised by their first names alone, are very present on social media and in the press, and all are active on Twitter. They have put their names to ranges of clothing, bed linen and cooking implements, but their television personas do not permit that their entrepreneurial abilities go anywhere beyond the expertise they present on their programmes. Brunsdon has argued that this persona involves a repudiation of feminism:

> . . . a housewife who is not a housewife. In her media - the media that she controlled - she exists within the domestic arena, but this domestic is devoid of

> the boredom, repetition and frustration characterized as the housewife's lot by 1970s feminism.[36]

Kirsty Allsopp is 'charmed' and 'excited' by domestic crafts, domesticity is represented in her programmes as 'fun'. The family and the home become a defence against the perceived dangers of modernity; that it is the woman's role to be homemaker is assumed and remains entirely unchallenged. There is no sense that in the twenty-first century the 'home' need not be entirely the domain of the woman. Men are almost entirely absent from the programme, except in their working role as craftsmen and artisans; Allsopp's partner and children never appear, although Meadowfield is insistently described in the programme as a family home. There is a bifurcation of gender roles here, in which the 'masculine' profit making of property development is distanced from the loving creation of a domestic environment, which remains the woman's province.

Micki McGee has identified a similarly gendered nostalgia in contemporary American self-help manuals, she describes:

> . . . a robust sort of nostalgia that appeals to scriptural wisdom, traditional metaphors, and American myths . . . a longing for an elusive past where it is imagined, men were governed by virtue rather than limited self-interest . . . and women supported their men and raised their children, putting first things first.[37]

That elusive past and longing for tradition is not restricted to American myths, it is very apparent in the British-made *Kirstie's Homemade Homes*. The programme's taste for 1950s prints and furnishings extends to the supposed role of women[38] as homemakers in the postwar period. The Making Do and Mending of the wartime and the postwar period (the period that is most regularly evoked in the styling and fashions of the 'vintage') is reconfigured as a period of craft and homely design, rather than as the moment of consumer culture, white goods and convenience food. The postwar world of consumption is reconstructed as homely and sustainable in a nostalgic rewriting of history.

A craft show on prime time television may not in itself be a significant cultural phenomenon, but *Kirstie's Homemade Home* belongs to discourses of both taste and politics that look backward. There is a dominant current fashion for 'vintage' clothes and household items, notably in the designs of Cath Kidston (who is, perhaps not entirely coincidentally, Kirstie Allsopp's cousin), which reference the cabbage rose chintzes of the decade of the 1950s.

Jim McGuigan has devised the term 'Cool Capitalism'. He explains:

> Cool capitalism is largely defined by the incorporation of signs of disaffection and resistance into capitalism itself, thereby contributing to the reproduction of the system and reducing opposition to it. . . . A programme such as *The Apprentice* then, performs an ideological role in projecting the values of free market business in a seductive manner that disarms criticism.[39]

Although apparently a long way from the corporate ambition of *The Apprentice, Kirsty's Homemade Home* could be seen as a feminised version of 'Cool Capitalism'. Kirstie Allsopp's television persona is precisely 'a seductive manner that disarms criticism'. The programme also performs an 'ideological role', which is profoundly gendered. While she claims to vaunt the value of the second hand and the home made, Kirsty herself sells craft kits which provide the means to make candles, soap, dolls and stationery at considerable expense to the consumer.[40] Craft is not here about making do with scraps of material (patchwork sets are available from Kirsty Allsopp's range and from Cath Kidston) and desisting from consumption, but about buying into a lifestyle.

Kirstie's Homemade Home directly references the Make Do and Mend campaign of the Second World War in its subtitle—but it has not earned the slogan. While the Make Do and Mend campaign was a publicly supported, collective effort to save resources in the service of the national interest, the focus *of Kirstie's Homemade Home* is entirely on the private and the domestic, the response to the economic downturn is to retreat into the home, where it becomes the woman's responsibility to 'make do and mend' in order to rescue the family finances.

In 1980, Richard Sennett described the romanticisation of hearth and home at the moment of industrialization:

> . . . the fragments of the old life which capitalism was shattering were being picked up and treasured as objects all the more precious because they were so vulnerable, too delicate and sensitive to survive the onslaught of material progress. Just as the village was idealized as a community, the stable family . . . was idealized as the seat of virtue.
>
> . . . The citizen was offered pastiche as a landscape of authority. Images of a broken world were pasted upon a canvas, tinted, and then presented as what trust, security, protection, safety, ought to be.[41]

The domestic fantasy of *Kirstie's Homemade Home* is precisely such a pastiche, in which literally broken objects are presented as what ought to be, and offered as a means of securing trust and safety in the domestic sphere. This is not a feminist assertion of the power and skill of traditionally 'feminine' crafts, but rather a post-feminist response in Angela McRobbie's understanding of the term, which reasserts the feminine as belonging in the sphere of the home and the family.

Kirsty Allsopp reconciles the domesticity and safety of traditional femininity with a corporate career and an embrace of late capitalism. *Kirstie's Homemade Home* may be a response to public disaffection with the globalised and neoliberal economy, and it does present itself as a bulwark against a 'broken world', but simultaneously it promotes self-help, enterprise and consumption. In a sleight of hand, a commercial venture is represented as a private family hobby and a professional woman is recast as a role model for a form of feminine domesticity that is not far removed from John Ruskin's 1865 assertion of what a woman's role should be:

> . . . a woman has a personal work or duty, relating to her own home . . . to secure its order, comfort, and loveliness. . . the woman is to be within her gates, as the centre of order, the balm of distress and the mirror of beauty . . .[42]

NOTES

1. Hugh Dalton, 'Foreword', *Make Do and Mend.* London: Ministry of Information (first published 1943), 1.
2. Asa Briggs, *The History of Broadcasting in the United Kingdom, Vol.III: The War of Words.* Oxford: Oxford University Press, 1995, 506.
3. George Osborne, speech, August 11, 2009, www.conservatives.com.
4. George Osborne, speech to the Conservative Party conference 2009, www.news.bbc.co.uk, October 6, 2009.
5. www.Channel 4. com. December 2010.
6. www.ons.gov.uk, December 2012.
7. Wayne Hemingway, quoted in Kim Stoddardt, 'Selling thrift by the pound'. *The Guardian*, September 28, 2013, p. 1.
8. The book, *Location, Location, Location: The Complete Guide to Buying and Selling Your Home* was ghost written by Fanny Blake, it was published 'in association with Kirstie Allsopp and Phil Spencer', the programme's presenters.
9. Fanny Blake, *Location, Location, Location: The Complete Guide to Buying and Selling Your Home.* London: Channel 4 Books, 2002.
10. Ibid., x.
11. Alice Thomson, 'Why Kirstie Allsopp's Kirstie's Homemade Home is my idea of hell', *The Times,* April 16, 2009.
12. Interview with Kirstie Allsopp, *The Times,* April 11, 2009.
13. Kirstie Allsopp, *Kirstie's Homemade Home,* ed. Lisa McCann. London: Hodder & Stoughton, 2010, 7.
14. *Radio Times*, October 30–November 5, 2010.
15. Phillip Blond, *Red Tory: How Left and Right have Broken Britain and How we Can Fix It.* London: Faber and Faber, 2010.

16. Asda is the British division of the American company Walmart.

17. Stephen Smith quoted in *The Observer*, November 17, 2013.

18. Diana Negra, *What a Girl Wants: Fantasizing the Reclamation of Self in Post-Feminism*. London: Routledge, 2009, 134.

19. Allsopp, 8.

20. Richard Sennett, *The Fall of Public Man*. Cambridge: Cambridge University Press, 1976, 12.

21. Eliane Glaser, 'Why Cameron's meat and potato act sticks in my craw'. *The Guardian*, March 30, 2012, p. 36.

22. Allsopp, 12.

23. Ibid., 96.

24. Sennett, 295.

25. Allsopp, 12 .

26. Rosie Millard, 'Her Indoors' *Radio Times* October 30–November 5, 2010, 22–23.

27. Other examples would include the 'teachers' of *Ladette to Lady*, broadcast from 2005, and Trinny Woodall and Susannah Constantine of *What Not to Wear*, broadcast from 2001.

28. Angela McRobbie, *The Aftermath of Feminism: Gender, Culture and Social Change*. London: Sage Publications, 2009, 143.

29. Esther Addley, 'Crafty Consumers roll out the dough'. *The Guardian*, December 10, 2011, p. 14.

30. Tania Lewis, 'Life Coaches, Style Mavens, and Design Gurus: Everyday Experts on Reality Television', in *A Companion to Reality Television*, ed. Laurie Ouellette, 402–420. Oxford: Wiley Blackwell, 2014.

31. Allsopp was a Conservative Party policy advisor on housing (news.bbc.co.uk, May 8, 2008).

32. See www. speakerscorner.co.uk.

33. McRobbie, 143.

34. Janice Winship, 'The impossibility of *Best*', in *Come On Down? Popular Media Culture in Post-War Britain*, eds. Dominic Strinati and Stephen Wagg, 82–115. London: Routledge, 1992.

35. Charlotte Brunsdon and Lynn Spiegel, 'Introduction', in *Feminist Television Criticism: A Reader*, Second edition. Milton Keynes: Open University Press, 2008, 1–19.

36. Charlotte Brunsdon, 'The Feminist in the Kitchen: Martha, Martha and Nigella' in *Feminism in Popular Culture*, eds. Joanne Hollows and Rachel Moseley, 41–56. Oxford: Berg, 2006.

37. Micki McGee, *Self-Help, Inc. Makeover Culture in American Life*. Oxford: Oxford University Press, 2005, 6.

38. This understanding of women's role in the 1950s has been challenged by feminist scholars, including Elizabeth Wilson in *Only Halfway to Paradise: Women in Postwar Britain: 1945–1968* (Tavistock Publications, London, 1980) and Deborah Philips and Ian Haywood, *Brave New Causes*, Cassell, 1998.

39. Jim McGuigan, *Cool Capitalism*. London: Pluto Books, 2009, 129.

40. See www. hobbycraft.co.uk/kirstie-allsopp.

41. Richard Sennett, *Authority*. London: Secker and Warburg, 1980, 50–51.
42. John Ruskin, 'Of Queen's Gardens', *Sesame and Lilies* (1865). New York: H.M.Caldwell & Co., 1902, 173.

BIBLIOGRAPHY

Addley, Esther. 'Crafty Consumers roll out the dough'. *The Guardian,* December 10, 2011.

Allsopp, Kirstie, ed. McCann, Lisa. *Kirstie's Homemade Home*. London: Hodder & Stoughton, 2010.

Blake, Fanny. *Location, Location, Location: The Complete Guide to Buying and Selling Your Home*. London: Channel 4 Books, 2002.

Blond, Phillip. *Red Tory: How Left and Right have Broken Britain and How we Can Fix It*. London: Faber and Faber, 2010.

Briggs, Asa. *The History of Broadcasting in the United Kingdom, Vol.III: The War of Words*. Oxford: Oxford University Press, 1995.

Brunsdon, Charlotte. 'The Feminist in the Kitchen: Martha, Martha and Nigella'. In eds. Hollows, Joanne and Moseley, Rachel, *Feminism in Popular Culture*. Oxford: Berg, 2006.

Brunsdon, Charlotte and Lynn Spiegel. 'Introduction' to *Feminist Television Criticism: A Reader,* Second edition. Milton Keynes: Open University Press, 2008.

Dalton, Hugh. 'Foreword' to *Make Do and Mend*. London: Ministry of Information (1943).

Glaser, Eliane. 'Why Cameron's meat and potato act sticks in my craw'. *The Guardian*, March 30, 2012.

Graham Alison, 'Interior Motives'. *Radio Times* April 11–17, 2009.

Lewis, Tania. 'Life Coaches, Style Mavens, and Design Gurus. Everyday Experts on Reality Television'. In ed. Ouellette, Laurie, *A Companion to Reality Television*. Oxford: Wiley Blackwell, 2014.

McGee, Micki. *Self-Help, Inc. Makeover Culture in American Life*. Oxford: Oxford University Press, 2005.

McGuigan, Jim. *Cool Capitalism*. London: Pluto Books, 2009.

McRobbie, Angela. 'Post-feminism and popular culture: Bridget Jones and the new gender regime'. In eds. Curran, James, and Morley, David. *Media and Cultural Theory*. London: Routledge, 2006.

———. *The Aftermath of Feminism: Gender, Culture and Social Change*. London: Sage Publications, 2009.

Millard, Rosie. 'Her Indoors'. *Radio Times,* October 30–November 5, 2010.

Negra, Diana. *What a Girl Wants: Fantasizing the Reclamation of Self in Postfeminism*. London: Routledge, 2009.

Ruskin, John. 'Of Queen's Gardens'. In *Sesame and Lilies* (1865). New York: H. M.Caldwell & Co., 1902.

Sennett, Richard. *The Fall of Public Man*. Cambridge: Cambridge University Press, 1976.

———. *Authority*. London: Secker and Warburg, 1980.
Stoddardt, Kim. 'Selling thrift by the pound'. *The Guardian*, September 28, 2013.
Thomson, Alice. 'Why Kirstie Allsopp's Kirstie's Homemade Home is my idea of hell'. *The Times*, April 16, 2009.
Winship, Janice 'The impossibility of *Best*'. In eds. Strinati, Dominic and Wagg, *Stephen Come On Down? Popular Media Culture in Post-War*. Britain, London: Routledge, 1992.

Chapter 11

Everyday Utopias, Technological Dystopias, and the Failed Occupation of the Global Modern

Dwell *Magazine Meets* Unhappy Hipsters

Joan Faber McAlister and Giorgia Aiello

At the turn of the twenty-first century, a new publication appealed to affluent consumers in the United States by combining aesthetics drawn from journals featuring artistic and architectural designs with themes common to popular "shelter" magazines guiding home décor. *Dwell: At Home in the Modern World* favored modernist urban housing over the traditional suburban homes found in decorating magazines, yet differed from its higher-end architectural counterparts by depicting and describing the residences it featured as overtly *occupied* spaces. The inaugural issue of *Dwell* characterized this combination of unique modernist architecture and domestic do-it-yourself (DIY) decorating as "a minor revolution," insisting that it was "possible to live in a house or apartment by a bold modern architect, to own furniture and products that are exceptionally well designed, and still be a regular human being."[1]

Called the "Fruit Bowl Manifesto," *Dwell*'s mission statement asserted its intentions to take up a position between elaborately staged domestic sets usually featured in magazine photographs and ubiquitous scenes of domestic life often imaged in marketing. *Dwell*'s manifesto thus not only focused on images of modernist dwellings, but also of modernist dwellers, blending machine aesthetics with messy organicism to create compelling portraits of both desirable environments and distinctive consumers to admire and emulate. Promising to offer a new, less purist and more livable version of modernism, *Dwell* distinguished its project from the empty elite environments of *Architectural Digest* and the vacant, pleasant scenes of *Better Homes and Gardens*. By combining an appreciation for both high culture's forms and the base demands of human nature, *Dwell's* visual portraits provided a bold alternative to the bland conventionality associated with the Martha Stewart set while mounting a defense against established critiques of the "modernist utopia" as dependent upon "the absence of human qualities such as desire, intuition, and feeling."[2] Moreover, the manifesto launching *Dwell*'s distinctive aesthetic cast this new version of modernism as adaptable and realistic, stating that "[h]ere at Dwell, we think of ourselves as Modernists, but we are the nice Modernists" insofar as "[t]o us the M word connotes an honesty and curiosity about methods and materials," together with "a certain optimism not just about the future, but about the present"; and that, in the end "no fantasy we could create about how people could live, given unlimited funds and impeccable taste, is as interesting as how people really do live (within a budget and with the occasional aesthetic lapse)."[3]

Differentiating the nicer modernist dwellings and dwellers as distinguished by their "honesty," "curiosity," and "optimism," and displaying an appreciation for the charms of products personally selected by real residents with budgets and tastes not dictated by professional stylists opened up new vectors for audience identification in *Dwell*'s heavy and tastefully muted pages. Indeed, the manifesto's declared departure from conventional shelter magazines in portraying both modernist dwellings and modernist dwellers in their intimate imagery branded the magazine's visual signature in distinctive ways for viewers.

Dwell's styling of this embrace of real modernist design (and real modernist dwellers) in the form of a "manifesto," as well as the links it drew between the beautiful and the mundane in the daily *milieu* of a society characterized by mass production and mass consumption, all link its visions of the architecture of the everyday modern to the utopianism of the radical French critics of modernity, such as Henri Lefebvre and the Situationist International. Michael Gardiner argues that contemporary scholars interested in utopian thought need to recover this strand in French theory, as Lefebvre's central project was "conjoining a critical utopianism with the analysis of everyday life,"[4] while the Situationists offered an "uncompromising critique of modern society and everyday life" from a perspective "firmly rooted in the utopian tradition."[5] Lefebvre (who was briefly associated with the Situationists) is a particularly key figure for scholars of utopia, as he is poised between a realist critique of a modernist machinic utopianism and an embrace of the potential for utopias to stimulate social transformation. A critic of the "abyss of negative utopias" offered by abstract critical thought divorced from daily practices,[6] Lefebvre nonetheless celebrated utopianism as crucial to the abstract visions guiding both social critique and the production of new spaces of everyday life. Declaring that there could be "no theory without utopia," he argued that "the architects, like the urban planners, know this perfectly well," as both the critique and creativity required for social transformations depend on the ability to imagine idealizations beyond the given social order and push toward these guiding visions.[7]

Moreover, Lefebvre's philosophy articulated a desire to bring together design/planning, everyday experience, and new (artistic yet *inhabitable*) possibilities—an aim that *Dwell*'s "minor revolution" seems to echo, bridging the gap between the "conceived" spaces represented by architects and the "perceived" spaces of readers' daily lives with "lived" spaces imaged/imagined through creative portraits of objects of beauty and the subjects who own them.[8] Illustrating the vision of "nice modernism" explicated in its mission statement, *Dwell*'s photographic portraits offered an idyllic fusion of enviable architecture and actual homeowners, replacing both sculptural design and ordinary environs with stylized spaces occupied by confidently casual modernist dwellers not only present on the scene but intimately so: distinctively portrayed "in their pajamas, in their sweatpants, in their best stay-at-home-and-do-nothing attire" in images that "conveyed the seemingly obvious but oft-obscured message: Real people live here."[9]

However, if a lack of "signs of life" and human subjects in visions of modernist architecture was a void *Dwell*'s imagery offered to fill, it did so through portraits that not only invited admiration of modernist dwellings, but also incited ridicule of modernist dwellers. The intimacy implied in *Dwell*'s promise to bring viewers closer to modernism by peering behind closed doors at optimistic fashion statements and real aesthetic imperfections also rendered its dwellings and dwellers vulnerable to critique. Spaces of everyday life are distributed, occupied, and perceived differently, which is one reason why Lefebvre placed such a premium on the creativity required to adequately capture lived spaces. In its attempt to bring modernist homes and homeowners closer to readers, *Dwell* also brought the objects and subjects visualized into intimate relation with one another, creating the possibility of surprising tropological inversions of object/subject relations via personification and objectification in its images. For, if enlivening utopian modern spaces was *Dwell's* aim, its portraits also provoked dystopian critiques via DIY recaptioning that rendered modernism's unique exteriors incongruous and its distinctive interiors dreary and uninviting. Such reversals underscore how perceptions and lives are shaped by perspectives, as viewers are positioned very differently in visual culture. As Kenneth Burke's account of consubstantiality makes clear, identification is created through a rhetorical process.[10] And rhetorical operations are notoriously contingent, uncertain, and capricious.

A website entitled *Unhappy Hipsters: It's Lonely in the Modern World* began a running joke of *Dwell*'s idyllic imagery of modernist environs and their occupants (both human and inanimate) with new text placing them in antagonistic relationship to one another. "The flowers began to wither under the rigorous interrogation," "Drink in hand, he settled into the numb nothingness of his self-imposed isolation," and "Never mind the fruit bowl, here's the empty pleasure of conspicuous consumption," serve as notable examples of the clever captioning found throughout the site. Such captions alter artistic portraits of modernist domestic life to suggest that the lives lived in *Dwell*'s world are both shallow and miserable. The website invites and celebrates (e.g., by holding contests for winning captions) a seemingly populist attack on elite architecture and public ridicule of its residents. If *Dwell* found the bowls of fruit that provide the organic matter for the domestic settings in other magazines to be staged and artificial, *Unhappy Hipsters* found *Dwell*'s images of domestic spaces to be austere and even anti-humanist, and saw the human subjects in the magazine's portraits as posers adopting a depressed affect as a fashion statement. The humorous revisions deploy *Dwell* imagery to illustrate the implausibility of combining machine aesthetics with organic embodiments into any place that might be called "home." Labeling *Dwell*'s residents "hipsters" also charged them with dwelling in melancholic spaces for the sake of appearances in a display of consumption that is conformist in its nonconformity and therefore worthy of derision.

We find the cultural commentary that emerges in the visual-textual interplay between *Dwell*'s photography of modernist interiors and *Unhappy Hipsters*' recaptioned revisions to be deeply entangled in the aesthetics of utopian and dystopian spatial imaginaries and the politics of DIY unmediated and mediated environments. This interplay takes place at the boundaries of envisioned architectures that are inherently both "*unredeemably utopian*" as they rely on and offer "powerful visions of making and unmaking the world,"[11] generating imagined spaces providing both new possibilities and new critiques of social realms. The visual and virtual productions of space at work in *Dwell* and *Unhappy Hipsters* are not only linked to utopianism, but also to DIY crafting that circulates via websites and blogs like those described above, connecting them to "a broader DIY culture and an activist community in a way that spatially and analogically links experiments in making futures differently."[12] For this reason, the making and unmaking of home happening in *Dwell*'s images and in *Unhappy Hipsters*' captions also illustrates the interdependence of the technological productions of global utopias and local dystopia required to open up new spaces for moving social space "beyond empire," as argued by Henri Lefebvre.[13] While Lefebvre was eager to explore the potential for spaces to escape the reach of global capitalism, we find his analysis helpful for considering how utopian and dystopian projects may also seek to displace the territorializing cartography of cultural imperialism.

Furthermore, we see the complex relations between *Dwell*'s and *Unhappy Hipsters*' re/productions to reveal some important ways that the aesthetics of homes and bodies are rendered and reworked through tensions between modern/postmodern, everyday/elite, and hip/hipster in contemporary visual culture. To account for the utopic and dystopic pleasures, politics, and possibilities of these DIY discursive re/figurations of images and texts, we examine the memetic tendencies, visual elements, and rhetorical functions of *Dwell* images and *Unhappy Hipsters*' captions that are re/circulated in digital form. Our focus is on how *Unhappy Hipsters* illustrates the failure of *Dwell* to image an everyday modernist utopia as an accessible and DIY lived domestic space for viewers refusing invitations to enter into its utopian imaginary. We explore how *Unhappy Hipsters* exploits the relationship between *Dwell*'s visual aesthetics, modernism's international aspirations, and globalizing communication genres (such as stock photography, design, and branding) and analyze how these aesthetics attain coherence by re/stylizing human and inanimate objects alike through highly generic semiotic resources.

Although the refashioning of modern spaces and modern subjects in *Unhappy Hipsters* clearly contains strains of postmodern critique, we contend that *Dwell*'s failure to convincingly image modernist houses transformed into lived space is more attributable to perspectives offered by postcolonial theory than those provided by postmodernist style. What the humorous appropriations of *Dwell*'s portraits indicate is that the subjects dwelling in elite architecture are not fragmented and decentered, but made visible as Western and affluent in ways that link the aspirations of modernism's "international style" of architecture to the hubris of its cultural architects. A key context for this critique emerges from the way that modernist architecture's elevation as high art was undermined in the face of a "post-Orientalist/postcolonial critique of the 'Western canon' in art and culture" in an era when this idealized aesthetic is the target of "postmodern attacks" found to have "an especially strong appeal outside the Western world, parallel to a mounting obsession with identity."[14] Such appeals are rendered more resonant after modernist architecture came to be associated with nationalistic and colonialist interests[15] and the "tragic" failure of modernist urbanism became the exemplar of the fall of "utopian thinking."[16]

Reading *Unhappy Hipsters* as pointing to a failed relation between *Dwell*'s subjects and globalization, we find that the magazine's attempt to make itself at home in the modern world takes place just as postcolonialism has rendered the "universal" spaces of Western affluence as uninhabitable dystopias and recast its privileged occupants as ridiculous posers. In sum, *Dwell*'s efforts to remake the world as a modernist utopia are out of place in an era witnessing critiques of the imperialist interests of globalization, which have made the dream of a globalized aesthetic via a modernist international style absurd. Ultimately, *Dwell*'s modernism is unable to comfortably reside in a global visual culture that is not only postmodern, but also postwestern. However, we also find intimate entanglements between the utopian and dystopian subjects and objects imaged and imagined in *Dwell* and *Unhappy Hipsters* that prompt important questions about the politics of the pleasures these visual and textual portraits offer their admirers and critics, while demonstrating how globalizing visions featuring everyday utopias prompt local responses in the form of technological dystopias—creating a critical exchange that may be crucial for social imaginaries to spark social change.

On January 25, 2010, *Unhappy Hipsters* made its debut on Tumblr with a scanned photograph from an issue of *Dwell* dating back to February 2008. The photograph shows a perspectival view of a hallway with a dark concrete floor. With floor-to-top, wall-size windows on the right side and primary blue, green, and red color-block walls on the left side and at the back, the hallway wraps around the internal courtyard of a squat and blocky modernist building. Leaning against one of the dark steel lighting poles that line the windowed side of the hallway, a bespectacled man in the background gazes at the walls with his arms crossed. Underneath the scanned image, the following caption humorously explains the remit of this image: "He is sad because his house looks like an elementary school. And all the children have died." Nearly 150 Tumblr users liked or reblogged *Unhappy Hipsters*' first post, with some of them adding comments like: "this is a shiny new thing," "new source of entertainment!" "I was recently re-reminded of how much fun it is to laugh at people trapped and lonely in their minimalist architecture…" and "Haha, I died. (and so did those children)." In the following days, *Unhappy Hipsters*' activity picked up quickly, with ten captioned images posted on January 26 and six on January 27 alone. After only a week online, the blog had received 122,000 hits.[17]

Over the next several months the anonymous authors continued to deliver their deadpan humor on modernist living regularly with captions like: "The stools huddled together, braced for another one of his incoherent solo poetry slams,"[18] "In their haste to score an original Damien Hirst, her parents had sped off to Art Basel without her,"[19] "The utopia of urban flight came with a price,"[20] and "He'd finally decided to eliminate the one thing that blemished the uninterrupted expanse of concrete and plywood—himself."[21] What emerged from the juxtaposition of these captions to images from *Dwell* and a handful of similar shelter magazines was a world made of disgruntled furniture, overpowering flooring and wall materials, utterly lonely if not desperate humans, and children neglected in the name of trendy art and design. In addition to its own carefully orchestrated parodies, over the first year *Unhappy Hipsters* started soliciting content from its readers, at first with caption contests and later also by encouraging them to produce their own *Dwell*-like imagery that would then be captioned by its authors. A year into its existence, *Unhappy Hipsters* opened up to full image and caption submissions by its "passionate, intelligent, and wildly good-looking readers,"[22] offering detailed guidelines on how to properly caption and credit images.

Unhappy Hipsters is a great example of social media DIY, both because of its bricolage, guerrilla approach to communication and its potential as an

Internet meme. As a short-form blogging platform, Tumblr enables users to post multimedia content that can be followed, liked, and reblogged by other bloggers. The platform also allows users to choose a unique domain name and access basic HTML code to customize the appearance of their blog. Each customized blog can then be connected to other social networking accounts, so that each time that a new post is added this update is also sent to Twitter or Facebook.

The political potential of the creative component inherent in such forums has prompted links between social media sites, "culture jamming" discourse, and a "do-it-yourself countercultural ethic" that can be traced to the Situationists' "psychogeography" as critique of the landscape of capitalism.[23] In an era when social media platforms like Tumblr have created virtual spaces for DIY everyday material productions as well as "psychogeographic aesthetic experiments" for publics whose "units of affinity can be small and local (harkening back to guilds and to contemporary affinity groups) and/or global (especially with virtual communities)."[24] Like other DIY fabrications and cultural crafts, *Unhappy Hipsters* is a stage for generating textual creations that share some of the aesthetics and ethics noted of the productions of the "citizen bricoleurs" Frank Farmer finds appealing. In line with Farmer's definition, *Unhappy Hipsters* interpellates counterpublics via a "collage aesthetic" and a "passionate allegiance to an ethics of 'do it yourself,' or DIY" while also promoting "a militant anti-copyright ethos and an oppositional stance toward all the established protocols of life under consumer capitalism."[25] While Farmer deems these textual creations to be "undeniably utopian" in the worlds they envision,[26] the culture jamming aesthetics and critical ethics characterizing *Unhappy Hipsters*' recaptioning also undercut *Dwell*'s images of DIY everyday domestic utopias (based on modernist designs articulated to international imperialism and global capital) with technological dystopias (relocating these modernist subjects and objects to specific cultural and classed localities).

In addition to being received warmly by social media users, who were compelled and then invited to submit their own content, *Unhappy Hipsters* was covered extensively in the press. Less than ten days after its debut, the *New York Times* reported that it "ricocheted in the blogosphere like a shuttlecock."[27] Just a few days later, the *LA Times* stated that *Unhappy Hipsters* "is the most welcome addition to the often self-serious world of architecture and design in recent memory, not to mention a pocket of satirical warmth in the middle of a soggy, recessionary, earthquake-wracked, Martha Coakley winter."[28] A host of other media outlets quickly took an interest in *Unhappy Hipsters*, including online trade magazines like *Ad Week* and *Creative Review* in addition to a myriad of design-related blogs. *Psychology Today* dedicated an online feature to *Unhappy Hipsters* asking the following question: "Are there elements of modern design that inherently make us feel gloomy?"

Taking *Unhappy Hipsters*' satirical critique seriously, the article expounded on the impact that color, light, texture, and form have on our mood and concluded that "modernism's restrained quality is fundamentally in tension with the idea of delight" and, in the end, "there must be something primal within us that understands such stripped down spaces as inhospitable—the emotional equivalent of dry desert, or fallow fields."[29]

At the most basic level, *Unhappy Hipsters* followed a fairly typical script in matters of viral communication. The authors were chased by literary agents and eventually got a book deal for a volume mimicking a proper architectural and interior design handbook. Following the hype, cofounder Molly Jane Quinn stated that the book deal and all of the media coverage the project received led people to believe that they had made a fortune off their project and that they were "rolling in Unhappy Hipsters cash." Instead, Quinn and her partner in crime Jenna Talbott "never made any money off of the site" and the book deal only "really funded one crazy summer of intense work." By the time the book was published, both Quinn and Talbott were onto other things.[30] In addition to its sudden if not short-lived success, *Unhappy Hipsters*' formula lent itself to being taken up by others through acts of recaptioning and remixing. As Limor Shifman[31] explains, an Internet meme is not simply an individual item that propagates well through digital means; rather, memes are groups of items that are aware of each other and share similarities most often due to imitation and transformation through the means of irony, parody or satire. While *Unhappy Hipsters* was not imitated or transformed by other digital authors, the Tumblr's creators actively integrated a memetic logic into their own highly regulated digital craft, not only by "remixing" *Dwell*'s imagery but also by inviting their readers to recaption the same imagery or submit their own modernist architectural photos to be captioned and published on the blog. It is in this sense that *Unhappy Hipsters* can be seen both as DIY utopia and dystopia, insofar as its quick rise to celebrity among social media users offered visibility to its authors but was not matched by a real opportunity for them to make a living out of this success. In parallel, *Unhappy Hipsters* offers a (humorous and potentially remixable) dystopic critique of yet another kind of DIY utopia: that of modernist architecture and interior design. With the subtitle "It's Lonely in the Modern World," *Unhappy Hipsters* parodies *Dwell*'s byline "At Home in the Modern World," hence establishing a clear linkage between prized, aspirational forms of contemporary dwelling and existential anomie.

A social semiotic approach to visual analysis[32] helps us to outline the representational, interactive and compositional meaning potentials of these images in order to examine the 'stories' they tell, the kinds of relationships that they establish with the viewer, and the ways in which they arrange their different components in relation to one another. In doing so, we are particularly interested in how the satirical captioning of these images draws out, reverses, and both radically and hilariously critiques some of the very rock-solid ideological assumptions underlying contemporary aspirational home design.

From a representational point of view, the architectural images featured in *Unhappy Hipsters* offer a combination of spaces with or without human presence. When humans are present, there is a prevalence of white adults in their 30s or early 40s. The sparse inhabitants of these carefully designed interiors are most often lone individuals engaged in activities such as standing in gardens and looking out of balconies, gazing outside wall-size windows with a mug or book in hand, tending to produce from behind open-plan kitchen counters, working on Apple laptops, and watering lawns against the backdrop of façades covered in concrete, glass, and wood paneling. Children feature regularly in these images too, but rarely in groups or in the company of adults. Pets, and in particular dogs, are sometimes present, mainly as décor rather than companions. When more than one individual is pictured, we typically see heterosexual couples or nuclear families with very few of these images representing larger groups of people, or any significant form of interaction between portrayed subjects. Most often couples are portrayed as they look away from each other or as they inhabit different spaces in the house.

From an interactive standpoint, these images tend to position the viewer as a distant participant. Eye-level, medium-long shots of exteriors and interiors alike suggest that the viewer's ability to dwell in these spaces is possible, though apparently still out of reach. The compositional outlook of these images privileges layouts that emphasize the separation, rather than continuity, of living spaces. The different quarters, levels, and corners of a house are often skillfully captured at once, with lone individuals inhabiting their own "boxes," which are marked by the lines drawn by window frames, stairwells, and doorless entryways. Through these framing devices, these images highlight a seemingly egalitarian potential for personal retreat and individual fulfillment within the safe boundaries of idyllic nuclear-family living.

The images that *Unhappy Hipsters* draws from *Dwell* magazine are stylized portraits, artfully displaying the modernist aesthetic appeals—such as clean lines, industrial materials, geometric shapes, and unusual textures—of its sculptural and brightly lit scenes and subjects. The tendency to treat architectural forms, artful objects, and their affluent owners as similar aesthetic features in these modernist environments, when paired with traditional critiques of modernist design as machine-like and anti-humanist, provides rich material for *Unhappy Hipsters'* captions that invert conventional subject/object relations to create rifts in *Dwell*'s utopic visions of modern life. These tropic inversions, clear in the earliest months of *Unhappy Hipsters*' appearance, tend to personify residential objects and environs, objectify residents, and invent or exploit tensions between *and within* nonhuman and human dwellers on the scene.

Personification of modernist décor, furniture, rooms, and even whole houses is a common trope in *Unhappy Hipsters* productions, a clever play on the shapes and styles common to abstract art (wherein a simple curve can suggest a human form). This trend was established from the start of *Unhappy Hipsters*' entry onto the virtual world of memes, as in the second image/caption it offered (a photograph of a bright bedroom with a stuffed animal on the bed over the words "The octopus was full of judgment"). Further posts frequently built on this theme, finding the modernist home littered with lurking lamps, hostile houseplants, and pretentious possessions. Examples of captions undermining attractive images with these dark personifications of the objects depicted include "For weeks the lamp had been creeping closer to the sofa, ready to engulf the man with its black lampshade of doom," "Flipping the pages hurriedly, he sensed that the potted plants were advancing," and "He couldn't stand another night with that smug hookah."

In other appropriations, *Unhappy Hipsters*' captions personify the architecture as a whole, attributing misery or malicious intent to the houses themselves. Modernist dwellings are described as despondent ("There. He felt it again. The whole house had unmistakeably slid toward the retaining wall, as if inching toward edificial suicide") or filled with unkind spirits ("At first, she had attributed the strange scribble on the blackboard to her forgetful memory. Now she descended the stairs each morning with dread, petrified of what the poltergeist wanted to communicate today"), and modernist façades are described as unfriendly faces ("The porthole windows seemed like a good idea. But now the house appeared to be leering at them, distinctly ominous"). In the midst of such frequent personification of modernist objects and structures, captions such as "She had this uncanny way of making him feel so, so small" (under an image of a couple dwarfed by the receding horizon of their extensive open floor plan) invite viewers to wonder whether the pronoun refers to an emotionally abusive human or house in the miserable cohabitation *Unhappy Hipsters* captures.

Not only do modernist objects become personified subjects in these visual-textual tropes, they also exert agency over their human owners, who become merely part of the décor in these dystopic settings. *Unhappy Hipsters*' captions describe residents reduced to minor contributions to the modernist color scheme ("He deeply resented her insistence that their wardrobes coordinate"), made slaves to the domestic aesthetic ("The frequent window washing and dry mopping required to keep the room sufficiently spartan became more than she could bear"), or converted into realist modern art, as below an image of a couple standing next to an enormous portrait featuring one of them: "Sober (and in the light of day), she realized that buying the companion sculpture to the photograph had been unwise."

Children in *Dwell*'s domestic scenes, always a sacred aspect of familial portraits in shelter magazine culture, are similarly reduced in status or even treated as pets. For example, a photograph of a small child and a large dog peering together over the metal railing of a rooftop balcony is given the sinister explanation: "Adding the roof deck to their cinder-block abode had been an afterthought. Now she thought of it more as an arena for natural selection." Other captions equate offspring with furnishings on the domestic scene, or even rank the needs of children below the modernist aesthetic imperative ("It occurred to her that in choosing the repurposed airplane ramp as a staircase, she hadn't considered the child"). Photographs of children at play in modernist environments are revised to evince a desire to flee their bizarre and bleak homes, as bunk-bed ladders, sidewalks, and slides are characterized as potential escape routes for trapped toddlers. These dark interpretations of modernist settings, as even less appropriate for families than they are for affluent couples or artistic singles, seem to exhibit a premodern (rather than postmodern) sensibility—one that ignores how the geometric shapes, bright colors, and durable materials of the modernist home might be more kid-friendly than the traditional models found in *House Beautiful* and *Good Housekeeping*. Running jokes about children forced by their aesthete parents to watch documentaries on design, sort swatches, or exhibit architectural knowledge drive home the idea that modernism is too severe for familial life.

In addition to these depressing accounts of modern parenting, the dystopic twists *Unhappy Hipsters*' captions add to *Dwell* imagery often find humor in imagined antagonisms and tensions between featured inhabitants (whether animate or inanimate) in modernist spaces. Implied flaws in personal or psychological dimensions of the lives of *Dwell*'s homeowners are projected onto these initially appealing portraits celebrating their style and taste, hinting that surface aesthetics conceal deeper problems. Attractive couples photographed in ideal modernist scenes are undermined by descriptions of the ugly reality of their relationships, through accompanying captions revealing fear, dread, and hostility hidden in these domestic settings. The tendency for *Dwell* photographers to capture residents in "natural" or unconventional poses rather than having them stand together and gaze into the camera (instead, they are often seen separated as they use different parts of the home or are seen relaxing/reading/eating alone) is exploited in captions listing reasons why household members are estranged. Many of these captions are "tagged" with one of the site's more extensive "file under" categories: "romance on the rocks" or "lonely" (tags frequently attached to pages of image/caption combinations).

Unhappy Hipsters also envisions modernist rooms and structures as cages or blinds, enclosing or obscuring occupants who conceal disappointment or desperation as an open secret via design choices. In some cases, the captions poke fun at the unrealistic color scheme of the scenes, as this caption under an image of a man whose knitting project seems tailored to suit his décor: "Trapped by the tawny palette, he struggled through yet another brown knit scarf." Others find modernist materials to be claustrophobic: "He tried to focus on the novel, and not how much his bedroom reminded him of a plywood coffin" and "The things that once so defined him—shag carpeting, Room & Board sofas, monogamy—now suffocated him." Still others hint that the impressive home décor is compensation for even more private failures ("Eames, Aalto—her most significant relationships were with dead designers").

Although the content and style of the images and text of *Unhappy Hipsters* were established during the first three months of online publication, opening up the site for submissions made room for very different kinds of DIY critiques of the utopian images in modernist magazines. Repeated warnings posted on the website make it clear that some contributions and comments were censored by the creators. The warning, "Hate speech of any type, directed at any race, gender, or orientation, will not be tolerated,"[33] indicates that some captions targeted more than the tastes of modernist dwellers. In addition to sexist, racist, and homophobic captions, profanity was removed from the website, generating some debate. Dismissing this controversy, while acknowledging the irony of *Unhappy Hipsters* editing captions, one visitor wrote (in response to complaints about censorship): "Maybe you are just shocked that something you thought was cool/funny/really hip is actually really square, and so now you are a real unhappy hipster." Both the censorship and the comment calling website visitors "hipsters" themselves raises some important questions about the specific types of critiques of modernism *Unhappy Hipsters* celebrates, and the viewers/readers who find them appealing. These questions are difficult to answer drawing on the Tumblr alone, but the book published by the creators offers more insights about the vulnerabilities and viewers the site targets.

The book version of the blog, *It's Lonely in the Modern World: The Essential Guide to Form, Function, and Ennui from the Creators of Unhappy Hipsters* is rhetorically significant, not only because its publication is a testament to the popularity of the website, but also because it fleshes out the lonely modernists skewered by the particular satirical tone that went viral via social media. In his introduction to the book, Andrew Wagner (editor of *Readymade*) charts the half-life of hipness as he writes about his own early days on the staff of *Dwell* when the magazine offered a bold alternative in 2000, as well as his own pleasures when *Unhappy Hipsters* challenged what had then become one of the established "purveyors of good taste" by 2010 by "deliver[ing] a swift kick to the groin of misappropriated modernism."[34] Despite the characterization of the Tumblr as aiming below the belt, the statement marking "hate speech" and obscenities as off-limits sharpens our attention to the identities and insults considered fair game in *Unhappy Hipsters*' attacks on modernist dwellers. Mimicking a DIY home design guidebook, the book has extensive textual portions and graphs (in addition to the familiar *Dwell* photographs and captions) that provide much more detail about its targets: unhappy hipsters are wealthy urbane Westerners who imagine themselves a "rare and superior breed of human" and who pursue the unattainable modernist ideal, seeking "a home that is a direct extension of [their] ego and ethos."[35] Replete with references to exorbitant expenses in modernist home design, eccentric European and American modernist icons, and the urgency of appearances in trendy urban areas of the United States, the book portrays unhappy hipsters as exceptionally privileged subjects who are aware of, and place a lot of stock in, their social standing. Advice for avoiding any semblance of suburban or mainstream tastes, and ways to score "points" by appearing more educated, wealthy, culturally literate, environmentally aware, and (of course) possessed of distinctively hip tastes are offered throughout the book. Like the blog, the book relentlessly hammers at hipsterism as hopelessly idealistic, impractical, superficial, and fundamentally unfulfilling.

Although *It's Lonely in the Modern World* also renders modernist dwellings and dwellers dystopian in their entrapment in utopian aesthetic ideals for homes and bodies, the book is (with a few notable exceptions) not as funny as the blog. We find the loss of the DIY character of the devastating and anonymous one-liner, now replaced by the unified propriety of an authored, edited, and published print volume, to be a key reason for this difference. The relative balance between text and images and the stable source and even production quality of all elements of the book is another factor. The beauty of a professional magazine photo scanned without permission and pasted above a satirical caption lies in the way that the strategies and resources expended in creating and imaging a utopian space are laid low by the tactical and temporary appropriations of anonymous authors. Finally, the memetic potential of blog postings to circulate among and be remixed by a broad public—all laughing at the private lives of hipster modernists—is also more provocative and wicked, giving the humor an appealingly cutting edge.

Our own relative pleasures in the humorous invitations the *Unhappy Hipsters* Tumblr and book make are important to consider, for in addition to finding these texts visually fascinating in their cultural commentary, we also find them funny. It is worth noting that rhetorical criticism analyzing the former without contending with the latter fails to address audience appeals at the most basic level. In other words, we cannot treat *Unhappy Hipsters* as solely a serious symptom of cultural malaise. We need to understand *why* we are laughing *and with (or at) whom* we are laughing. Despite its mass-circulated and memetic form, we find *Unhappy Hipsters*' humor to be built on imbricated layers crossing categories for spaces of lived/perceived, imaged/

imagined, and subject/object dwelling. Overall, these complex cultural constructions invite humor with a sharp flavor drawn from contrasts between modern and postmodern styles, elite and everyday experiences, and visual and textual modes of sense- and place-making.

The type of humor *Unhappy Hipsters* employs, and the pleasures it offers, are both overt and subtle, pointing to both simplistic and complex ways to consider *who* is laughing and *why*. Its humor seems to adhere to the directional valence of satire, in that it appears to allow those with less access to conventional modes of power (supplemented with anonymous populist posting online) to poke fun at those with more social privilege (model owners of model homes depicted in elite modernist magazines). Thus, the appeal of *laughing at* is most evident in these DIY captions converting utopian images into dystopian imaginaries. This said, the captions evince an intimate familiarity with the designers and scenes and sensibilities showcased in the photographs they parody. References to Eames, ennui, and ecru are unlikely to be appreciated by outsiders of this elite world of modernist living. In order to *get* the jokes, you need a complex understanding of the cultural capital on display—the kind of understanding that only comes with careful study and/or extended exposure.

The elite vocabulary and concepts represented through these connections between the original images and the added captions suggest humor appealing to "insiders" rather than outsiders. More importantly, the captions are not voiced as *outside* observations, but as insights drawn from internal dialogues attributed to the subjects portrayed. Grammatically, the captions are written in the third person, but they express intimate knowledge of the inner fears, hopes, desires, and experiences of the modernist dwellers depicted in the photographs. Rather than observing that the hipsters appear to be unhappy in these images, the captions publicly confess their private unhappiness—usually drawing on intimate self-knowledge that it would be difficult for any other person (even a friend or family member) to know for certain. In other words, they perform observing the self *as other*. For example, a photograph of a woman seated in a wire chair bears the caption "Secretly, she enjoyed the grids imprinted on her skin. In the new DSM, the American Psychiatric Association gave her disorder a name: 'Bertoia butt.'" Another caption, under a family scene, reads "Creative parenting meant allowing the wee one his own boundaries, but it didn't mean they couldn't secretly mock him." Of course, these attributions of misery and pathology are only humorous because they are fictional emotional realities projected onto the model spaces and bodies by a knowledgeable figure excluded from the frame: a witty and resentful viewer with intimate knowledge of modernism and hip taste, but without the home or body that would make for a model of modernist style . . . or perhaps a viewer who would be too self-conscious to pose (without appearing to pose) for a magazine shoot. Yet despite the differences captions draw between *Unhappy Hipsters'* fans and *Dwell* models, the affective appeals of the dystopian recaptioning seem to draw on a heightened *self*-awareness that links the negative feelings attributed to and about the subjects in the photographs. The DIY global modernist utopia provokes a DIY local modernist dystopia, as both contributors and viewers are not satisfied with the generally beautiful private spaces depicted until they have imagined specific ugly private thoughts dwelling within these model homes and bodies. The strong negative affect bespeaks a subjective entanglement. *Unhappy Hipsters'* critique is not a random hit and run. It's personal.

Moreover, the intimate relationship between the images and the captions has a formal structure. In a tropological sense, the image and caption operate in antithetical relation to one another, since the textual reversal relies on the visual fashion statement the image makes. In other words, it is both the DIY and utopian character of these visual statements on domestic style that fuel the satirical twist and provide its humorous appeals; it is not the appearance of the styled modern dwelling and dwellers that is funny, but it is instead the way in which they are exposed in public magazine spreads of their private spaces. The sheer hubris of holding out one's home and body as a model of taste and style galls and provokes resentment. The bold fashion statements render these subjects more vulnerable because they lack the backing of normative domestic conventions. These elements—resentment and vulnerability—combine to offer considerable *Schadenfreude* when the prestige of having your home and your body featured in a magazine is negated via ridicule. However, we suspect that these may also involve a substantial degree of *self*-ridicule.

A 2011 interview with Molly Jane Quinn, one of the creators of *Unhappy Hipsters* and the author of the written portions of *It's Lonely in the Modern World*, is quite revealing of the role of reflexive ridicule in the critiques of modernism her work offers. In response to the question "Having imagined the secret lives of unhappy hipsters, what closeted vice would you most like to attribute to them?" Quinn responds: "I would love if they had a secret guilty pleasure, like Velveeta. Something crappy they wouldn't want to admit they ate. I love the idea that you have this kitchen that's presented as if you're making these amazing gourmet meals, but really you're alone in a chair eating frozen TV dinners and reading *US Weekly*. Like my life." This insight into the pleasures *Unhappy Hipsters* offers its creator is significant. If the impulse to shred the glamorous images of modernist dwellings stems from a failure (or refusal) to relate to the utopian subjects and spaces depicted, the pleasure comes through a dystopian darkness that establishes a point of connection, rather than further distances viewers from the private homes imaged. There is a yearning to take modernist models down a peg or two, to bring them down to the viewer's level. The gap between the perceived spaces of viewers' daily lives and the lived spaces imaged in *Dwell*'s portraits is bridged by projecting dystopian emotional realities onto a utopian aesthetic scene.

Despite its satirical tone, *Unhappy Hipsters* does not ultimately observe the directional grain of satire, dethroning privileged statures via populist perceptions. The sources for its humor are not located in working class ridicule of affluence or attacks on white privilege by people of color. Rather than operating as a critique from below, *Unhappy Hipsters* is a critique *from within*. The frequent name-dropping of famous modernist designers, the display of art terminology, the recognition of elite brands in its one-liners all suggest a target audience intimately immersed in the kind of cultural capital on display in *Dwell*'s modernist utopias.

Likewise, *Unhappy Hipsters*' creations do not critique *Dwell*'s wealthy Western subjects in ways calling global capitalism into question or pointing to the colonial histories shaping Euro-American art and fashions. Nevertheless, they quite vigorously resist the aspirations of an earlier modernism imagining its forms as universal and timeless, truly utopian (or placeless) modes for living. The writers and readers who create and celebrate dystopic visions of modernist dwellings exhibit a heightened awareness of the specific (geographical, socioeconomic, and cultural) place of these homes and homeowners, as captions with frequent references to US cities, designer brands, and famous figures can attest. *Unhappy Hipsters*' followers recognize Euro-American affluence, education, and social practices in *Dwell*'s photographs in ways that are only possible after postcolonial critiques and political movements have rendered such privileged subjects hyper-visible as such. Followers recognize *themselves* in these portraits, even as they draw on their own elite cultural capital to peddle hipster humor in the form of the newest meme.

It is clear that *Unhappy Hipsters*' captions both poke fun at and perform an unhappy hipsterism that is gleefully masochistic in locating misery in its own pleasure, and pleasure in its own misery. The DIY dystopia of unhappy home that these appropriations create to undercut the intimacy and optimism of a "nice modernism" reflects an intimate self-knowledge that situates beautiful objects and tasteful subjects within a field of power relations that Western affluence both attacks and utilizes in its mediated (self)portraits of the cultural elite. These acts of visual self-destruction are performed as if they could assuage the guilt of markers of bodily and economic racial, ethnic, national, and class privileges only superficially displaced. In these ways, *Unhappy Hipsters* exhibits a post*western* sensibility, even as it stages a complex cultural performance that both embraces and distances itself from modes of cultural capital in visual culture.

Paradoxically, we find the dark DIY recreations of modernism in *Unhappy Hipsters* to be somewhat idealist in their yearning for an intimate and strange confrontation with a post-hipster social privilege enacted through staged encounters with the cultural capital wielded by the tech and style literate. The "nice modernism" this exchange between *Dwell* magazine and *Unhappy Hipsters* enables is the reflexive intimacy of a self-critique that makes economic, social, and cultural capital visible, even as it retains the privileges and pleasures of its (post)hipster denizens. In other words, *Unhappy Hipsters* is a DIY dystopia with utopian aspirations that are more selfish than satirical. The visual and textual signature of a new, postmodern, postwestern modernist sensibility may be the pleasure of laughing with others at the self *as other.* At the risk of presuming to claim that Henri Lefebvre anticipated the current state of a visual culture shaped by both Tumblr and postcolonial critiques, we cannot ignore his observations about the interdependence of utopia/dystopia and global/local fashioning of place via technologies with the potential to open new social imaginaries and social spaces beyond the reach of both capitalism and imperialism:

> Perhaps the most promising response to the newest iteration of a globalizing mode of production for a "technological utopia" is a radically localized technological dystopia, for between these might lie the very real possibility of transformed and transcendent social space beyond empire.[36]

If Lefebvre's hope is well-founded here, we may begin to see how the latest critiques of modernism are opening pathways to a kind of dwelling in the everyday that is reflexive and, rather than relying on the occupation of others, relocates the globalized other to the interior of a localized self.

NOTES

1. Karrie Jacobs, "Fruit Bowl Manifesto," *Dwell Magazine*, October 2000. Accessed January 3, 2016, http://www.dwell.com/info/about-dwell.
2. Lara Schrijver, "Utopia and/or Spectacle? Rethinking Urban Interventions Through the Legacy of Modernism and the Situationist City." *Architectural Theory Review* 16:3 (2011): 249.
3. Jacobs, "Fruit Bowl Manifesto."
4. Michael Gardiner, "Utopia and Everyday Life in French Social Thought." *Utopian Studies* 6:2 (1995): 97.
5. Ibid., 103.
6. Henri Lefebvre, *The Production of Space* (Malden, MA: Wiley-Blackwell, 1992), 60.
7. Henri Lefebvre, *State, Space, World: Selected Essays*, eds. Neil Brenner and Stuart Eldon, trans. Gerald Moore, Neil Brenner and Stuart Eldon (Minneapolis, MN: The University of Minnesota Press, 2009), 178–179.

8. Henri Lefebvre, *The Production of Space* (Malden, MA: Wiley-Blackwell, 1992), 38–41.

9. Andrew Wagner, "Foreword," in *It's Lonely in the Modern World: The Essential Guide to Form, Function, and Ennui from the Creators of Unhappy Hipsters*, ed. Molly Jane Quinn (San Francisco: Chronicle Books, 2011), 7.

10. Kenneth Burke, *A Rhetoric of Motives* (Oakland, CA: University of California Press, 1969), 46.

11. Lynda H. Schneekloth, "Unredeemably Utopian: Architecture and Making/Unmaking the World." *Utopian Studies* 9:2 (1998): 23.

12. Jack Z. Bratich and Heidi M. Brush, "Fabricating Activism: Craft-Work, Popular Culture, Gender." *Utopian Studies* 22:2 (2011): 234.

13. Henri Lefebvre, *The Production of Space* (Malden, MA: Wiley-Blackwell, 1992), 423.

14. Sibel Bozdoğan, *Rethinking Modernity and National Identity in Turkey* (Seattle, WA: University of Washington Press, 1997), 134.

15. Kathleen James-Chakraborty, "Beyond Postcolonialism: New Directions for the History of Nonwestern Architecture." *Frontiers of Architectural Research* 3 (2014): 3.

16. David Pinder, "In Defence of Utopian Urbanism: Imagining Cities after the 'End of Utopia'." *Geografiska Annaler. Series B, Human Geography* 84:3/4 (2002): 233.

17. Penelope Green, "Mischievous Bloggers Take on Dwell Magazine," *The New York Times*, February 3, 2010. http://www.nytimes.com/2010/02/04/garden/04online.html.

18. *Unhappy Hipsters: It's Lonely in the Modern World* (blog), February 23, 2010, http://www.unhappyhipsters.com.

19. Ibid., July 30, 2010, http://www.unhappyhipsters.com.

20. Ibid., last May 4, 2010, http://www.unhappyhipsters.com.

21. Ibid., July 24, 2010, http://www.unhappyhipsters.com.

22. Ibid., last February 14, 2011, http://www.unhappyhipsters.com.

23. Christine Harold, *OurSpace: Resisting the Corporate Control of Culture* (Minneapolis, MN: The University of Minnesota Press, 2009), 28.

24. Jack Z. Bratich and Heidi M. Brush, "Fabricating Activism: Craft-Work, Popular Culture, Gender." *Utopian Studies* 22:2 (2011): 242

25. Frank Farmer, *After the Public Turn: Composition, Counterpublics, and the Citizen Bricoleur* (Logan: Utah State University Press, 2013), 47.

26. Farmer, *After the Public Turn*, 50.

27. Penelope Green, "Mischievous Bloggers Take on Dwell Magazine."

28. Christopher Hawthorne, "Unhappy Hipsters Parody Website Is a Hit," *Los Angeles Times*, February 6, 2010, http://articles.latimes.com/2010/feb/06/home/la-hm-hipsters6-2010feb06.

29. Ingrid Fetell, "Unhappy Hipsters: Does Modern Architecture Make Us Gloomy?" *Psychology Today*, February 6, 2010, http://www.psychologytoday.com/blog/design-and-the-mind/201002/unhappy-hipsters-does-modern-architecture-make-us-gloomy.

30. Rob Walker, "The Social Media Phenoms of Yesteryear: Where Are They Now?" *Yahoo! Tech*, August 20, 2014, https://www.yahoo.com/tech/the-social-media-phenoms-of-yesteryear-where-are-they-95240862559.html.

31. Limor Shifman, "The Cultural Logic of Photo-Based Meme Genres," *Journal of Visual Culture* 13:3 (December 1, 2014): 340–58. doi: 10.1177/1470412914546577.

32. Gunther Kress and Theo van Leeuwen, *Reading Images: The Grammar of Visual Design*, 2nd edition (London: Routledge, 2006).

33. *Unhappy Hipsters: It's Lonely in the Modern World* (blog), April 9, 2012, http://www.unhappyhipsters.com.

34. Molly Jane Quinn, *It's Lonely in the Modern World: The Essential Guide to Form, Function, and Ennui from the Creators of Unhappy Hipsters*. San Francisco: Chronicle Books, 2011.

35. Ibid.

36. Lefebvre, *The Production of Space*, 423.

BIBLIOGRAPHY

Bozdoğan, Sibel. *Rethinking Modernity and National Identity in Turkey*. Seattle: University of Washington Press, 1997.

Bratich, Jack Z., and Heidi M. Brush. "Fabricating Activism: Craft-Work, Popular Culture, Gender." *Utopian Studies* 22:2 (2011): 234.

Burke, Kenneth. *A Rhetoric of Motives*. Berkeley, Calif.: University of California Press, 1969.

Delahoyde, Steve. "Chronicle Publishes 'Unhappy Hipsters' Book, *It's Lonely in the Modern World*." *FishbowlNY*, October 11, 2011. http://www.adweek.com/fishbowlny/chronicle-publishes-unhappy-hipsters-book-its-lonely-in-the-modern-world/288594.

———. "'Unhappy Hipsters' Makes Us Happy." *FishbowlNY*, January 28, 2010. http://www.adweek.com/fishbowlny/unhappy-hipsters-makes-us-happy/278998.

Farmer, Frank. *After the Public Turn: Composition, Counterpublics, and the Citizen Bricoleur*. Logan: Utah State University Press, 2013.

Fetell, Ingrid. "Unhappy Hipsters: Does Modern Architecture Make Us Gloomy?" *Psychology Today*, February 6, 2010. http://www.psychologytoday.com/blog/design-and-the-mind/201002/unhappy-hipsters-does-modern-architecture-make-us-gloomy.

Gardiner, Michael. "Utopia and Everyday Life in French Social Thought." *Utopian Studies* 6:2 (1995): 116.

Green, Penelope. "Mischievous Bloggers Take on Dwell Magazine." *The New York Times*, February 3, 2010. http://www.nytimes.com/2010/02/04/garden/04online.html.

———. "The Unhappy Hipsters on Their New Book — Q&A." *The New York Times*, October 12, 2011. http://www.nytimes.com/2011/10/13/garden/the-unhappy-hipsters-on-their-new-book-qa.html.

Harold, Christine. *OurSpace: Resisting the Corporate Control of Culture*. Minneapolis, MN: The University of Minnesota Press, 2009.

Hawthorne, Christopher. "Unhappy Hipsters Parody Website Is a Hit." *Los Angeles Times*, February 6, 2010. http://articles.latimes.com/2010/feb/06/home/la-hm-hipsters6–2010feb06.

Jacobs, Karrie. "The Fruitbowl Manifesto." *Dwell*, October 2000. http://www.dwell.com/info/about-dwell.

James-Chakraborty, Kathleen. "Beyond Postcolonialism: New Directions for the History of Nonwestern Architecture." *Frontiers of Architectural Research* 3 (2014): 3.

Kress, Gunther and Theo van Leeuwen. *Reading Images: The Grammar of Visual Design*. 2nd edition. London: Routledge, 2006.

Lefebvre, Henri. *The Production of Space*. 1st edition. Malden, Mass: Wiley-Blackwell, 1992.

———. *State, Space, World: Selected Essays*. Edited by Neil Brenner and Stuart Eldon. Translated by Gerald Moore, Neil Brenner and Stuart Eldon. Minneapolis: The University of Minnesota Press, 2009.

Pinder, David. "In Defence of Utopian Urbanism: Imagining Cities after the 'End of Utopia'." *Geografiska Annaler. Series B, Human Geography* 84:3/4 (2002): 233.

Quinn, Molly Jane. *It's Lonely in the Modern World: The Essential Guide to Form, Function, and Ennui from the Creators of Unhappy Hipsters*. San Francisco: Chronicle Books, 2011.

———. "Unhappy Hipsters: The Cult Satirical Design Bloggers Play Guest Editors With the Nowness Archive." *Nowness*, November 7, 2011. https://www.nowness.com/story/unhappy-hipsters.

———. *Unhappy Hipsters: It's Lonely in the Modern World* (blog), last modified May 28, 2015. http://www.unhappyhipsters.com.

Schneekloth, Lynda H. "Unredeemably Utopian: Architecture and Making/Unmaking the World." *Utopian Studies* 9:2 (1998).

Schrijver, Lara. "Utopia and/or Spectacle? Rethinking Urban Interventions Through the Legacy of Modernism and the Situationist City." *Architectural Theory Review* 16:3 (2011): 249.

Shifman, Limor. "The Cultural Logic of Photo-Based Meme Genres." *Journal of Visual Culture* 13:3 (December 1, 2014): 340–58. doi: 10.1177/1470412914546577.

Walker, Rob. "The Social Media Phenoms of Yesteryear: Where Are They Now?" *Yahoo! Tech*, August 20, 2014. https://www.yahoo.com/tech/the-social-media-phenoms-of-yesteryear-where-are-they-95240862559.html.

Chapter 12

"Change Your Underwear, Change the World"

Entrepreneurial Activism and the Fate of Utopias in an Era of Ethical Capital

Lisa Daily

In "The End of Utopia," Herbert Marcuse writes: "Today we have the capacity to turn the world into hell, and we are well on the way to doing so. We also have the capacity to turn it into the opposite of hell. This would mean the end of utopia, that is, the refutation of those ideas and theories that use the concept of utopia to denounce certain socio-historical possibilities."[1] Whereas Marcuse situates utopia within a historical continuum—one which may require a rupture—he also acknowledges its impossibility for material social change. I open with Marcuse because he provides insight into the concept of utopia as it functions within the source of this chapter, which focuses on the contemporary capitalist utopian vision of ethical capital.

Each year for the past eight years, hordes of people have opted to go barefoot for an entire day to raise awareness about the fact that millions of faraway children go without shoes every day. Many of these humanitarian-activists are college students or working Millennials, but the event also enfolds celebrities, bands, business executives, and even the US Embassy of Armenia in 2013.[2] Appearing more like a simulacrum of a social movement, "One Day Without Shoes" is hosted by TOMS Shoes, a for-profit company that started in 2006 by ex-*The Amazing Race* participant, Blake Mycoskie—now closer to a charismatic leader or international celebrity than a business owner. TOMS Shoes started by selling a now trendy slip-on shoe, which mimics the traditional Argentinian *alpargata* shoe but is "made for the American market," meant to be "more comfortable and durable . . . but also more fun and stylish."[3] The company has long surpassed selling merely one style of shoe, now expanding to include everything from "desert wedge" heels and "Nepal" boots, to sunglasses, bags, coffee, and hosting the TOMS Marketplace, a venue for the company to showcase other socially minded companies' products.[4] TOMS even partnered with Target for the 2014 holiday season, releasing a collaborative collection under the mantra, "One for One, for All," a play on the TOMS trademarked business model, "One for One" wherein a consumer buys a product and a like product is given to someone in need.

An exemplar of ethical or "conscious" capitalism, along with similar configurations that have emerged of late, TOMS attempts to transform the dominant capitalist paradigm toward one that is softer, kinder, and more concerned with societal benefit, 'doing good,' and social responsibility. Although the trademarked term "Conscious Capitalism" stems from organizations associated with John Mackey, an outspoken libertarian and the founder and co-CEO of Whole Foods, other terms embody the same vision that privatized business and free markets provide the best-possible defense against the detrimental effects of the capitalist system itself—growing inequality, the continuation of impoverishment and hunger, and environmental decay, for example.[5] In this model, success is supposedly defined not through the accumulation of capital, but through a deeper commitment to making the world a better place, although the two become co-constitutive, enacting something like a spiritual meritocracy.[6] Such ethical positions are ubiquitous within the United States today as evidenced not only in Product (RED) and Pink commodities, raising awareness about AIDS in Africa and breast cancer in the United States respectively, but also the wildly popular TOMS Shoes, B-Corp legislation, and mission-driven businesses such as Honest Tea, Thinx, and Whole Foods. The idea that one can "change the world" through the quotidian act of shopping or embodying the entrepreneurial spirit is pervasive today and each of these companies sells not only a particular product or service, but also a concrete idea about a future idyllic world that is achievable only if we collectively "harness the power of private enterprise for public benefit."[7]

What Adam Arvidsson and Nicolai Peitersen call *ethical capital* becomes a model for the incorporation of ethical value into economic processes of value-creation and capital accumulation. For the authors reputation and virtue are crucial in that they "function as a kind of capital," much like the Bourdieuian *cultural capital.*[8] But the subjective nature of ethics and virtue bring about troublesome interpretations of Utopia in this model, envisioned as a neoliberal capitalist paradise driven primarily by what Michel Foucault theorizes in his *Birth of Biopolitics* as *homo oeconomicus,* or what Wendy Brown sees as a guiding rationality of marketization and entrepreneurialism.[9] Despite the seeming newness of ethical capitalism and its revolutionary engagement with social causes, it does little to reform existing modes of accumulation, instead producing and reproducing an 'empowered' yet docile citizen-subject who is understood only in terms of his/her economization as a moral entrepreneurial figure, a consumer, and/or a laborer or recipient of a company's "good." This chapter builds upon these sentiments by interrogating the construction of utopian longings for a better world and how their promises transpire within the contemporary spirit of capitalism. As the opening Marcuse quote may suggest, the chapter argues that a utopian futurity must see its way *beyond* existing ethical capitalism inasmuch as its development limits social imaginings to the confines of capitalist reproduction. In so doing it naturalizes a faulty form of ready-made solutions that inevitably secures the continuation of excessive consumption (often without the consideration for the production of environmental destruction), perpetuates the myth of individualized private sector solutions to structural inequalities, and cements existing hierarchical social relations despite appearances of empowerment and solidarity through the rhetoric of freedom, voluntary exchange, and competition. Whereas entrepreneurship predates the rise of capitalism, its evolution has brought it to a moment of embodying the ethos of social welfare (or social entrepreneurship). Such historical shifts continually ask spectators, consumers, and citizens alike to "buy into a better world" not only as a series of ideological movements, but also as achievable political, social, and economic acts. Hence, one may change the world through consumerist and entrepreneurial activities that simultaneously privilege the market while also attaching to it a claim of public benefit, thereby focusing the gaze on a distant other in need of support. In this model, utopian actuality has never being so simple with images, social media, and advertising providing the concretization of imagining one's place within this (capitalist) future—evidenced in mantras such as Thinx's "change your underwear, change the world," a company selling women's underwear while also advocating for the elimination of taboos surrounding menstruation and female empowerment, certainly a worthy cause.[10]

The chapter opens by delineating what some scholars refer to as the ethical turn and its relation to existing capitalism, especially the infiltration of *homo oeconomicus* and Brown's assertion that it undermines democracies and one's political role within them.[11] The chapter then turns to what is actually utopian about ethical capitalism as demonstrated in a multitude of companies, highlighting two key characteristics: first, a proliferation of empowerment discourses often partnered with poverty alleviation and second, the belief in global interconnectedness, which materializes through proclamations of solidarity. Within these characteristics, there are four crucial actors who maintain the utopian impulse—the charismatic and 'heroic' entrepreneurial-activist who constructs the idea, the commodity-form and its subsequent mediations that become the site of a symbolic use-value or commodity activism, the conscientious consumer, and the recipient of 'good,' who is often most visually present in company or commodity advertisements. The chapter relies heavily on images in so much that they serve as the material indices of utopian longing—cementing entrepreneurs, commodities, and thereby consumers with solvable crises involving particular people in specific (often far away) places. Different than imagery of earlier philanthropic endeavors such as Sally Struther's commercials with Christian Children's Fund, the images of ethical capital are future-oriented, envisioning 'poverty porn' as the joys of empowerment and solidarity rather than the devastation of a current or past crisis.[12] Thus, the chapter concludes by considering the ways that ethical discourses, emotion, and affect contribute to an activism bound by markets and cautions against the fate of utopian longing when rationalized within the economic calculus of capitalism.

THE ETHICAL TURN AND HOMO OECONOMICUS

New spaces of sociality and capitalist reproduction emerge daily with the explicit purpose to remake capitalism, but the new twist brought about by 'the ethical turn' is that it recasts the mechanisms of capitalism—its modes of value creation and accumulation—on its transformative powers of public benefit and envisages ethics in a way unforeseen by early eras, building such ideas upon the decaying edifices of crisis-ridden global capitalism and using not only the wreckage of unilateral agreements about rising inequality, but also the bad name capitalism has received in recent decades with backlash against the Washington Consensus, market-driven globalization, trenchant corporatization, banking fraud, incessant commodification, precarious labor, and environmental ruin. Authors of *The Ethical Economy* openly declare: "The Naomi Klein era is over, replaced by the likes of Umair Haque and John Grant, who preach a reformed capitalism ready to address wider social concerns."[13] The dismantling of the Naomi Klein era, however, does not just bring about new politics as guided by free-market ideology rather than progressive Keynesianism, but also further casts a fissure between competing notions of social responsibility—guaranteed by the social safety net of the state or individualized by corporations, people, and nonprofit organizations. In this new iteration of capitalism, the private sector stands in as social actor and governing body, becoming the legitimizing force for particular causes and social positions. As John Mackey and Raj Sisodia argue in *Conscious Capitalism: Liberating the Heroic Spirit of Business,*

> We humans can choose to exist at a caterpillar level, consuming all we can, taking as much as possible from the world and giving little back. We are also capable of evolving to a degree that is no less dramatic than what happens to a caterpillar, transforming ourselves into beings who create value for others and help make the world more beautiful. The same is true for corporations.[14]

Hence, the corporation ought to transmorph itself away from a hungry caterpillar, accumulating all it can, and should instead ensure the longevity of the world and its peers. Conversely, Wendy Brown reads these seemingly altruistic shifts critically: "the conduct of government and the conduct of firms are now fundamentally identical; both are in the business of justice and sustainability, but never as ends in themselves."[15] She continues by exemplifying the popularity of social responsibility, "which must itself be entrepreneurialized" as it "is part of what attracts consumers and investors."[16] What Brown means here is not that all spheres become monetized as markets, although this certainly occurs in some spaces, but rather that "neoliberal rationality disseminates the *model of the market* to all domains and activities—even where money is not an issue—and configures human beings exhaustively as market actors, always, only, and everywhere as *homo oeconomicus.*"[17] The idea of *homo oeconomicus* classically refers simply to economic man or "the partner of exchange and the theory of utility based on a problematic of needs."[18] Yet, for Foucault neoliberalism fundamentally alters *homo oeconomicus* in so much that the "partner of exchange" becomes an "entrepreneur of himself, being for himself his own capital, being for himself his own producer, being for himself the source of [his] earnings."[19] Related to ethical capitalism, this is seen within numerous seemingly contradictory ways: the insistence of the activist-turned-entrepreneur, social justice campaigns and worthy causes circulating as marketable commodities and subjected to competitive forces, and the very notions of consciousness, mindfulness, happiness, and enlightenment furthering one's credibility as human capital or an "entrepreneur of the self."[20] In the case of TOMS' "One Day Without Shoes," the company and its participants sell an image of the self as good and concerned with the plight of others.

Melissa M. Brough, in "Fair Vanity: The visual Culture of Humanitarianism in the Age of Commodity Activism," details some of these developments as they relate to the nonprofit organization Invisible Children. The organization first drew attention to itself with its *Global Night Commute: A Musical to Believe in,* a musical released on YouTube that sought to bring awareness to global night commuting by youths in Uganda. According to Brough, Invisible Children embodies a new pop-aesthetic humanitarianism that focuses more on the construction of the young humanitarian and his/her personal growth than older conceptions. Claiming Bono's utterance of the term "fair vanity" in the 2007 "Africa Issue" of *Vanity Fair* magazine, Brough says the term epitomizes the idea that philanthropy ought to be not just about style and commodification, but "also about adventure and spectacle."[21] Within Invisible Children however it occurs only through an ahistorical narrative of self-discovery, ignoring any structural or historical contextualization of the crisis in Uganda. Like Invisible Children, TOMS Shoes enacts a "participatory spectacle," which Brough links to Stephen Duncombe's *ethical spectacle*—an activist tactic that relies upon "the collective, carnivalesque, self-reflexive enactment of a social change 'dream,' performed as a spectacle but tied to real material goals and actions."[22] While the *ethical spectacle* contains within it the possibility for social transformation, it is utilized within the entrepreneurial-activism of TOMS and Invisible Children in such a way that they fail to ever see beyond their own futurity, bound to the model of the market and thereby lacking the politicization that Duncombe evokes.

Assuredly a contentious issue, the infiltration of overtly moralistic discourses into capitalism teeters between one the one hand, politicizing markets and on the other, economizing the political, thereby diminishing its efficacies. Whereas the introduction of moralistic claims into economic exchange does not necessarily entail a retreat from politics, it subjects such politics to the logic (or illogic) of capitalist markets, cementing the idea's worth to its marketability and financial value like any other commodity. Hence, companies and commodities that promote causes such as Breast Cancer Awareness or the combating of AIDS in Africa are doubly "worthy" in that they are both 'doing good' *and* are highly marketable, although ample scholarship criticizes the commodification of these causes and contradictions between their goals and economization.[23] In "Ethical Ambivalence," Judith Butler reveals a cynical approach to the topic:

> I do not have much to say about why there is a return to ethics, if there is one, in recent years, except to say that I have for the most part resisted this return, and that what I have to offer is something like a map of resistance and its partial overcoming . . . I've worried that the return to ethics has constituted an escape from politics, and I've also worried that it has meant a certain heightening of moralism and this has made me cry out, as Nietzsche cried out about Hegel, 'Bad air! Bad air!'[24]

Chantal Mouffe argues that the popularity of humanitarian causes and "ethically correct" crusades may be understood as the "triumph of a sort of moralizing liberalism that has increasingly filled the void left by the collapse of any project of real political transformation."[25] She continues, "This moralization of society is in my view a consequence of the lack of any credible political alternative to the current dominance of neoliberalism."[26] The erosion of viable democratic politics is echoed by other scholars as well, including Ella Myers in *Worldly Ethics* and Wendy Brown in *Undoing the Demos: Neoliberalism's Stealth Revolution*. When surveying the landscape of conscious or ethical capitalism, the retreat from politics as such often appears much like a simulacrum of the political, with civic engagement broadening in scope to include (rather than simply be replaced by) forms of economic activism—that is to say, consumerism, entrepreneurship, and the creation of seemingly politically charged commodities.

TOMS' "One Day Without Shoes" is a prime example of this. In the spring of 2015, the company changed its tactic: instead of a call to arms for its consumer-activists to march barefoot the entire day—a hardship perhaps too much to endure for its consumers—it merely asked them to take a picture of their bare feet and post it to the social media site Instagram with the hashtag *#withoutshoes.* With the elimination of the physicality of walking without shoes for an entire day, solidarity became one of mere mediated spectacle, asking even less of consumers. Perhaps building off of other ethical mediated events such as the ALS Ice Bucket Challenge that went viral in the summer of 2014, TOMS incorporated its "One for One" model in a new way, giving a pair of shoes to a child in need for each photograph posted to Instagram between May 5 and May 21, 2015. According to the company's website, 296,243 new pairs of shoes will be given because of the event, which simultaneously politicizes something as trivial as bare feet due to the textual accompaniment linking the image of the feet to a cause, while also depoliticizing (and importantly, ahistoricizing) any understanding of the cause. Only in its giving of shoes is this TOMS event any different from other slacktivist campaigns, which are useful for bringing international recognition to particular events or crises, while also circulating via social media as the visualization of one's ethics.[27]

Many scholars who discuss the turn to ethics note these eroding tendencies, often framed as the "shattering" of the liberal democratic social contract.[28] Wendy Brown sees this as an example of how "rights themselves can be economized" wherein citizen-subjects are incessantly reproduced as human capital.[29] Put another way, *homo oeconomicus* is holistically supplanting *homo politicus,* which Brown argues occurs at the behest of a guiding neoliberal rationality. Whereas Brown understands these developments as detrimental to the viability of *demos,* advocates of ethical or conscious capital argue that economizing possibilities serve the best possible chance of preserving liberal democracies, citizen-rights, and the reproduction of 'good.' It is, in fact, much more complicated than either of these dichotomies and instead the contemporary transformative 'spirit' of an ethically minded capitalism blurs previously familiar antinomies of the political and economic, but also between the public and private, and individual and collective.

Within all of this, the role of critique in the changing landscape of capitalism and "moralizing liberalism" is also further eroded, a point echoed in John Mackey's closing comments in the 2005 *Reason Magazine* debate: "I believe if economists and business people consistently communicated and acted on my message that 'the enlightened corporation should try to create value for all of its constituencies,' we would see most of the resistance to capitalism disappear."[30] Certainly, it is not a new argument to say that capitalism co-opts dissent by making it into a marketable commodity and subcultural identity formation.[31] More recently, scholars Jason Hickel and Arsalan Khan ask: "How have we arrived at a place where the Left's only plan for change is to further facilitate market deregulation and advance the consolidation of monopoly capitalism?"[32] The insistence of the ethical turn pushes the atomized individual to go beyond mere consumerist politics and instead to seek the "heroic" status of entrepreneurship and the insistence that business is "a force for good in the world," as stated by former Twitter Chairman and CEO Evan Williams.[33] While "changing the world" is central to the utopian impulse within ethical capitalism, it also advocates a more moralistic version of the American Dream wherein one can have it all—riches, private property, happiness, *and* a better world. Any contradiction of these ideals is erased and capitalist competition continues to be celebrated with any potential for brutality erased by the karmic.

The point of critique made by the ethical turn rarely falls on capitalist structures themselves and instead on a 'wrongly practiced' capitalism or the naturalization of the problem entirely. Hence, children without shoes potentially suffering from podoconiosis or being at risk to other soil-transmitted infections and unable to attend school is not a problem *of capitalism*—too much or too little—but rather a solvable crisis seemingly eradicated by 'dropping' loads of shoes into communities, often at the detriment of local communities, which then allows impoverished children in the developing world "a better chance of improving the future of their entire community."[34] For TOMS, breaking the poverty cycle is as simple as a pair of shoes. Why? Because shoes allow for access to education and to better health.[35] While something as simple as shoes is certainly a crucial marker of success and even potentially hinders one's access, it is not the gatekeeper of impoverishment. TOMS has heard some of the criticisms of its "One for One" model and responded accordingly by expanding to liken particular commodities to other societal needs: each 12 ounce bag of TOMS Coffee provides safe drinking water to someone for one week, with every TOMS bag purchased, the company "will provide a safe birth for a mother and baby in need."[36] TOMS is not alone in these commodified forms of aid, but they are one of the most popular, even drawing enough attention so that Skecher's started a copy-cat brand, BOBS, which even has a similar logo. While it is easy to deride these developments as mere branding strategies, there is much more going on here; these companies and entrepreneurs are not only responding to a need within markets, but also soothing the anxieties of individuals about the contemporary status of the world. What is most significant is that these anxieties are best assuaged through one's naturalization within market relations (as consumers and entrepreneurs) with the caveat being that this 'new economy' rooted in higher-purpose, consciousness, and a path toward progress that is fulfilled by utopian promise, is better than those other capitalisms of the past.

This simplification of utopian actuality fails to ever deliver, but such failures become individualized rather than attributed to broader failures of a capitalist futurity.

"CAPITALISM IS DEAD. LONG LIVE CAPITALISM": UTOPIAN LONGING IN ETHICAL CAPITALISM

The embedding of the utopian impulse within ethical capitalism exists in a dialectic precariousness that is best articulated in the opening sentences of Umair Haque's *The New Capitalist Manifesto*: "Capitalism is dead. Long live capitalism."[37] The statement simultaneously mandates the death and longevity of capitalism, but the capitalism in the first sentence differs from the capitalism of the second sentence. For Haque, the capitalism that is dead is a hegemonic global capitalism as connected to its industrial model of the nineteenth and twentieth centuries, which must be replaced by a new system that actually maintains the privileging of the very same mechanisms of private property, accumulation, and divisiveness according to the standard lines of class, race, sex, sexual preference, and so forth. Now, it should be said that ethical capitalism certainly does not reflect upon itself in this way, rather seeing itself as a revolutionary vanguard for what is just, empathetic, and spiritually enlightened. That is not to say, however, that ethical capitalism is doing no good. Quite the contrary, many of these companies are actually providing material impact on others around the world—often quantifiable alongside the number of commodities sold—but as a Smithian interpretation of capitalism would suggest, "By pursuing his own interest [an individual] frequently promotes that of the society more effectually than when he really intends to promote it. I have never known much good done by those who affected to trade for the public good."[38] What Adam Smith means here, a sentiment that Milton Friedman supported and defended in a debate with Conscious Capitalist and Whole Foods founder, John Mackey, is that by merely pursuing the entrepreneurial spirit and self-interest, one will *unintentionally* benefit society. To overtly consider "public good," according to Smith is merely an "affectation," unnatural in market relations. Each individual instead will *naturally* find "the most advantageous employment for whatever capital he can command," which will "naturally, or rather necessarily, [lead] him to prefer that employment which is most advantageous to the society."[39] This equilibrium relies upon conditions of an abstracted perfection between markets, governments, corporations, and individuals acting in their own self-interest but also contributing to societal development.

Smith is useful here not because I concur with him in terms of profit maximization or self-interest representing a more beneficial model for societies, but instead because it is in the difference between Smith's understanding of entrepreneurship and ethical capitalism's that we may understand the latter's utopian impulse. It ultimately comes down to the reinvestment of capital for both parties, or, to Marx's formula of M-C-M'.[40] For Smith, this system naturally achieves an equilibrium that transcends any conspicuous attempts at public good. This too is where many contemporaries of *laissez-faire* find themselves. Yet, an emergent trend of ethical capital, supported by those finding themselves both to the right and left on the political spectrum, suggests a new path forward that accounts for the M' taking on some sort of explicit reinvestment in society. For Whole Foods, this may mean the establishment of its Whole Planet Foundation, which seeks to provide poverty alleviation in developing countries through microloans.[41] For TOMS, it occurs through a direct "One for One," giving like products to those in need. For Thinx, it provides reusable menstrual pads for girls in Uganda. Each conscious business envisions the reinvestment in society differently, acting together as some vague conception of an "ambiguous utopia."[42] Yet, this ethical M' is a false difference in that, as I mentioned earlier, ethical capitalism integrally links the accumulation of wealth with the accumulation of metaphysical enlightenment. Partly, this strategy is necessary when attempting to *sell* ethical capitalism to businesses that might otherwise not consider it, making it more of a branding gimmick than a meaningful approach to business. Yet, ethical capital operates within the realm of the karmic (in theory)—one cannot falsely worship at the altar of ethical capital unless he/she is an authentic practitioner.[43] The point is that whether surplus-value (the M') recirculates within markets as monies or as a more directed reinvestment in society ('doing good'), both secures the expansion of capital, as ultimately the goal of 'doing good' is to help those in need to better participate in the creation and circulation of capital.

Take for example Whole Foods' investment in its private nonprofit organization, the Whole Planet Foundation. The premise is that the organization invests money in microfinance institutions, which then give out microloans turning impoverished communities into hubs of entrepreneurial frenzy and thereby ending what the Father of Microfinance and founder of the Grameen Bank, Muhammad Yunus, deems a "financial apartheid."[44] These microfinance schemes incorporate the borrowers into a system of calculability while also creating new spaces for capital accumulation and cycles of debt. Although there is ample evidence of microfinance working in some instances and not working in many others, the most famous backlash against it came in late 2010 to early 2011 when Yunus, was accused of "sucking blood from the poor" by the Prime Minister of Bangladesh, Sheikh Hasina.[45]

Much like the Smithian characterization of capital, this instance demonstrates Whole Foods' public good simply existing as an expansion of capital, folding in those outside its grip, but being framed as an overt altruistic project of poverty alleviation. Yet, it is important to remember that ethical capitalism emerges from a position of critique, ousting the "bad" capitalism of today and replacing it with a capitalism that is entirely based on linking such mechanisms of accumulation to entrepreneurial heroes who are enlightened and rich in spiritual wealth.[46] Although there are countless visions of utopianism within ethical capitalism, the chapter now turns to two examples to concretize its argument—the idea of empowerment, which is often packaged with poverty alleviation, and the belief in a global citizenry or global interconnectedness that works with conceptions of solidarity and compassion.

"WE BLEED FOR FEMALE EMPOWERMENT:" SOLIDARITY, AGENCY, AND INTERCONNECTEDNESS

Miki Agrawal and her twin sister Radha—both self-acclaimed "serial" social entrepreneurs—started Thinx to design and sell "period proof underwear" while also promoting female empowerment through donations to AfriPads, a for profit limited liability company with a nonprofit foundation in Uganda that designs reusable maxi-pads for girls who are otherwise unable to attend school during their "week of shame."[47] The idea emerged when Miki visited South Africa for the 2010 World Cup and encountered a girl who was not in school because of her period. Miki returned home and with the help of her sister and friend began researching the troubling statistics for girls in the developing world missing school because of their lack of feminine hygiene products.[48] The founders then realized the potential for these "magic period underwear to support these girls."[49] Thinx originally prided itself on the slogan, "change your underwear, change the world," but has since switched to perhaps an even more provocative statement: "we bleed for female empowerment."

Within Thinx, empowerment works at multiple registers affecting the entirety of the commodity-circuit. First, the girl who is given reusable pads is gifted empowerment materializing as reusable pads because she is now allowed to attend school during her "week of shame." Second, other girls are able to purchase their reusable pads in Uganda, feeling the "power of the purchase" much like the consumers of Thinx under-garments and similar to the AfriPads donors. Third, AfriPads empowers its employees (90% women) in Uganda with employment while Thinx empowers its underwear producers—women in Sri Lanka at a "family-run factory that has an outstanding commitment to providing supplementary education and training to its female employees, empowering them to become leaders in their communities."[50] Finally, the entrepreneurs themselves are empowered to "help" or "do good" by seeing a problem in the world and solving it with entrepreneurial frenzy. More broadly, Thinx seeks a new world:

> We see a world where no woman is held back by her body. We will work proudly and tirelessly until every single girl has an equal opportunity for the brighter future she deserves. By reimagining feminine hygiene products to provide support, comfort, confidence, and peace of mind, we aim to eliminate shame, empowering women and girls around the world.

Certainly well intentioned, this utopian narrative of female empowerment is easy to support, as are most empowerment narratives. After all, to stand against "empowerment" veers toward diabolical and assumes a position of supporting the continuation of a lack of power for some people throughout the world. However, like other discourses within ethical capitalism, empowerment narratives work in particular ways that simultaneously give the appearance of opening up spaces of new self-power while also enforcing certain modes of governance, or what Foucault calls the "conduct of conduct" by creating management systems for poverty.[51] In *The Will to Empower,* Barbara Cruikshank challenges the term's invocation as a "noble or radical political strategy," seeing it as linked to the privatization strategies of the 1980s and 1990s:

> The will to empower may be well intentioned, but it is a strategy for constituting and regulating the political subjectivities of the 'empowered.' Whether inspired by the market or by the promise of self-government and autonomy, the object of empowerment is to act upon another's interests and desires in order to conduct their actions toward an appropriate end; thus, 'empowerment' is itself a power relationship and one deserving careful scrutiny.[52]

Certainly a contentious point, one that some scholars within this very anthology may take issue with, Cruikshank makes a particularly compelling case for the utility of this narrative as a mechanism of social control. Within the contemporary epoch and specifically within the ethical turn, the construction of empowerment circulates drawing new masses into the capitalist mode of production and its reproductive ideologies with its seemingly new consciousness. According to Google's Ngram, the very use of the words "empower" and "empowerment" have rapidly ascended since the 1980s with the earlier term "impower" becoming virtually obsolete by the mid-1800s.[53]

Although the reproduction of empowerment discourses and practices are required for its continuation, it also works in and through the visual within ethical capitalism to further the imagining of the utopian impulse. For example, the images of Thinx rely on both a textual and visual utterance of empowerment in order to concretize the company's social imperative. In a banner image that is no longer on the Thinx website, the spectator sees three female models—only visible from torso to knee—modeling elegant black underwear. These women are all of a lighter skin tone and possess the quintessential slender physique normalized within American beauty standards. Over this image, supporting text reads: *Change your underwear, Change the world. Thoughtful underwear with hidden powers.* Another image on the website, a part of the same sliding banner, instead shows the faces of at least two-dozen dark skinned girls, each wearing an ivory button-down shirt, smiling, and holding up what appears to be baby pink and blue cotton-candy, but upon further inspection is actually a packet of reusable menstrual pads. A similarly bolded text reads: *join the movement to keep girls in school. For every pair of Thinx you buy, you fund 7 pads to help 1 girl.*

While these images are no longer on the website, each reinforces what E. Ann Kaplan refers to as an "imperial gaze" in so much that the visualization of difference promotes a one-directional looking that privileges the Western female—typically white and affluent—who not only portrays her sexuality and desirability in the images of Thinx, but also articulates her benevolence by being a part of the Thinx movement to change the world.[54] In the images mentioned above, the consumer-spectator has all the agency for action whereas the African girl is portrayed as in need of saving. The new content on the website is equally troubling and despite its best intentions, reinforces yet again a hegemonic relationship wherein the western consumer or entrepreneur stands in as the savior of the 'uncivilized.' To date, the home screen image shows a Caucasian woman sitting on a bed reading a book and wearing a midriff top and lacey black underwear. The background provides a warm and comforting space—plants, candles, art on the walls, and natural light. A text-over reads: *How modern women do periods.* A clear comparison exists between this woman and the Ugandan girls in need of saving who are antithetical to modern women.[55] Similarly, under the "power of the purchase" section of the website—which users get to by clicking a small icon with outlines of the US country and African continent—a group photo captures Thinx founder Miki and her friend sitting among approximately thirty presumed Ugandan women. All are smiling and raising their hands with the focal point of the image centering on Miki and her light-skinned partner. Structurally, the image replicates the metropole-periphery relationship of the colonial era and in case the image is not clear enough, the white text-over reads: *We bleed for female empowerment. Every Thinx purchase has the power to help a woman in Uganda.* The embodiment of empowerment is shared in this instance through an interconnectedness that ultimately hierarchizes the western consumer as the one with power (as a consumer) and the Ugandan woman as the powerless. Any empowerment that comes to the Ugandan female occurs through a gift from the already powerful western female consumer despite the assumption of solidarity. This solidarity comes across as a cast-off form of empowerment in that it toys with the tension between similarity and difference with a juxtaposition of image and word working to forge a point of commonality between the visual foreign-ness of the bodies and the shared corporeal reality that everybody bleeds. Relatedly, TOMS relies on the same bodily qualities linking diverse peoples together through the solidarity of understanding that it is painful to walk without shoes.

The gift of empowerment works in tandem with poverty alleviation efforts through a belief that if one is empowered, (s)he will not be impoverished. A false binary in its simplicity, it ignores the broader structural forces of poverty and as Cruikshank emphasizes, serves as a device to manage 'the poor,' funneling any antagonism that could manifest as a collective political form of power into individualized market-led empowerments. In the cases of Thinx and TOMS, empowerment does not function as a mechanism of political agency despite its earliest derivations as such and instead promulgates *homo oeconomicus* and its incessant need for the expansion of the model of the market, markets themselves, and a guiding rationality that supports these demands. Poverty, according to both Thinx and TOMS, is solvable through work, gifts, and education. For both companies, a simple commodity—reusable menstrual pads, shoes, eyewear, or water—hinders the powerless' access to empowerment and thereby poverty alleviation because the commodity is all that seemingly stands between the child's potential for power.[56] These simple quotidian objects impede access to education, which according to both Thinx and TOMS is the route for one to lift him/herself out of poverty. Yet, a simple pair of flimsy shoes, water for even a week, or eyewear may *better the odds* for an impoverished individual, but does not address the broader societal and historical causes of poverty. For example, what if instead of giving water to someone for a week, TOMS fought the privatization of precious water resources by countries devastated by such developments and resisted the commoditization of water (a thing that should be a human right)? The website indicates that the company's efforts go beyond water for one week and that its Giving Partners also "support local business development and government investments to create sustainable water systems and solutions for widespread, long-term impact."[57] However, with little transparency, consumers are left only with slogans such as "Coffee for You, Water for All" and a simplified and quantifiable equation:

12 Ounce Bag of Coffee = Safe Drinking Water for Someone
in Need for One Week.

Already implicit within the examples above—"we bleed for female empowerment" or "coffee for you, water for all"—is a discourse of solidarity, interconnectedness, and public benefit, that links those already with some degree of power, typically economic, with the person or communities in need. In the case of ethical capitalism, a muddying of public mindedness and individual self-care occurs with notions of collectivity, solidarity, and interconnectedness working at the behest of the individual ethical actor. Self-care thus includes the emotional well-being and the "moralization of . . . freedom"[58]—the good feelings of helping others, of the mindfulness and consciousness that comes from recognizing the crisis of global capitalism, but also believing that the solutions are found within actualizable individualized everyday practices of consumption and social entrepreneurship. Yet, this imagined collectivity requires not only the calculability and rationality of the neoliberal order that Brown discusses wherein all is reduced to the economic, but also highly affective media cultures that interpellate subjects as empathetic (globally conscious) consumer-citizen-maybe-entrepreneurs who must "change the world" or stand in solidarity with those far away (and typically racialized) people 'in need.'

Krochet Kids, a trendy nonprofit organization that looks just like a private firm selling products takes solidarity a step further by urging its consumers to: "Scan this [QR code] and search for the lady that made this item." You can even "write her a thank you note."[59] The imagined bonds of collectivity are fun and compassionate for those with the freedoms and power—economic or otherwise—to participate, while potentially being either nonexistent or a matter of sheer survival for others. While the entrepreneur or consumer can *choose* to "change the world" by quotidian acts of changing her/his underwear, scanning a QR code, or purchasing a bag of coffee, it actually places some communities and individuals in a place of further *dis*-empowerment, becoming reliant on the possibly fleeting goodwill and purchasing trends of the faraway consumer or entrepreneurial-activist. Moreover, by proffering simplistic market-based solutions to complex historical and social crises, it entrenches a neoliberal rationality of *homo oeconomicus* that ultimately naturalizes the inherent goodness of a capitalism guided by higher purpose, consciousness, and market-led activism that diminishes its political possibilities. Furthermore, the utopian longing of ethical capitalism relies upon an individualizing tendency that also presents an image of togetherness, solidarity and interconnectedness. As evidenced in several images by Thinx—merely one example of these trends—solidarity and empowerment despite their best efforts remain bound to the confines of existing hierarchies and are unable to envision a more egalitarian relationship—one free of racial, geopolitical, gendered, or classed implications.

CONCLUSION

In the opening of "Utopia Now," Fredric Jameson states that, "our imaginations are hostages to our own mode of production," suggesting that Utopias may be best utilized through their failure and "serve the negative purpose of making us more aware of our mental and ideological imprisonment."[60] Elsewhere, Jameson writes about the "blind spots" of utopian longings, which are always bound by the current situation of the imaginer. For Thomas More who was writing in the early 1500s, this was, as Jameson says, an "inability to imagine capitalism and the market."[61] Today, however, it is unimaginable to see outside of capitalism and *homo oeconomicus*. Within the ethical capitalist movement, often (but not always), efforts are well-intentioned, missions noble. Yet, ethical capitalism remains always already committed to a twofold set of purposes, which often operate in contradiction: the reproduction and expansion of market-led capitalism and a social mission to "change the world" and rebuild the dereliction of existing capitalism. These two cannot always work in tandem and often do not. By subjecting public benefit and the vision of a better world to the whims of capitalism, the real needs of communities and individuals are limited to the imagination of what is entrepreneurial and marketable.

This chapter has argued that a utopian futurity must be able to see beyond existing ethical capitalism, which might mean challenging the ideological training of our imaginations that incessantly look for ready-made solutions to complex problems within simplistic acts of economization. But, it may be as Jameson suggests, ethical capitalism as a utopian project and collection of theories, for-profit companies, nonprofit organizations, commodities (and associated advertisements), and consumer habits may need to serve its negative purpose first—working to alert us to our current mode of imaginative failures or as Jameson says, "our mental and ideological imprisonment."[62] And yet, the moment that awareness becomes known, without a doubt some entrepreneurial-minded person will make a T-shirt about it.

NOTES

1. Herbert Marcuse. "The End of Utopia." (First published in *Psychoanalyse und Politik*; lecture delivered at the Free University of West Berlin in July 1967.) Accessed March 2, 2015. https://www.marxists.org/reference/archive/marcuse/works/1967/end-utopia.htm

2. On April 16, 2013, John Heffern (@AmbHeffern)—then US Ambassador to Armenia—was tweeting about TOMS' #onedaywithoutshoes and a photograph of sugar cookies in the shape of bare feet with TOMS written on each cookie in orange-red icing. The tweet reads: "Feet cookies for @toms one day #withoutshoes at embassy yerevan."

3. Blake Mycoskie, *Start Something That Matters* (New York: Spiegel & Grau Trade, 2011), 8.

4. My own university, George Mason University (GMU), has a record of being particularly smitten with TOMS and broader ideas of social entrepreneurship. In 2013, its Common Read Program, which seeks to build a community for off-campus freshman and thereby secure higher retention rates, featured Mycoskie's book, *Start Something That Matters,* asking students to visualize what it is that could matter to them at GMU and how they could become involved in campus clubs or begin thinking about their own future endeavors into entrepreneurship or leadership. Faculty mentors—myself among them—were not monetarily compensated, but instead gifted a pair of none other than TOMS shoes. GMU's campus frequently participates in events such as "One Day without Shoes" or its foray into World Sight Day, which on October 10, 2013, asked consumer-activists to #BESHADY: "What's that mean? Wear your shades inside—something typically reserved for rock stars (and people who want to be rock stars)! When you catch coworkers or classmates giving you a funny look, take advantage of the conversation starter. Tell them you're doing this for World Sight Day. To raise awareness. To be part of something bigger than yourself." (Blake Mycoskie. "World Sight Day." *The Huffington Post* (October 10, 2013), accessed October 30, 2013, http://www.huffingtonpost.com/blake-mycoskie/world-sight-day-2013_b_4073653.html.) The campus even allowed (temporarily) for a TOMS student group to be formed—receiving access to state funds—with its logo consisting of founding father (and slave-owner) George Mason flaunting a pair of red TOMS shoes. The organization's goal was to "spread the message and perpetuate the goals of TOMS Shoes. This includes, but is not limited to, promoting the One for One Movement and active participation in a collegiate setting." (TOMS Shoes Campus Club Constitution, George Mason University, 2012–2013.) Never had a privately held company successfully stood in as a nonprofit organization or a social justice movement and certainly the university would never allow for a more overtly corporate entity—Walmart or Dow Chemical—to have a student club on campus, but due to the continuing slippage between previously distinct categories of for- or nonprofit, and social movements, TOMS was able to successfully brand itself "a movement."

5. Conscious Capitalism is a trademarked term that is associated with John Mackey, the founder and co-CEO of Whole Foods. The trademark was first secured through the now defunct organization, Freedom Lights Our World (FLOW). Conscious Capitalism, Inc. has also secured the rights to such basic phrases as "Liberating the entrepreneurial spirit for good" (serial number: 77407666). It should also be noted that TOMS Shoes has trademarked the term "One for One," which is the foundation of its business model wherein a consumer buys a commodity and a like commodity is given to someone in need. Although other companies may practice this One for One™ model, they do not use the phrase.

6. Shawn Van Valkenburg, "The Dangerous American Myth of Spiritual Meritocracy." *Salon* (October 26, 2014), accessed October 26, 2014, http://www.salon.com/2014/10/26/the_dangerous_american_myth_of_corporate_spirituality/

7. This is the guiding principle of Benefit Corporation (B-Corp) legislation within the United States, which since 2010 has been altering state corporate law to account for corporations who wish to focus the company on what good it does for society rather than the traditional model of profit maximization. While this sounds like a

positive change, it lacks any real oversight and only loosely defines "public benefit," allowing for corporations to interpret the term in any variation of ways. Any oversight comes from the third-party certifying organization, B Labs. To date, 27 states have passed legislation with another 14 considering it.

8. Adam Arvidsson and Nicolai Peitersen, *The Ethical Economy: Rebuilding Value after the Crisis* (New York: Columbia University Press, 2013), xvi.

9. Wendy Brown, "Neoliberalism and the End of Liberal Democracy." *Theory & Event* 7, no. 1 (2003). Also see *Undoing the Demos: Neoliberalism's Stealth Revolution* (2015).

10. The term "commodity activism" comes from Roopali Mukherjee and Sarah Banet-Weiser's (eds.) *Commodity Activism: Cultural Resistance in Neoliberal Times* (2012).

11. The term "the ethical turn" is utilized by Adam Arvidsson and Nicolai Peiterson in *The Ethical Economy* (2013) and also by Ella Myers' *Worldly Ethics: Democratic Politics and Care for the World* (2013). While both texts employ the term in an effort of historicization, it ultimately takes on differing characteristics wherein Myers is more concerned with liberal democratic politics and Arvidsson and Peiterson are focused on ethical-economic value creation, which ought to be linked to productive publics and financialization. Finally, *The Turn to Ethics* is an edited volume that considers what such a turn means politically, morally, structurally, and culturally (2000).

12. This is very possibly in response to the idea of the "aestheticization of suffering," which risks overproduction creating what Luc Boltanski in *Distant Suffering: Morality, Media, and Politics* sees as a "crisis in pity" (1999).

13. *The Ethical Economy*, viii.

14. *Conscious Capitalism: Liberating the Heroic Spirit of Business*, 25.

15. *Undoing the Demos: Neoliberalism's Stealth Revolution*, 27.

16. Ibid.

17. Ibid., 31.

18. Michel Foucault, *Birth of Biopolitics* (March 14, 1979), 225.

19. Ibid., 226.

20. This term is utilized in Foucault's *Birth of Biopolitics,* although he commonly says "entrepreneur of himself."

21. *Commodity Activism: Cultural Resistance in Neoliberal Times*, 180.

22. Brough, Melissa. "Fair Vanity," 186. The idea comes from Stephen Duncombe's *Dream: Re-imagining Progressive Politics in an Age of Fantasy,* 2007.

23. For more on these issues, see Samantha King's *Pink Ribbons, Inc.: Breast Cancer and the Politics of Philanthropy* (University of Minnesota Press, 2008). Also see Lisa Ann Richey and Stefano Ponte's *Brand Aid: Shopping Well to Save the World* (Quadrant Books, University of Minnesota Press, 2011), which discusses in detail (RED) products and their work to eradicate AIDS in Africa. A crucial point of each book is uncovering the contradiction inherent within the commodification of these causes and the individualization of any philanthropic and consumerist activism. The Susan G. Komen Foundation for instance markets breast cancer awareness and raises funds for research often by working with sponsors who are likely to inevitably be contributing to the breast cancer epidemic. For (RED) products, the branding of fighting

AIDS in Africa ultimately turns the entirety of the African continent into a passive victim in need of rescue by the affluent western consumer through the purchasing of trivial objects: vodka, condoms, computers and cell phones, GAP T-shirts, and even Starbucks coffee. Celebritydom also works to promote the cause with a trinity of celebrities promoting (RED): Bono of U2 ("the guarantor of cool"), Jeffrey Sachs, and Paul Farmer. Importantly, both Pink and Red products remove the image of death and suffering, replacing it with a sexy-coolness—"save the tatas" or "save 2nd base" branding of Breast Cancer Awareness. As Richey and Ponte state: "RED takes a new twist in which sexuality is being reclaimed by the West as healthy. Bono provides the healthy and sexy body to contrast with the 'African woman dying from sex' body. In the role of the totemic celebrity, he redeems sex, while reclaiming masculinity, and restoring a social hierarchy where cool, rich, white men save poor, voiceless African women and children." [From their plenary paper entitled "Better (RED) Than Dead? Celebrities, Consumption, and International Aid" (65), which was initially published in *Third World Quarterly* 29, no. 4 (2008): 711–729.]

24. In *The Turn to Ethics,* eds. Majorie Garber, Beatrice Hanssen, Rebecca L. Walkowitz. NY: Routledge, 2000: 15.

25. "Which Ethics for Democracy." In *The Turn to Ethics*, 85–86.

26. Ibid. Also see Brown, Wendy. "Moralism as Anti-Politics," in *Materializing Democracy: Toward a Revitalized Cultural Politics.* Duke University Press, 2002.

27. Slacktivism has become a term to describe the turn to "armchair activism" that increasingly rely on social media and/or consumerism. For instance, with the June 26, 2015, Supreme Court legalization of same-sex marriage many Facebook users very quickly turned their profile pictures rainbow-colored. The Facebook App that put existing profile pictures through a rainbow filter was used in the days following the SCOTUS decision by approximately 26 million Facebook users and by June 30 "garner[ed] more than half a billion likes and comments all over the world," including celebrities and politicians such as Russell Simmons, Arnold Schwarzenegger, Leonardo DiCaprio, California Attorney General Kamala Harris, and Brazilian president Dilma Rousseff. [Heather Kelly, "Facebook Rainbow Profiles used by 26 Million," *CNN Money* (June 30, 2015), http://money.cnn.com/2015/06/29/technology/facebook-rainbow-profile/.]

The use of Facebook "likes," hashtag campaigns, and reposting photos on Instagram are common slacktivist strategies, but what is key in any of these armchair activist techniques is minimal effort. As a *Washington Post* article proposes, "Slacktivists don't have to spend a Saturday doing hard labor to build a home or sacrifice a portion of their monthly entertainment budget to a cause. They don't even have to move from behind the screens of their electronic devices." [Laura Seay, "Does Slacktivism Work?" *The Washington Post* (March 12, 2014), http://www.washingtonpost.com/blogs/monkey-cage/wp/2014/03/12/does-slacktivism-work/.]

28. Adam Arvidsson and Nicolai Peiterson in *The Ethical Economy* (2013), ix.

29. Brown, *Undoing the Demos,* 38.

30. "Rethinking the Social Responsibility of Business: A Reason Debate Featuring Milton Friedman, Whole Foods' John Mackey, and Cypress Semiconductor's T.J.

Rodgers." *Reason Magazine* (October 2005), accessed December 12, 2014, http://reason.com/archives/2005/10/01/rethinking-the-social-responsi

31. Within cultural studies, these ideas came about with Birmingham School scholars Paul Cohen, Stuart Hall, and Dick Hebdige's studies of postwar youth cultures. See Cohen, Paul. "Subcultural Conflict and Working Class Community," in *Culture, Media, Language: Working Papers in Cultural Studies: 1972–1979* (Article originally published in 1972, London: Routledge, 1980), 66–75. Stuart Hall and Tony Jefferson, *Resistance through Rituals: Youth Subcultures in Post-War Britain.* (London: Taylor & Francis e-library edition, 2003). Hebdige, Dick. *Subculture: The Meaning of Style* (New York: Routledge, 1979).

32. *Anthropological Quarterly* 85, no. 1 (2012): 204.

33. Evan Williams was interviewed by Umair Haque at the 2010 SXSW, a keynote that has gained the infamous reputation as being "The Keynote from Hell," due to no apparent reason other than its tediousness. See David Peisner's "What Really Happened During Evan Williams's Worst SXSW Moment?" which is part of the SXSW Oral History. http://www.fastcompany.com/3026992/what-really-happened-during-evan-williams-worst-sxsw-moment

34. TOMS Giving Report, 2012.

35. Ibid.

36. http://www.toms.com/women/womens-bags

37. Gary Hamel, Foreword to *The New Capitalist Manifesto*, by Umair Haque (Boston: Harvard Business Review Press, 2011), ix–xv.

38. Adam Smith, *Wealth of Nations*, Originally published 1776 (New York: Bantam Publishing, 2003).

39 Ibid., 569–570.

40. Marx writes of the formula in *Capital, Volume One,* Chapter Four: "The General Formula for Capital." Most simplistically, M-C-M represents how money is invested in commodities and then sold, resulting in the final M. Yet, capital thrives on the second "M" resulting in more money than the first "M," what Marx defines as M', where the change in difference is what Marx calls surplus value. As he states, "Value, therefore now becomes value in process, money in process, and as such, capital. It comes out of circulation, enters into it again, preserves and multiplies itself within circulation, emerges from it with an increased size, and starts the same cycle again and again." ("The General Formula for Capital," 256.)

41. For more on Whole Foods reinvestment of capital, see its "core values," where you can learn about how it helps local communities. http://www.wholefoodsmarket.com/mission-values/core-values/we-serve-and-support-our-local-and-global-communities; http://www.wholefoodsmarket.com/mission-values/caring-communities/whole-planet-foundation

42. Fredric Jameson, "Utopia and Its Antinomies," in *Archaeologies of the Future* (London: Verson, 2005), 156.

43. The idea of authenticity is central to ethical capitalism with leaders seeking to overturn the previous eras of blind or unconscious leadership that lead to the crumbling of faith in the corporation. In *Authentic Leadership,* a book written by Bill George in 2003, the new leaders must be guided by stewardship to corporations and the people they serve.

44. Muhammad Yunus, "Opening Speech at 1997 Microcredit Summit" (Washington, DC, February 2, 1997).

45. Fahira Karim, "Nobel Laureate Muhammad Yunus Leaves Microfinance Bank." *The Guardian* (May 12, 2011), accessed May 20, 2013, http://www.guardian.co.uk/world/2011/may/13/nobel-laureate-muhammad-yunus-microfinance. For more, see Anis Chowdhury, "Microfinance as a Poverty Reduction Tool—A Critical Assessment." *DESA Working Paper 89,* United Nations Department of Economic and Social Affairs (December 2009).

46. Despite these sentiments, Whole Foods continually pops up in the news for its bad behavior, most recently being accused of overcharging customers. As a *Gothamist* article states: "The investigation looked at products that are weighed and labeled and found a 'systematic problem' whereby customers were routinely overcharged for things like nuts, snack foods, poultry and other grocery products. Eight packages of chicken tenders—priced at $9.99 per pound—were inaccurately priced and labeled to the tune of a $4.13 overcharge to the customer per package, a store profit of $33.04 for the set. DCA says one package was overpriced as much as $4.85. 'Additionally, 89 percent of the packages tested did not meet the federal standard for the maximum amount that an individual package can deviate from the actual weight, which is set by the U.S. Department of Commerce.'" [Nell Casey, "Investigators Say Whole Foods has been Ripping Us Off More Than We Realized," *The Gothamist* (June 24, 2015), accessed June 24, 2015, http://gothamist.com/2015/06/24/whole_foods_ripoff.php.]

47. AfriPads was started in 2009 by Paul Grinvalds and Sophia Klumpp, a North American couple, after traveling to Uganda in 2008 and witnessing the hardship girls and women go through due to their menstrual cycle. What is noteworthy is that AfriPads was not set up as a nonprofit organization, but rather a limited liability for-profit company. As the website declares: "With the success of the pilot project, AFRIpads was ready to start addressing the acute need for affordable menstrual products on a nation-wide scale. But rather than establishing a charity, the founders decided to take a new approach to addressing development problems, and in late 2009 AFRIpads Ltd. was incorporated as a social business. By blending the power of business with the social objectives of charity, AFRIpads is utilizing the power of the market to provide the best and most sustainable menstrual product solution," http://afripads.com/blog/theissue/history/

48. Both Miki and Radha were listed on *Forbes* 2013 list of "Top Millennials on a Mission," having also started a healthy pizza chain in New York City and a children's multimedia nutrition education company. Additionally, Miki spoke at the 2012 World Youth Summit at United Nations, was awarded the 2013 Tribeca Disruptive Innovation Award, and invited on the exclusive Summit at Sea, an invite-only "schmooze cruise" conference that has previously featured Zappos founder Tony Hsieh, TOMS Shoes founder Blake Mycoskie, Richard Branson, Russell Simmons, and even billionaire philanthropist Ted Turner. She chronicles some of this in her bestselling book, *Do Cool Sh*t: Quit Your Day Job, Start Your Own Business & Live Happily Ever After.* Her current project, which has an IndieGoGo page seeking to raise $20,000 in capital, is Tushy: For People Who Poop—a bidet attachment that seeks to advocate for a toilet-paperless world. https://www.indiegogo.com/projects/tushy-for-people-who-poop#/story

Also see Bertoni, Steven. "Schmooze Cruise: Summit Series Takes the Party to the Open Seas." *Forbes*, April 6, 2011. http://www.forbes.com/sites/stevenbertoni/2011/04/06/schmooze-cruise-summit-series-takes-the-party-to-the-open-seas/

49. Thinx Website, FAQs "What Made Them Actually Do It?" http://www.sheThinx.com/pages/faq

50. http://www.sheThinx.com/pages/about-us, accessed June 1, 2015.

51. The term "conduct of conduct" is widely attributed to Foucault's "The Subject and Power," *Critical Inquiry* 8, no. 4 (Summer 1982): 777–795. In its English version, the term as such does not appear, but is alleged to appear in the original French: Foucault M (1994) *Dits et* écrits *IV* (Paris: Gallimard), 237.

52. Barbara Cruikshank, *The Will to Empower* (New York: Cornell University Publishing, 1999), 68–69.

53. Google's NGram works through its quickly growing collection of published books, Google Books, to historically trace particular words over time. Although it is still a new technology, it provides useful data sets for words within its catalog of over 30 million, according to several reports back in 2013. If nothing else, NGram is an enjoyable way to see within Google's archive the fluidity of language. For more on NGram, see: https://books.google.com/ngrams/info

Also see Ben Zimmer, "Google's NGram Viewer Goes Wild." *The Atlantic* (October 17, 2013), accessed May 1, 2015, http://www.theatlantic.com/technology/archive/2013/10/googles-ngram-viewer-goes-wild/280601/. Also see Cade Metz, "8 Years Later," Google's Book Scanning Crusade Ruled "Fair Use." *Wired Magazine* (November 14, 2013), accessed May 1, 2015, http://www.wired.com/2013/11/google-2/

54. E. Ann Kaplan, *Looking for the Other: Feminism, Film, and the Imperial Gaze.* (New York: Routledge, 1997). Also see Anne McClintock's *Imperial Leather: Race, Gender, and Sexuality in the Colonial Conquest* (New York: Routledge, 1995).

55. http://www.sheThinx.com, accessed June 5, 2015.

56. Referencing TOMS' other products: eyewear, but also eye exams and surgeries, if consumers purchase TOMS glasses; and water for one week if consumers purchase TOMS Coffee.

57. Quote from TOMS website, accessed June 10, 2015, http://www.toms.com/water-partners. It should be emphasized that although TOMS presents a simple progression to poverty alleviation via water in this case, its partners actually do good work, it's just that TOMS does not always publicize this, perhaps due to a fear that over information may turn consumers off to its causes. For example, one of TOMS' Giving Partners is Aguayada, an organization that works to build sustainable water and sanitation systems for communities. http://www.aguayuda.org/index.php/about-aguayuda/vision/

58. Wendy Brown actually says: "Neo-liberal subjects are controlled *through* their freedom—not simply, as thinkers from the Frankfurt School through Foucault have argued, because freedom within an order of domination can be an instrument of that domination—but because of neo-liberalism's *moralization* of the consequences of this freedom." ("Neoliberalism and the End of Liberal Democracy.")

59. From product material 2014.

60. Fredric Jameson, "Utopia Now." *Archaeologies of the Future: The Desire Called Utopia and Other Science Fictions* (London: Verso, 2005), xviii.
61. "Comments." *Utopian Studies* 9, no. 2 (1998): 75.
62. Ibid.

BIBLIOGRAPHY

Agrawal, Miki. *Do Cool Sh*t: Quit Your Day Job, Start Your Own Business & Live Happily Ever After.* New York: HarperCollins, 2013.

AfriPads Company, accessed April 12, 2015, http://afripads.com/blog/theissue/history/

Aguayuda Organization, accessed May 10, 2015, http://www.aguayuda.org/index.php/about-aguayuda/vision/

Arvidsson, Adam and Nicolai Peitersen. *The Ethical Economy: Rebuilding Value After the Crisis.* New York: Columbia University Press, 2013.

Bertoni, Steven. "Schmooze Cruise: Summit Series Takes the Party to the Open Seas." *Forbes,* April 6, 2011, accessed May 10, 2015, http://www.forbes.com/sites/stevenbertoni/2011/04/06/schmooze-cruise-summit-series-takes-the-party-to-the-open-seas/

Boltanski, Luc. *Distant Suffering: Morality, Media and Politics.* Cambridge, UK: Cambridge University Press, 1999.

Brough, Melissa. "Fair Vanity: The Visual Culture of Humanitarianism in the Age of Commodity Activism." In *Commodity Activism: Cultural Resistance in Neoliberal Times,* eds. Roopali Mukherjee and Sarah Banet-Weiser, 17411–94. New York: New York University Press, 2012.

Brown, Wendy. "Moralism as Anti-Politics." In *Materializing Democracy: Toward a Revitalized Cultural Politics,* eds. Dana D. Nelson and Russ Castronovo, 36833–92. Durham, NC: Duke University Press, 2002.

———. "Neoliberalism and the End of Liberal Democracy." *Theory & Event* 7, no. 1 (2003).

———. *Undoing the Demos: Neoliberalism's Stealth Revolution.* Brooklyn, NY: Zone Books, 2015.

Butler, Judith. "Ethical Ambivalence." In *The Turn to Ethics,* eds. Garber, Marjorie, Beatrice Hanssen, and Rebecca L. Walkowitz, 1522–8. London: Routledge, 2000.

Casey, Nell. "Investigators Say Whole Foods has been Ripping Us Off More Than We Realized." *The Gothamist* (June 24, 2015), accessed June 24, 2015, http://gothamist.com/2015/06/24/whole_foods_ripoff.php

Chowdhury, Anis. "Microfinance as a Poverty Reduction Tool—A Critical Assessment." *DESA Working Paper 89,* (December 2009). United Nations Department of Economic and Social Affairs.

Cohen, Paul. "Subcultural Conflict and Working Class Community." In *Culture, Media, Language: Working Papers in Cultural Studies: 197211–979*, 6677–75. London: Routledge, 1980.

Cruikshank, Barbara. *The Will to Empower: Democratic Citizens and Other Subjects.* New York: Cornell University Press, 1999.
Duncombe, Stephen. *Dream: Re-imagining Progressive Politics in An Age of Fantasy.* New York: New Press, 2007.
Foucault, Michel. "The Subject of Power." *Critical Inquiry* 8, no. 4 (Summer 1982): 77777–95.
———. *Birth of Biopolitics: Lectures at the College de France, 197811–979.* Trans, Graham Burchell. New York: Palgrave Macmillan, 2008.
Garber, Marjorie, Beatrice Hanssen, and Rebecca L. Walkowitz, eds. *The Turn to Ethics.* London: Routledge, 2000.
George, Bill. *Authentic Leadership: Rediscovering the Secrets to Creating Lasting Value.* San Franscisco, CA: Jossey-Bass, 2003.
Hall, Stuart and Tony Jefferson. *Resistance through Rituals: Youth Subcultures in Post-War Britain.* London: Taylor & Francis e-library edition, 2003.
Hamel, Gary. Introduction to *The New Capitalist Manifesto,* ed. Umair Haque, ix–xv. Boston: Harvard Business Review Press, 2011.
Haque, Umair. *The New Capitalist Manifesto.* Boston: Harvard Business Review Press, 2011.
Hebdige, Dick. *Subculture: The Meaning of Style.* New York: Routledge, 1979.
Hickel, Jason and Arsalan Kahn. "The Culture of Capitalism and the Crisis of Critique." *Anthropological Quarterly* 85, no. 1 (2012): 204.
Jameson, Fredric. "Comments." *Utopian Studies* 9, no. 2 (1998): 7477–7.
———. "Utopia Now." In *Archaeologies of the Future: The Desire Called Utopia and Other Science Fictions*, xi–xvi. London: Verso, 2005.
———. "Utopia and its Antinomies." In *Archaeologies of the Future,* 14211–69. London: Verso, 2005.
Kaplan, E. Ann. *Looking for the Other: Feminism, Film, and the Imperial Gaze.* New York: Routledge, 1997.
Karim, Fahira. "Nobel Laureate Muhammad Yunus Leaves Microfinance Bank." *The Guardian* (May 12, 2011), accessed May 25, 2012, http://www.guardian.co.uk/world/2011/may/13/nobel-laureate-muhammad-yunus-microfinance
Kelly, Heather. "Facebook Rainbow Profiles used by 26 Million," *CNN Money* (June 30, 2015), http://money.cnn.com/2015/06/29/technology/facebook-rainbow-profile/
King, Samantha. *Pink Ribbons, Inc.: Breast Cancer and the Politics of Philanthropy.* University of Minnesota Press, 2008.
Kunkel, Benjamin. *Utopia or Bust: A Guide to the Present Crisis.* London: Verso, 2014.
Mackey, John and Raj Sisodia. *Conscious Capitalism: Liberating the Heroic Spirit of Business.* Boston: Harvard Business Review Press, 2014.
Marcuse, Herbert. "The End of Utopia." (First published in *Psychoanalyse und Politik*; lecture delivered at the Free University of West Berlin in July 1967.) Accessed March 2, 2015, https://www.marxists.org/reference/archive/marcuse/works/1967/end-utopia.htm
Marx, Karl. *Capital, Volume One,* Introduction by Ernest Mandel, Trans, Ben Fowkes. London, Penguin, 1976.

McClintock, Anne. *Imperial Leather: Race, Gender, and Sexuality in the Colonial Conquest.* New York: Routledge, 1995.

Metz, Cade. "8 Years Later, Google's Book Scanning Crusade Ruled 'Fair Use.' *Wired Magazine* (November 14, 2013), accessed April 12, 2015, http://www.wired.com/2013/11/google-2/

"Millennials on a Mission: 2013." *Forbes* (May 9, 2013), accessed May 13, 2015, http://www.forbes.com/special-report/2013/millenials/millenials.html

Mouffe, Chantal. "Which Ethics for Democracy." In *The Turn to Ethics*, eds. Garber, Marjorie, Beatrice Hanssen, and Rebecca L. Walkowitz, 8599–4. London: Routledge, 2000.

Mukherjee, Roopali, and Sarah Banet-Weiser, eds. *Commodity Activism: Cultural Resistance in Neoliberal Times.* New York: NYU Press, 2012.

Mycoskie, Blake. *Start Something that Matters.* New York: Spiegel & Grau Trade, an imprint of The Random House Publishing Group, 2011.

———. "World Sight Day." *The Huffington Post* (October 10, 2013), accessed October 10, 2013, http://www.huffingtonpost.com/blake-mycoskie/world-sight-day-2013_b_4073653.html

Myers, Ella. *Worldly Ethics: Democratic Politics and Care for the World.* Durham, NC: Duke University Press, 2013.

NGram, "About," https://books.google.com/ngrams/info

Peisner, David. "What Really Happened During Evan Williams's Worst SXSW Moment?," *Fast Company* (March 5, 2014), accessed May 18, 2015, http://www.fastcompany.com/3026992/what-really-happened-during-evan-williams-worst-sxsw-moment

"Rethinking the Social Responsibility of Business: A Reason Debate Featuring Milton Friedman, Whole Foods' John Mackey, and Cypress Semiconductor's T.J. Rodgers." *Reason Magazine* (October 2005), accessed January 22, 2015, http://reason.com/archives/2005/10/01/rethinking-the-social-responsi

Richey, Lisa Ann and Stefano Ponte. *Brand Aid: Shopping Well to Save the World.* Quadrant Books, University of Minnesota Press, 2011.

Seay, Laura. "Does Slacktivism Work?" *The Washington Post* (March 12, 2014), http://www.washingtonpost.com/blogs/monkey-cage/wp/2014/03/12/does-slacktivism-work/

Smith, Adam. *The Wealth of Nations.* Originally published 1776. New York: Bantam Publishing, 2003.

THINX website, accessed June 5, 2015, http://www.sheThinx.com

———. THINX Indiegogo website, accessed June 5, 2015, https://www.indiegogo.com/projects/tushy-for-people-who-poop#/story

———. FAQs, "What Made them Actually Do it?" accessed June 1, 2015, http://www.sheThinx.com/pages/faq

TOMS Shoes Campus Club Constitution, George Mason University, 2012–2013.

———.TOMS Giving Report, 2012.

———. Giving Partners, accessed June 10, 2015. http://www.toms.com/water-partners.

———. TOMS Bag Collection, accessed June 10, 2015, http://www.toms.com/women/womens-bags

Wegner, Phillip. "Horizons, Figures, and Machines: The Dialectic of Utopia in the Work of Fredric Jameson." *Utopian Studies* 9, no. 2 (1998): 5877–3.

Whole Foods Market, "Core Values," accessed May 22, 2015, http://www.wholefoodsmarket.com/mission-values/core-values/we-serve-and-support-our-local-and-global-communities

Yunus, Muhammad. "Opening Speech at 1997 Microcredit Summit." Washington, DC, February 2, 1997.

Van Valkenburg, Shawn. "The Dangerous American Myth of Spiritual Meritocracy." *Salon* (October 26, 2014), accessed February 12, 2015, http://www.salon.com/2014/10/26/the_dangerous_american_myth_of_corporate_spirituality/

Zimmer, Ben. "Google's NGram Viewer Goes Wild." *The Atlantic* (October 17, 2013), accessed June 3, 2015, http://www.theatlantic.com/technology/archive/2013/10/googles-ngram-viewer-goes-wild/280601/

Index

About the Contributors

Giorgia Aiello is an associate professor in Media and Communication at the University of Leeds (United Kingdom). Her research focuses on the nexus of globalization, social and cultural difference, and both visual and urban communication. She has written about branding, photography, and the urban built environment, and on institutions like the EU and Magnum Photos, and corporations such as Starbucks and Getty Images. Dr. Aiello is the current Chair of the International Communication Association's Visual Communication Studies Division.

Clovis Bergère is a PhD candidate and adjunct professor in Childhood Studies at Rutgers University—Camden. His dissertation focuses on emergent digital cultures among urban youth in Guinea. He is particularly interested in the impact of social media on the social constructions of youth. He has recently conducted research on street corners as sites of youth sociability in Guinea and coauthored (with Lauren J. Silver, Rutgers University) a chapter on the politics of global urban youth research in Kennelly, J., & Poyntz, S. (eds.) *Phenomenology of Youth Cultures and Globalization* (2015). At Rutgers, he teaches childhood studies and urban education. His academic work builds on his experience working as a teacher in Guinea and in London, United Kingdom, where he worked in sports development, children's play, and education.

Lisa Daily is a current Cultural Studies PhD candidate at George Mason University (Fairfax, Virginia). Her dissertation is tentatively titled, "Ethics Incorporated: Ethical Commodity Formations & the Rise of a Conscious Capitalism (TM)," which examines how discourses of ethics and morality are mobilized within the "Conscious Capitalism"™ and the commodity form. She has taught for both cultural studies and global affairs departments at George Mason University and is currently associate faculty at New York University's Gallatin School of Individualized Study.

Amber Day is an associate professor in the English and Cultural Studies Department at Bryant University. She is the author of *Satire and Dissent: Interventions in Contemporary Political Debate*. Her research focuses broadly on the intersections of popular culture and political speech, including ironic and satiric communication, political performance and activism, and public debate. She has published on parody news shows, satiric documentaries, ironic activism, internet memes, and comedians in the public sphere.

Linda Doyle is the director of CONNECT/CTVR and an associate professor in Trinity College Dublin. She works with a team of researchers at Trinity. They focus on cognitive radio, reconfigurable networks, dynamic spectrum access, spectrum management regimes, and spectrum policy. They have a very large interest in experimental work and pride themselves on taking their ideas from concept to prototype. The group also includes a number of researchers who focus on art- and technology-related research.

Stephen Duncombe is a professor of Media and Culture at New York University. He is the author and editor of six books, including *Dream: Re-Imagining Progressive Politics in an Age of Fantasy*. He is also the creator of the Open Utopia, an open access, open source, web-based edition of Thomas More's Utopia, and is currently working on a book on the art of propaganda during the New Deal. Duncombe is a life-long political activist, and is presently cofounder and director of the Center for Artistic Activism, a research and training institute that helps activists to think more like artists and artists to think more like activists.

Catherine D'Ignazio is an assistant professor of Civic Media and Data Visualization Storytelling in the Journalism Department at Emerson College. She is a researcher, artist, and software developer whose work focuses on data literacy, media innovation, and civic art. D'Ignazio has codeveloped a suite of tools for data literacy (DataBasic.io), developed custom software to geolocate news articles, and is currently working with the Public Laboratory for Technology and Science to explore the possibilities for journalistic storytelling with DIY environmental sensors. Her art and design projects have won awards from the Tanne Foundation; Turbulence.org; the LEF Foundation; and Dream It, Code It, Win It. Her work has been exhibited at the Eyebeam Center for Art & Technology, Museo d'Antiochia of Medellin, and the Venice Biennial.

Jessica Foley is an artist and academic whose work is concerned with how forms of writing and speech can be developed to critically explore, engage, and practice cultures of communication and thought. She crafts ways to bring people together to reconsider ideas, words, customs, objects, and practices, and to catalyze apperception through this work. She has exhibited throughout Ireland and internationally. She is a member of Difference Engine (2009–present), an artist-led touring exhibition of iterative mixed media work with artists Gillian Lawler, Wendy Judge, and Mark Cullen. Her educational background is in Graphic Design (B.Des, LSAD), Art and Design Education (H.Dip LSAD), and Contemporary Art Theory (MA Art in the Contemporary World, NCAD).

Lorenzo Giannini is a research fellow at the Department of Communication Science, Humanities, and International Studies of the Urbino University (Italy). His research interests are in sociology of consumption and cultural studies, with a methodological approach based mainly on ethnography and historical research

Jeremy Hunsinger holds a PhD in Science and Technology Studies from Virginia Tech. He is an Assistant Professor in Communication Studies at Wilfrid Laurier University. His research agenda analyzes the transformations of knowledge in the modes of production in the information age. His current research project examines innovation, expertise, knowledge production, and distributions in hacklabs and hackerspaces. He was coeditor of the journal *Learning Inquiry* and has published in *FastCapitalism*, *The Information Society*, *Social Epistemology*, and recently published a special issue on the Democratization of Hacking and Making in *New Media & Society*.

Martha Kuhlman is a professor of Comparative Literature in the Department of English and Cultural Studies at Bryant University, where she teaches courses on the graphic novel, critical theory, and Central European literature. She edited *The Comics of Chris Ware: Drawing Is a Way of Thinking*, published by the University Press of Mississippi (2010), and contributed chapters to a number of works, including *Drawn from the Classics: Essays on Graphic Adaptations of Literary Works*, *Comics and Abstraction*, and the *Cambridge Companion to Comics*.

Chenjerai Kumanyika is a scholar, journalist, organizer, and artist who holds a creativity professorship in Clemson University's Department of Communication Studies. He is a contributor to Transom, NPR Codeswitch, All Things Considered, VICE, and a news analyst for RisingUp Radio on KPFK. Starting in the fall of 2014, Dr. Kumanyika pulled in international audiences with his livestream coverage of protests in a number of cities including Ferguson, New York, Philadelphia, and South Carolina. His January 2015 article on Vocal Color in Public Radio produced for Transom.org was featured on *NPR*, *The Washington Post*, and *BuzzFeed*, trending nationally on Twitter, and spawning a nationwide discussion of diversity in public media. Dr. Kumanyika is also a founding member of the hip-hop group Spooks whose first album, S.I.O.S.O.S. Vol. 1 (2000) produced singles that reached gold-selling status in four countries and placed highly on top ten charts around the world. Dr. Kumanyika serves as a board member for several youth mentoring programs. You can learn more about his work at Chenjerai.net.

Joan Faber McAlister is an associate professor of Rhetoric, Media, and Social Change at Drake University in Des Moines, Iowa. Her research draws on feminist, queer, and critical theory to analyze visual and spatial cultures, and focuses on the relationships between rhetoric, aesthetics, and social location. The status, function, and material character of home, dwelling, and belonging in daily life are persistent themes in her writing. Dr. McAlister is currently the Editor of *Women's Studies in Communication*.

Deborah Philips is a professor of Literature and Cultural History at the University of Brighton. Her books include *Fairgound Attractions* (Bloomsbury, 2013), *Women's Writing 1945–2014*, and with Garry Whannel *The Trojan Horse: The Growth of Commercial Sponsorship*.

Rob Walker is a writer in Savannah, Georgia. His books include *Buying In* and *Letters from New Orleans*, and his additional side projects have included Significant Objects and the Unconsumption project.

www.ingramcontent.com/pod-product-compliance
Lightning Source LLC
LaVergne TN
LVHW011524200926
848484LV00001B/144